RECEIVED

3 0 MAY 2014

Moreton Morrell Site

£42.95

KT-556-300

GRE
(D23)

WARWICKSHIRE
COLLEGE
LIBRARY

WITHDRAWN

Warwickshire College

00780166

MANAGING
SPORT EVENTS

T. Christopher Greenwell, PhD

University of Louisville

Leigh Ann Danzey-Bussell, PhD

University of West Georgia

David J. Shonk, PhD

James Madison University

WARWICKSHIRE
COLLEGE
LIBRARY

HUMAN KINETICS

Library of Congress Cataloging-in-Publication Data

Greenwell, T. Christopher, 1967-
  Managing sport events / T. Christopher Greenwell, Leigh Ann Danzey-Bussell, David J. Shonk.
    p. cm.
  Includes bibliographical references and index.
  1. Sports--Management. 2. Sports administration. 3. Special events--Management. I. Danzey-Bussell, Leigh Ann, 1965- II. Shonk, David J., 1969- III. Title.
  GV713.G65 2014
  796.06'9--dc23

                    2012038835

ISBN-10: 0-7360-9611-6 (print)
ISBN-13: 978-0-7360-9611-9 (print)

Copyright © 2014 by T. Christopher Greenwell, Leigh Ann Danzey-Bussell, and David J. Shonk

All rights reserved. Except for use in a review, the reproduction or utilization of this work in any form or by any electronic, mechanical, or other means, now known or hereafter invented, including xerography, photocopying, and recording, and in any information storage and retrieval system, is forbidden without the written permission of the publisher.

The web addresses cited in this text were current as of February 2013, unless otherwise noted.

Acquisitions Editor: Myles Schrag; **Developmental Editor:** Melissa J. Zavala; **Managing Editor:** Amanda S. Ewing; **Assistant Editor:** Amy Akin; **Copyeditor:** Patricia L. MacDonald; **Proofreader:** Red Inc.; **Indexer:** Susan Danzi Hernandez; **Permissions Manager:** Dalene Reeder; **Graphic Designer:** Joe Buck; **Graphic Artist:** Dawn Sills; **Cover Designer:** Keith Blomberg; **Photograph (cover):** © Glyn Kirk/Action Images/Icon SMI; **Photo Production Manager:** Jason Allen; **Art Manager:** Kelly Hendren; **Associate Art Manager:** Alan L. Wilborn; **Illustrations:** © Human Kinetics, unless otherwise noted; **Printer:** Sheridan Books

Printed in the United States of America   10 9 8 7 6 5 4 3 2 1

The paper in this book is certified under a sustainable forestry program.

Human Kinetics
Website: www.HumanKinetics.com

United States: Human Kinetics
P.O. Box 5076
Champaign, IL 61825-5076
800-747-4457
e-mail: humank@hkusa.com

Canada: Human Kinetics
475 Devonshire Road Unit 100
Windsor, ON N8Y 2L5
800-465-7301 (in Canada only)
e-mail: info@hkcanada.com

Europe: Human Kinetics
107 Bradford Road
Stanningley
Leeds LS28 6AT, United Kingdom
+44 (0) 113 255 5665
e-mail: hk@hkeurope.com

Australia: Human Kinetics
57A Price Avenue
Lower Mitcham, South Australia 5062
08 8372 0999
e-mail: info@hkaustralia.com

New Zealand: Human Kinetics
P.O. Box 80
Torrens Park, South Australia 5062
0800 222 062
e-mail: info@hknewzealand.com

E5207

Warwickshire College
Library
Moreton Morrell Centre

Class No: 658.91.

Acc No: 00780166

To my supportive parents, Zack and Leigh, and my wonderful family, Donna, Sam, and Molly.

—T. Christopher Greenwell

This book is proof that sometimes dreams do come true! This dream would not have been achieved without the support of my meticulous proofreader and husband, Tim Bussell; my best girl and daughter, Sophie Grace Bussell; my life-long supporter, my dad, Fritz E. Danzey; and my guardian angel, my mother, Barbara W. Danzey. Thank you to all who have supported me, tolerated me, and most of all encourage me along this journey, especially my students who have impacted my life more than they will ever know. I also owe a big debt of gratitude to Myles Schrag at Human Kinetics who put up with my persistent nagging before helping to make this dream a reality. Finally, thank you to my coauthors, Chris Greenwell and David Shonk, for allowing me to contribute to this amazing book.

—Leigh Ann Danzey-Bussell

I dedicate this book to six instrumental teachers in my life:

1. My father, the late coach and professor of physical education, William E. Shonk, who taught me how to teach and the important lessons of life.

2. My mother, Mary Aretta Shonk, whose unselfish love and persistent determination inspire me every day.

3. My brother, William S. Shonk, who taught me the importance of leadership and teamwork.

4. My wife, Jennifer R. (Brady) Shonk, who is my love, inspiration, and the natural born teacher in our household.

5. My uncle, James H. Shonk, who inspired me to write and taught me about team development.

6. My mentor, Chella, who always expected excellence and has given so much to the field of sport management.

—David J. Shonk

CONTENTS

CHAPTER 12 EVENT-DAY MANAGEMENT 185

CHAPTER 13 POSTEVENT DETAILS AND EVALUATION 205

PREFACE

To have a successful career in sport, it is important to have some proficiency in sport event management because just about everyone involved in sport will be engaged in planning, promoting, or managing a sporting event at one time or another. Sport event management is unique among the many areas of sport management in that it integrates various areas of the sport industry including, but not limited to, marketing, sponsorship, budgeting, risk management, and personnel management. In addition, running a sporting event requires the skills to plan, organize, lead, and communicate. Users of this textbook should be able to demonstrate an understanding of event management principles unique to sport.

Managing Sport Events is written for those either working in or aspiring to work in the sport industry. One does not necessarily need to be working in event management per se, as everyone working with sporting events should be able to draw something from this text. This textbook is designed to familiarize readers with principles and practices related to effective event management. The text approaches sport event management from a practical standpoint, integrating theory to support suggestions for practice, and it takes readers through the entire process of organizing events, from event conception through postevent evaluation.

SCOPE OF THE BOOK

Considering the breadth of sporting events, this book covers a wide variety of competitions, from local grassroots events such as a youth soccer tournament to mega-events such as the Olympic Games. The reader should be able to glean relevant information that applies to events large and small, local and international. Further, *Managing Sport Events* accounts for the various purposes events serve (e.g., competition, revenue, tourism, promoting a cause) and for the various stakeholders

sporting events may serve (e.g., athletes, governing bodies, sponsors, communities). Whether the reader is working in parks and recreation or in high school, college, amateur, minor league, professional, or international sports, this book should be a resource for anyone involved in sporting events, regardless of size or scope.

ORGANIZATION

Each chapter covers key sport event management principles, and relevant examples from the sport industry are woven into each principle to illustrate how it applies to practice. In addition, each chapter begins with a profile of an industry professional in the form of an interview. These profiles give an industry insider's perspective into each concept being discussed. Each chapter ends with learning activities that apply what has been learned in the text. Numerous checklists, templates, and worksheets are provided throughout the book to illustrate tools that can be used to successfully plan and implement events.

Managing Sport Events covers the main topics necessary to plan, organize, implement, and evaluate an event. The book opens with an overview of the sport event industry and a chapter that educates readers on how to conceive and develop an event. Next, the book covers key planning areas such as staffing, budgeting, marketing, promotion, sponsorship, and legal and risk management. These chapters illustrate how different disciplines within sport management specifically apply to planning sporting events. Key operational areas such as event services and logistics and managing the event are then presented to encompass what happens during the event itself. The final chapter discusses what needs to happen after the event.

eBook available at HumanKinetics.com

BENEFITS OF THE BOOK

Managing Sport Events is intended for practitioners within the sport industry and students preparing to enter the industry. It provides a strong conceptual, theoretical, and practical basis for understanding the sport event industry and for selecting, planning, implementing, and evaluating a sporting event. The textbook helps the reader to better understand the conceptual aspects of a sporting event that form the basis of how the event will ultimately be run. Conceptual skills are vitally important to all managers, especially event planners, and help to differentiate top-level managers from middle- and staff-level managers and leaders.

Students

This textbook is written with the understanding that the primary audience will be undergraduate students. The majority of students will be studying sport management. However, the text is also applicable to students within any discipline of study who desire to learn more about the nuts and bolts of selecting, planning, implementing, and evaluating an event. Students interested in areas such as hospitality, entertainment, physical education, business, and nonprofit or public administration may also find the textbook useful.

Event management is an important course for almost every sport management program. More important, employers within the sport industry expect students to enter the field as young professionals with an understanding of event management and possessing the necessary skills to immediately engage in event production. Although not every student will have the title of event planner, every student within the sport industry will most likely be engaged in some type of event planning, even if it is only a meal function at your place of business. Our hope is that this will not be one of those books that students buy and sell back at the end of the semester. Instead, this text should serve as a continual resource as you graduate and enter the industry.

Professors

This textbook is written to assist faculty in teaching important theoretical and conceptual issues within the context of sport event management. These are important concepts that add to conceptual and cognitive skill development in each student. At the same time, the authors of the book recognize the practical nature of event management. We have extensive experience within the industry in the area of event management, and because we are also current faculty, we understand the challenges of bringing fresh and relevant practical material into the classroom.

Handy resources such as an instructor guide, test package, and PowerPoint presentation are included in the package for professors. Specific instructions are provided should the faculty member want to engage the students in the process of putting on an actual event. Chapters are organized to follow the process of staging an event, and all chapters contain learning activities to assist the faculty member in engaging students. All chapters contain summaries that review key concepts. Furthermore, each chapter provides a short biography of a current industry professional that may assist professors in experiential learning using case studies.

Current Industry Professionals

Those currently working within the sport industry may need a refresher course in event management, and this text serves as an important resource. Those needing additional training or going back for a graduate degree will find the textbook helpful. In addition, the text is useful as an independent study and as a resource for writing industry reports or proposals. It will help industry professionals brush up on key definitions and is a refresher for key theoretical concepts. Every sport industry professional should keep this text on his bookshelf because of its practical nature.

NEED FOR THE BOOK

Most of us who attend an event do so as an invitee, not fully understanding the vastness of what it takes to host an event. *Managing Sport Events* provides a comprehensive look at what it takes to produce a successful event from conception to fruition to evaluation. As a dynamic field, sport management encompasses traditional business segments (administration, finance, and marketing) requiring expertise. The uniqueness of the sport industry must be understood and applied to event management. This book marries the business side with the unique traits of sport to provide a fresh perspective on event management.

Marketing, risk management, staffing, budgeting, and sponsorship are just a few areas of concern for event managers. Being knowledgeable about these topics and the role each plays in the bigger picture is imperative for today's sport management students. This textbook provides a distinctive perspective on the "how to" aspects of sport management and its intricacies. The years of experience expressed throughout this book and the industry profiles found in each chapter offer the students great perspectives and real-life examples to contemplate and critically analyze. Many textbooks focus on singular aspects of the sport management field, such as sport marketing, sport finance, or sport media relations, but this text represents an inclusive look at event management and how those singular aspects work together to provide a strong foundation for students considering careers in this segment of the industry. We have taken great effort to ensure this textbook addresses all pertinent areas of event management. Upon completion of this course, readers will have a comprehensive knowledge of event management and will be prepared to accept the challenges of the field.

CHAPTER 1

Understanding the Sport Event Industry

Chapter Objectives

After completing the chapter, the reader should be able to do the following:

- Appreciate the role of sporting events from a historical perspective.
- Identify various types of sporting events.
- Recognize the employment opportunities in sport event management and the skills and knowledge necessary for success within the industry.
- Compare and contrast sporting events versus nonsporting events.
- Understand the relationship of sport event management to sport facility management and sport tourism.

Talty O'Connor is the founder and president of Covey Communications Corporation, a media company that publishes nationally distributed magazines for targeted markets. Among its titles are *ConventionSouth*, one of the leading magazines in the United States for meeting and convention planners; *SportsEvents*, a magazine for planners of all types of sporting events held throughout the United States; *Condo Owner* magazine (Northern Gulf Coast Edition); *Coastal Design*, a high-end home-design magazine; and *Crossties* magazine, an internationally known railroad industry publication. Covey Communications also publishes *Skater's Edge Sourcebook*, an ice skating directory, and has also produced two additional sport facilities directories, *Soccer Fields & Facilities Directory* and *Baseball/Softball Fields & Facilities Directory*.

Q: How has the sport event industry changed over the years?

A: Organized sport competitions are simply big business these days. While we once based youth sports on local league championships, the industry now revolves around travel teams and elite athletes. Parents, coaches, and players spend enormous amounts of time and money participating in sport competitions, often traveling on a weekly basis to compete. The loss of "sports sampling" is another significant change and is a casualty of modern-day sports specialization. Rather than changing sports with the seasons, today's young athletes tend to settle on one sport on a year-round basis. Whether this is detrimental to the development of well-rounded athletic skills and conducive to early burnout are topics of hot debate and lengthy discussion. The industry shifts and changes slightly with each generation. Male athletes dominated the generation of Baby Boomer sports participants. Young female athletes did not have the opportunities to participate that they have today. Generation X tended to be more individualistic and less team oriented. They opened the door to extreme sports and introduced us to BMX racing and snowboarding. Generation Y are more team oriented and

are the force behind today's travel team sports. As for Gen Z, they are more social and connected than any generation. The jury is out as to whether we can attract them to organized sports, and the industry acknowledges the fact that we need to change our events in order to engage these digital natives.

Q: What skills are most important to students who would like to work in the sport event industry?

A: Although sport management revolves around modern technology and social media connectivity, it remains a business of relationships. In my opinion, the fundamentals for success are unchanged in that effective managers need excellent communication and people skills as well as good business management skills. If anything, excelling with these skills will be an even greater asset as we continue to slide into the digital world.

Q: How important is facility management within the industry?

A: Excellent facilities are available throughout the country. The differentiating factor is how well they are managed. Build it and they will come doesn't work. Build it and manage it better than the other facility is the key to success. I have been a member of the United States Olympic Committee's PLAYS committee. PLAYS is an acronym for Pipeline Leadership for America's Youth Sports. The question asked was "What is the best way to get more sport competitions at our sport facility?" The answer was universal: "Run excellent sport events at your facility, and the word will spread throughout the pipeline!"

Q: How has sport tourism affected the industry?

A: The revenue from sport tourism is the funding source for most modern sport facilities. Communities typically invest in new sport complexes with a goal of drawing visitors into the city. The visitors spend significant amounts of money staying in hotel rooms, dining out at restaurants, visiting local attractions, and shopping in local stores. This direct spending circulates through the local economy long after the visitors return to their hometowns. If it wasn't for the economic impact of sports, most communities wouldn't be able to cost-justify the sport facilities they enjoy. Many local leagues don't like sharing their facilities with outside competitors, but the fact is, they probably would not have those nice facilities if it wasn't for revenues from sport tourism. Sport visitors include not only the participating athletes but also the family members, league officials, and other spectators. The industry exceeds $7 billion annually in direct spending in local economies. This figure does not include spending for professional major league events or fixed events such as the Kentucky Derby or the Masters golf tournament. If you include most professional sport, TV, and network sponsorships, the revenues exceed $170 billion annually. But that is not direct spending from sport tourism in local economies.

Q: **What types of sporting events have gained in popularity?**

A: Many people tend to think of traditional sports such as baseball, basketball, or soccer, but those are merely the tip of the iceberg when it comes to sport competitions. Sport events are held by hundreds of different sport organizations and range from well-known sports such as tennis, gymnastics, and archery to niche sports such as horseshoe pitching, disc golf, and cup stacking. There are also extreme sports (Tough Mudder, extreme laser tag) and even weirder events such as street bowling, wife-carrying obstacle races, and underwater hockey. Running sports

are gaining popularity after several years in decline. Half marathons are the most popular running events being held throughout the United States. Lacrosse is one of the fastest-growing sports and is now spreading from the Northeast throughout the country. Tennis has starting growing again. Traditional sports such as baseball, softball, and basketball are struggling to stay even. The most-played sport on earth surprises many people in the United States. It is badminton, which is the national sport of China and is being promoted heavily throughout Asia and now in the United States.

Q: **What are some emerging trends in the industry?**

A: The number of sport events being held in the United States has grown consistently throughout the last decade in spite of the economic woes our country has faced. However, what has not grown is the athlete base or the sponsorship base. Sport event planners are struggling to acquire funding as well as to grow the number of competitors in their events. Compounding the issue is the fact that 7 out of 10 kids who start playing organized sports quit completely by age 14. In addition, the number of kids who are completely inactive doubled between the years 2008 and 2011. Until we reverse this trend, we will continue to struggle to grow our events. Also, an adult is four times more likely to play organized sports if she competed as a youth athlete. So the challenge for the long-term health of our industry as well as our overall physical health is to grow our athlete base for the long term by keeping kids involved in sports.

The Pan-Hellenic Games in 776 BC, one of the earliest documented examples of a sporting event, attracted more than 40,000 spectators who traveled from all parts of Greece to be in attendance (Weed and Bull 2004). This festival was held in Olympia and was celebrated once every four years in accordance with the Greek calendar, occurring after the crops had been gathered and there was a

lull in which men could relax from a hard year's work (Swaddling 1999). Most cities in Greece had their own stadiums during this time, and touring was an important aspect of sport because athletes received awards for participating.

Today, sports participants as well as spectators engage in sport-related activities for numerous reasons. For active participants, playing in a softball tournament is a means of relieving stress, and in a similar manner fans and spectators flock to professional sporting events on a weekend to relax after a long week of work. Even in the early years, stress relief was a motivational factor for those participating in various sport events. Sport derives its meaning from the word *disport*, meaning "carry away from"; as a noun the word means "diversion" or "display" or "amusement" (Struna 2009). The implications are that sport diverts a person's attention away from the rigors and pressures of everyday life (Kurtzman and Zauhar 2003).

Many of today's contemporary sporting events derive from England's system of club sports managed by the wealthy elite (Masteralexis, Barr, and Hums 2009). When European settlers arrived in Virginia and Massachusetts, the only sports were those of Native Americans, who participated in activities such as archery, running, horse riding, and lacrosse (Gems, Borish, and Pfister 2008). However, as life became easier and values changed, the European settlers began to engage in various pastimes and later became concerned about health and fitness (Swanson and Spears 1995). The festive culture of 17th- and 18th-century Britain became a central component of sport in America (Rader 2009). Gambling became an important recreation, and many settlers in Virginia wagered on horses because of the excitement of the competition (Breen 2010). Harness racing soon became the sport of the common person and America's first national pastime and professional sport.

The outgrowth of the success of harness racing was the various profit-oriented leagues we see today. Leagues such as the National Football League, the National Basketball Association, Major League Baseball, the National Hockey League, Major League Soccer, and others were created to develop a system for sport that would work in the United States. In addition, tournament sports such as tennis and golf evolved from England's system of club sport brought to the United States (Masteralexis, Barr, and Hums 2009).

Over the years, the modern sport industry has seen tremendous growth. In 2011, Plunkett Research estimated the industry at $411 billion, and this figure comprises components such as sporting goods, advertising and marketing, professional sport, fitness and recreation, golf courses, racetracks, amusement and recreation, other spectator sports leagues, and NCAA sports (Miller and Washington 2012). Revenues for the top four professional sports leagues (i.e., NBA, MLB, NFL, NHL) in the United States were in excess of $21 billion. Major sporting events such as the Super Bowl, NCAA basketball finals, World Series, NBA Finals, and Kentucky Derby attract millions of viewers. *Forbes* magazine assessed the value of professional teams such as the Dallas Cowboys (NFL), New York Yankees (MLB), and Washington Redskins (NFL) as being more than $1.5 billion (Miller and Washington 2012). In addition, professional athletes such as Tiger Woods, LeBron James, Alex Rodriguez, and Peyton Manning earn millions of dollars in salary and endorsements for playing their respective sports.

The future of the sport event industry seems bright. As the nature of sport evolves, so do the various events that make up the industry. New sports, such as Trangleball, have recently entered the market with hopes of gaining popularity and distribution through large sporting goods companies. The objective of Trangleball is to throw a ball off the face of a pyramid in such a way that your opponent cannot catch it (Trangleball.com).

Technology has changed how sporting events are marketed. Social media sites such as Facebook, Twitter, YouTube, and Foursquare are now used to promote and market many sporting events. As new technologies emerge, sport marketers will continue to reach out to new consumers through these new mediums. The impact of the media allows sport marketers to promote their product to a global audience. In addition, as the sport industry continues to grow, there may be a greater focus on specialization within event management. Although many organizations currently employ a limited number of employees responsible for event planning, this may change as the roles and duties become more specialized in one or more areas within the industry.

Although the future is bright, there are also some concerns regarding the future of sporting events. As noted by Talty O'Connor in the industry profile, one of the primary concerns within the sport event industry is the dropout rate of youth sports participants. Research suggests that many youth drop out because of injury or a lack of enjoyment. Sport event planners must continue to examine new ways to build sport identity in youth. Often, sport identity is carried by a person throughout his life span, and parents will pass the torch of a favorite sport or team to a child.

Opponents also note the commercial nature of sport and the ever-increasing need for sponsorship. As the number of events continues to increase, the competition for sponsorship dollars becomes more competitive, with the largest events having a considerable advantage. The increasing level of commercialism within sport is also evident when considering the impact of the media on sport. Televised sporting events are now scheduled according to the timing of commercial breaks and for peak audiences. Moreover, this commercialism has led to the development of some sports at the expense of others. For example, in the United Kingdom, the top 10 sports receive 90 percent of all the money spent on sponsorships (Masterman 2009).

CAREER PATHS IN SPORT EVENT MANAGEMENT

As the sport industry continues to grow, so do the number of sport-related event management jobs. Almost every professional sport franchise and collegiate athletic program hires some type of event manager. Jobs with titles such as special events coordinator, game-day event staff, director of events, and associate athletic director for event management can commonly be found in an organization's marketing department, event department, or facilities management department. For students seeking entry into event management within the sport industry, there are an increasing number of opportunities for employment. Almost every organization within various segments of the sport industry recognizes the importance of individual employees who specialize in planning and implementing different types of events.

According to the National Association of Sports Commissions (NASC) website (2011), more than 300 cities across the United States currently have a sports commission or a similar type of entity focused on attracting small-scale, youth, or amateur sporting events, and although many of these organizations are small, their employees spend a large amount of time involved in event planning. In fact, the NASC offers a certified sports event executive (CSEE) designation for those members who complete educational sessions related to sales and marketing, strategic planning, event management, technology, revenue generation, and the bid process. The enormous growth in the number of sports commissions is evident when considering that in 1993 there were only 30 such organizations in existence (Kelly 2000). Sport governing bodies and international federations offer potential applicants various event management opportunities. Organizations such as the International Olympic Committee (IOC), United States Olympic Committee (USOC), U.S. Masters Swimming, USA Volleyball, USA Swimming, and U.S. Lacrosse employ event managers. Also, amateur sanctioning bodies such as high school state athletic commissions (e.g., Ohio High School Athletic Association), Little League Baseball, Babe Ruth League, Amateur Athletic Union (AAU), Pony Baseball and Softball, American Youth Football, and American Youth Cheer are involved in planning events and championships.

Students and others seeking event management jobs should be flexible and think creatively as to the types of organizations to which they may apply and where to find these jobs. For example, organizations such as Disney's Wide World of Sports and Universal Studios in Florida offer sport event management jobs. Numerous nonprofit associations (e.g., NCAA national office, National Association of Collegiate Directors of Athletics) hire people to plan their conferences and seminars. Recreational sport jobs are another consideration because almost every locality has a parks and recreation department, and most college campuses employ event managers at their campus recreation facility. Some of the best free websites to consult for finding sport event management jobs include www.teamworkonline.com; www.ncaa.org; www.sportscommissions.org; www.aahperd.org/careers; www.bluefishjobs.com; and www.nrpa.org/careers. In addition, there are a number of fee-based websites such as http://sportsjobboard.com/index.html and www.workinsports.com.

SKILLS, KNOWLEDGE, AND TRAITS FOR SUCCESS

Beyond the sport- and event-specific knowledge necessary to run an event, a number of skills are critical for success in sport event management. Perhaps the most important skill is the ability to manage and maintain a strong personal life. The long hours required by many jobs within the industry can have a detrimental effect on an event planner's personal life. In fact, you may not have a professional career if you do not effectively manage issues such as interpersonal relationships and finances. The ability to organize, prioritize, supervise, and delegate is second to the ability to manage your time and professional resources efficiently and effectively (Goldblatt 2011).

Staging an event requires a multitude of management and business skills, and event managers encompass skills that derive from a multitude of disciplines. Among others, event managers may have backgrounds in law, marketing, accounting, and human resource management (Masterman 2009). Event planning requires a great amount of attention to detail, and event planners must have the ability to conceptualize, recognize, and implement all the key details of the event. More important, these details must be coordinated within a limited time frame. Thus, you must be able to effectively manage your time and resources. As new technologies continue to emerge, the ability to manage and use these technologies is critical for the implementation and marketing of an event. Event planners work within a network of people and companies and must effectively manage a wide variety of interpersonal relationships. This section highlights some skills that all students should work to further develop.

Interpersonal and Communication Skills

Interpersonal skills allow a person to work effectively with others. Vitally important is the ability to get along with others and to span diverse relationships. As will be discussed later in the chapter, event planners must network with a wide variety of people and organizations. Interpersonal skills also include written and verbal communication. Event planners are required to make numerous telephone calls and attend personal meetings. Developing written reports and proposals is a common task. The ability to listen is another important skill that allows the event planner to more effectively meet the needs and wants of a client.

Time Management Skills

When we suggest that an event planner should be an effective manager of his time, we are essentially saying he should have the ability to multitask. Graham, Neirotti, and Goldblatt (2001) claim the most common traits of sport event managers include the following:

- Comfortable with preparing and managing a checklist of activities
- Projects a positive attitude
- Can work independently or as a member of a team
- Accurate and quick at details
- Articulate on the telephone and in written and oral communication
- Creative and flexible
- Capable of working under extreme pressure for long hours
- Good at working with all levels of people, including volunteers
- Effective at balancing multiple projects simultaneously
- Excellent time manager
- Effective negotiator
- Finance- and budget-conscious
- Possesses good typing, word processing, and other office skills

- Has leadership ability
- Quick problem solver
- Good motivator
- Has the desire to learn and grow

A number of these traits involve the ability to multitask and manage one's time. Many event planners enjoy their jobs because of the variety of duties for which they are responsible. For example, one day may entail traveling to a destination for a site visit, while another day consists of negotiating a contract, writing a proposal, or attending meetings. Because of this wide variety of duties and the deadlines imposed by an event, planners must be good managers of their time. Remember, once the date of the event arrives, an event planner is either prepared or not. At this point, it is often too late to arrange for busing, order decorations, prepare extra food, or negotiate a hotel contract. These tasks must be done in advance and require strong organizational and time management skills.

Technology Skills

Students graduating from colleges and universities in the 21st century should possess proficient technology skills; moreover, they are often expected by their more senior coworkers to be highly advanced in these areas. Of course there are expectations that students will graduate with an advanced working knowledge of social media such as Facebook, Twitter, YouTube, and Foursquare. In addition, students should be familiar with various software packages such as Microsoft Office and other types of media such as blogs, videoconferencing, and mobile applications. However, students may graduate without learning about the various software packages unique to their particular industry. For example, many sport organizations use ticketing packages such as Ticketmaster, SRO4, or Paciolan, which are not taught in detail by most college or university sport management programs. In addition, an event planner may need to be able to mine for data, use various project management and customer relationship management (CRM) software packages, manage and develop websites, and understand some aspect of information technology (IT) security.

Students who know the type of jobs they will be seeking after graduation should do some research while they are still in school to determine the technology skills required for their jobs of choice. Research can be done online through the Internet, by visiting trade journals, or even during informational interviews that many students are required to complete during their course work.

SPORT EVENTS VERSUS NONSPORT EVENTS

An event is a carefully crafted experience delivered to make an impact on the person in attendance. The event is staged and choreographed with such precision and polish that the mechanics are imperceptible to the consumer (Silvers 2004). Regardless of the type, event planning requires people who can design the event, manage human and material resources, plan strategically, conceptualize the logistics of the event, manage time effectively, and forecast and budget finances. People who have these types of skills can effectively manage a sport or nonsport event. For example, event planners are needed for nonsport events such as corporate board meetings, business meetings, client appreciation events, executive retreats, fund-raising galas, incentive travel and premium programs, product launches, professional conferences, special events, teleconferences, webcasts, conventions and expositions, corporate shows, and trade shows (Allen 2009). The fundamental skills necessary for planning these types of events are no different from the skills needed for planning a sporting event.

Sporting events are different from nonsporting events in the sense that some form of competition involving physical prowess is involved. They are planned and organized throughout the world for disabled and nondisabled men and women, using single and multisport formats, offering various competition formats (e.g., one-day tournaments to year-round championships), and catering to various levels of ability (e.g., elite athletes to recreational users), and they are marketed to both active participants and passive spectators (Masterman 2009). The emotional element of sport is also a unique characteristic that distinguishes it from various other types of events. Sport marketers use this emotional element in their advertising by focusing on the drama of a sporting contest or matchup between star players. Depending on the type of sport, external factors such as the weather at an outdoor event may have a considerable impact on the success of the event. Sport is also a cultural phenomenon and can differ based on geography. For example, North Americans are apt to consider jogging and walking as recreational and fitness pursuits, whereas Europeans may consider them sporting pursuits (Weed and Bull 2004). In addition, geography and culture also dictate the types of sporting events that are popular in certain regions. Events such as skiing and snowboarding may be more popular in mountainous areas, whereas surfing and fishing events are more popular in coastal regions.

Unlike the competitive and physical nature of sport, events such as meetings and conventions often revolve around a particular trade and are educational in nature. Most corporate meetings and events are discretionary and are held only if management deems them necessary. For example, incentive trips, recognition programs, and product introductions can be canceled if employees fall short of quotas, if nobody is worthy of recognition, or if products are not innovative enough to be introduced. In contrast, association conventions are more mandatory and predictable than corporate meetings and events. The bylaws for an association such as the National Association of Collegiate Directors of Athletics (NACDA) may require an annual convention for members that revolves around board and leadership meetings and concurrent educational sessions.

Depending on economic conditions, corporate and association meetings and events also differ. In tough economic times, fewer corporate events may be planned, whereas association events are more resilient and may be greater in number (Hoyle 2002). Sporting events are not resistant to the challenges of tough economies. However, sport has often been considered recession-proof and a form of stress relief for active participants and spectators alike during tough times. Furthermore, in cases where governing bodies are involved, such as the Olympics, there are certain requirements for participation.

SPORT TOURISM

Sport tourism has become a global phenomenon and an increasingly important topic of study in the field of sport management. In the United States, sport tourism is a $27 billion per year industry, and it has become a significant economic activity for many regions (Kurtzman and Zauhar 1998; Eugenio-Martin 2003). As suggested earlier in the chapter, sporting events have required some form of travel since the early days in Greece. Today, the majority of sporting events are family-oriented or youth events which travel between various destinations (O'Connor and Martin 2009). Sport tourism is defined as leisure-based travel that takes people temporarily outside of their home communities to participate in or watch physical activities or to revere attractions associated with physical activities (Gibson 1998, p. 49). Sport tourism has also been defined as "travel to and participation in or attendance at a predetermined sport activity" (Turco, Riley, and Swart 2002). The destination receives many economic, social, and psychological benefits from hosting an event.

At this point, it may be helpful to explain sport tourism by breaking it into two separate parts, one focused on sport and the other on tourism. Sport has been defined as a range of competitive and noncompetitive active pursuits involving skill, strategy, and chance in which human beings engage simply for enjoyment and training or to raise their performance to levels of publicly acclaimed excellence (Standeven and DeKnop 1999). It has also been described as a pursuit that builds character, teaches values, encourages healthy competition, provides an outlet for aggression, and promotes international friendship and understanding (Kurtzman and Zauhar 2003). Three characteristics are unique to sport: (1) Each sport has its own set of rules; (2) sport encompasses a continuum from elite competition to recreational sport or sport for all; and (3) sport is characterized by its playful nature (Higham and Hinch 2003).

Tourism has been defined in many ways, but it generally refers to travel away from a person's place of residence. Thus, tourism has the following characteristics: (1) It entails traveling to and from a destination along with an overnight stay outside of one's permanent residence; (2) a tourist's movement to and from a destination is temporary, is short term, and includes an intention to return to a permanent place of residence; (3) the destination is visited for purposes other than taking up permanent residence or employment; and (4) the activities the tourist engages in are distinct from those of the local resident and working populations of the place visited (Reisinger 2001). For the destination, there are a number of benefits such as enhancing economic impact and the social and psychological benefits of hosting an event.

Types of Sport Tourism

According to Gibson (1998), there are generally three types of sport tourism: (1) event sport tourism, (2) active sport tourism, and (3) nostalgia-based sport tourism. Examples of event sport tourism include mega-events such as the Olympic Games, Pan American Games, Super Bowl, World Series, and World Cup. It may also encompass tournaments hosted by the Professional Golf Association (PGA), Amateur Athletic Union, or college sport clubs (e.g., hockey). Active sport tourism refers to resorts and other segments of the hospitality industry such as golf courses, ski resorts, and country clubs. There has been a growing demand for active vacations since the 1980s, and the highest rates of participation for these activities generally stem from people between 25 and 34 years of age with household incomes between 50 and 75 thousand U.S. dollars. The active sport tourist is likely to be male, affluent, and college educated; is willing to travel long distances to participate; tends to participate in the sport repeatedly; and is likely to engage in active sport tourism well into retirement. Nostalgia sport tourism includes sport-related attractions such as a hall of fame, sport museum, or stadium. According to Fairley (2003), nostal-

gia and memory are inextricably linked because you cannot have feelings of nostalgia without the memory or perceptions of how things used to be. Many professional sports teams market the concept of nostalgia with old-timers games and nostalgic uniforms from days gone by in an effort to reattract an older demographic of people who grew up watching those teams.

Whether you recognize it or not, you have probably consumed some type of sport tourism during the course of your life. Can you identify what type of tourism the following people are consuming?

- A spectator traveling to the Super Bowl in New Orleans, Louisiana
- A skier traveling to Vail, Colorado
- A marathon runner traveling to Massachusetts for the Boston Marathon
- A fan traveling to Cooperstown, New York, to the Baseball Hall of Fame
- An AAU basketball player traveling to Chicago, Illinois, to play in a tournament
- Parents of the AAU basketball player traveling to watch the tournament in Chicago

Motivation for Sport Tourism

A tourist's decision to travel may be influenced by a number of social factors such as family, reference groups, social classes, culture, and subculture (Moutinho 2000). Sport event planners should take these factors into account when marketing their events. For example, the sport of quidditch is marketed in a unique way based on its subculture. Although you will not find this sport often on television, it was made popular because of the Harry Potter books and movies and is marketed to thousands of young people via Facebook (Carbonell 2012). Schools such as Harvard, UCLA, and Texas A&M have quidditch teams.

Tourists can also be segmented based on their purposes for traveling. Robinson and Gammon (2004) distinguish between *sport tourism*, where the major purpose of a visit is sport, and *tourism sport*, where the tourist engages in sport as a secondary pursuit. For example, many people will travel to places like Miami or New Orleans with the primary purpose of attending the Super Bowl, while others will travel to Augusta, Georgia, for the Masters golf tournament or Churchill Downs in Louisville, Kentucky, for the express purpose of witnessing the Kentucky Derby. However, another traveler may be visiting Boston for a business convention but have enough discretionary time to attend a Boston Red Sox Major League Baseball game. A wide variety of motivational factors can be attributed to why a tourist consumes sport. These motivational factors include alleviating stress, group affiliation, escape, drama, aesthetics, vicarious achievement, gaining knowledge, or interacting with family and friends.

Sport is also widely marketed as entertainment, and many spectators attend for reasons beyond just watching the players on the field. Major sporting events also include fancy halftime shows, on-field contests, and promotional giveaways. Relaxation and pleasure are common motivational factors for many tourists, and some fans may use sport tourism as a way to escape from understimulation and boredom, while others use it to escape from overstimulation and stress (Moutinho 2001; Wann, Allen, and Rochelle 2004).

Actors in Sport Tourism

Sport tourism has been described using a theatrical analogy suggesting that players represent the actors, sport spectators are the audience members, and the stadium or arena is the theater (Thwaites and Chadwick 2005). However, by digging deeper we find that a number of other actors engage in sport tourism, starting with the event planner. An event planner may be employed by a variety of different organizations, many of which include rights-holder organizations (RHOs) and destination marketing organizations (DMOs). Rights holders are organizations that own the rights to one or more events and are usually responsible for planning, organizing, and controlling the event. For example, the National Football League owns the rights to the Super Bowl, and the American Cancer Society owns the rights to the Relay for Life event. A number of events rights holders are classified as governing bodies, which are sport organizations that have a regulatory or sanction-ing function. USA Table Tennis is an example of a governing body that owns multiple events; this organization controls four events but sanctions more than 300 different table tennis competitions. DMOs are organizations that represent a specific destination and thus help the long-term development of communities through a travel and tourism strategy (Destination Marketing Association International 2012). DMOs include organizations such as sports commissions, convention and visitors bureaus, chambers of commerce, and other similar entities that serve as a link or point of contact for convention, business, and leisure travelers. These organizations are often referred to as host organizations. Chapter 3 provides more information about these types of organizations, especially sports commissions.

The integration of sport and tourism means event planners must be capable of collaborating with a network of different organizations or actors. These sport event networks may include event rights-holder organizations, destination marketing organizations, tourist attractions (e.g., local museums, battlefields), rental companies (e.g., rental cars), airlines, sport venues, accommodation providers (e.g., hotels, motels, campgrounds), local businesses, media, sponsors, stadium authorities, and sport governing bodies (e.g., IOC, USOC). This network of organizations must be committed to working together to plan and implement a successful event. To create a committed network, each organization within the network must provide resources and exhibit trust toward each other (Shonk and Bravo 2010).

All actors within the network seek to leverage the event. Leveraging an event begins by encouraging visitor spending and retaining the visitors' expenditures within the host economy by fostering the tourists' spending and lengthening their stay (Chalip 2004, p. 230). For this reason, many events have other activities surrounding the larger event to encourage multiple-night stays and increased spending at restaurants and other attractions. For example, the National Football League owns the rights to the NFL Experience, which they market as an exciting continuous event surrounding the Super Bowl. It has an interactive theme park offering participatory games, displays, entertainment attractions, kids' football clinics, free autograph sessions, and the largest football memorabilia show ever.

RELATIONSHIP BETWEEN SPORT EVENT MANAGEMENT AND SPORT FACILITY MANAGEMENT

All sporting events require a functional host facility. For event rights holders (e.g., AAU, NCAA), the event venue is the most important factor for determining the site of a nonfixed sporting event that travels between venues (O'Connor and Martin 2009). Event planners are often responsible for negotiating the type of venue to be used for the sporting event. As the event planner negotiates with potential host facilities, she must maintain a realistic image of the prestige of the event. Event venues are generally either public or privately owned facilities. The public facilities may include venues such as armories, municipal stadiums and arenas, convention centers, and fairgrounds, and they may be more flexible in negotiations (Supovitz 2005). An example of a public facility is the Kentucky Exposition Center. Privately owned facilities are generally in the business of making money and are less flexible. Joe Dumars Fieldhouse in Shelby Township, Michigan, is a good example of a privately owned sport facility.

Facility managers are key stakeholders within the sporting event network, and event planners spend a significant amount of time working with them. A facility manager may work for a stadium authority, arena, convention center, armory, or any other of a number of facilities. He is responsible for coordinating all the employees and entities involved in the facility to ensure they meet both short- and long-term goals. In some cases, the facility manager must work with outside vendors or government entities to secure permits. The facility manager may also be responsible for building design and thus may choose material color schemes or purchase new equipment. He may also need to ensure that contracts are fulfilled in addition to maintaining the building and all

corresponding equipment (Fried 2009). Before an event, the facility manager may need to provide certain field specifications to the event planner and help coordinate the design and layout of the sport venue. In addition, issues such as security and concession and merchandise layouts may be discussed. The facility manager may also be responsible for coordinating the walk-through for a site visit before the sporting event.

TYPES OF SPORTING EVENTS

Because of the broad scope of sport, numerous types of sporting events can be planned. The various types of events may differ based on their scope and scale along with the type of market they target. In this section, we discuss the following types of events: mega-events, multisport events, multiple-location events, cross-cultural events, international events, youth events, events for people with disabilities, senior events, family events, and extreme events.

Mega-Events

Mega-events are large short-term, high-profile events capable of having a significant impact on their host communities or countries (Hiller 2000). Sporting events such as the Olympics and the FIFA World Cup are large enough to qualify as mega-events because of their size in terms of prestige, public involvement, social and political influence, media coverage, and economic impact (Getz 2005).

Mega-events can have a significant economic impact through tourism, infrastructure improvements, and economic development. Mega-events also attract interest far beyond the event itself. For example, it is estimated that 50,000 people travel to the Super Bowl's host city each year who will not attend the game (Super Bowl XLVII New Orleans Host Committee 2012). These people travel to attend meetings, parties, and other festivities that surround the event. Beyond the economic impact these events generate, mega-events often create a legacy in the city or country where they are held. For example, local organizers of the 2010 FIFA

World Cup in South Africa hoped the event would leave a lasting legacy much more important than soccer. According to Danny Jordan, executive director of the organizing committee, the event was about nation building and country branding. Through the event, they hoped to drive trade, investment, and tourism to the country (Allmers and Maennig 2009).

Events of this nature involve extensive logistical planning and require significant political and taxpayer support to be successful. For example, the bidding process for the Olympic Games is lengthy and costly. Brazil spent approximately $50 million (U.S.) just on its bid for the 2016 Olympic Games and plans to spend $14.4 billion hosting the games (Courcoulas and Hay 2009).

Multisport Events

Multisport events feature competitions in a host city or host region in a variety of sports. These events often bring together participants from different sports competing under a common theme or organized for a specific community. Although the Olympics are the most notable multisport event, numerous others exist to serve different purposes. Examples of multisport events include the following:

- Pan American Games: an event open to countries in North, South, and Central America
- Maccabiah Games: an event for Jewish athletes
- World Police and Fire Games: an event for active and retired police officers and firefighters
- Amateur Athletic Union's Junior Olympic Games: the largest national multisport event for youth in the United States

Hosting a successful multisport event requires long-term planning, a variety of competition venues, available hotel space, and willing community partners. Although the logistics of managing several different sporting events can be daunting, the advantages of having all the athletes competing in one location can be substantial. Specifically, these events tend to draw more participants and spectators, creating a more exciting event and a

better economic return for the host (Chavis 2008). The Louisville Sports Commission, host of the 2010 NCAA Division II National Championships Festival, estimated the event would attract 70 teams and 800 athletes competing for six national championships, generating an economic impact of $3.5 million (Grant 2009).

Multiple-Location Events

Events spanning multiple locations present special challenges. Competition may take place in several different cities (e.g., soccer's World Cup) or in the same city but in multiple venues (e.g., the Olympics). Smaller events can also take place in multiple venues. For example, a volleyball tournament may be staged in multiple gyms, and ancillary events such as practices, banquets, and awards ceremonies may take place in additional facilities. The complexity of managing multiple sites makes it difficult for one person, or one group of people, to efficiently manage all operations at once.

To manage multiple-location events, event organizers often assign a management team to each venue, creating events within an event. This type of structure allows for more immediate decision making and tighter control over activities. Venue-specific staffing allows the flexibility to deal with issues unique to that location or activity. Typically, venue staff are given the authority to deal with local issues. Larger issues are the responsibility of the main event staff.

Cross-Cultural Events

Cross-cultural events involve interactions between members of different cultural groups. These types of events bring people of different backgrounds together or give people of one culture an opportunity to experience another culture. When staging a cross-cultural event, it is important to understand the cultural norms of the participants and the location. Event organizers need to appreciate differences between cultures because something acceptable in one country may be unacceptable in another. For example, religious differences may prohibit play on Sundays or limit dietary options.

International Events

Many major sporting events are international in nature. It is now easier than ever for athletes to play in other countries and for fans to access events taking place in other countries (Lizandra and Gladden 2005). Some events such as the Olympics, Asian Games, Pan American Games, and Commonwealth Games have different countries competing in multiple sports. Other international competitions bring together multiple countries competing in one sport, such as world championship events. Others, such as the Tour de France and the British Open, feature the best individual athletes from around the world.

From a marketing standpoint, the global appeal of these sports can be very attractive to broadcasters and sponsors. For example, Formula One, an auto racing series featuring drivers and race teams from around the world, can be watched either live or by tape delay in more than 200 countries. Races attract millions of viewers across Europe and in other major markets such as China and Brazil.

International events can also be used to promote a sport or sport entity. American sports have extended their reach beyond borders through international exhibitions or tournaments. The World Baseball Classic, created by Major League Baseball in 2006 and sanctioned by the International Baseball Federation, provides a format for the top players from around the world to compete while promoting the sport internationally. The National Football League hosted international exhibitions, called the American Bowl, from 1986 to 2005 in countries such as Great Britain, Ireland, Germany, Japan, Spain, Australia, and Canada to promote the sport abroad. Since then the NFL has hosted regular-season games in Mexico City and London.

Youth Events

The youth sport market has been steadily growing over the last decade, making youth sports a lucrative industry. According to the National Council of Youth Sports, participation in youth sports has grown from 23 million in 1997 to 44 million in 2008. In addition to the participants, youth sports also tend to attract significant numbers of coaches and family members, which can generate significant business for restaurants and hotels as well as organizers. For example, the Columbia Invitational Memorial Day soccer tournament attracts approximately 9,000 youth athletes to Maryland, generating a sizeable economic impact (Sharrow 2009). Indianapolis attracted 155,000 visitors for amateur sport events from 2009 to 2011 who paid for approximately 62,000 hotel room nights and spent an estimated $62 million (Cutter 2009).

Sponsors also see opportunities with youth sports. The inaugural ESPN Rise Games featured competitions for athletes 10 to 19 years old in the sports of baseball, basketball, field hockey, and track and field at Disney's Wide World of Sports Complex in July of 2009. Media companies such as ESPN, along with sponsors Target, Champion, Powerade, and Under Armour, saw this event as an opportunity to reach young consumers while they are making brand decisions (Mickle 2009).

Management of youth sport events can differ significantly from adult sporting events. Martens (2001) identifies several issues that affect sport programs. First, the needs of the participants must be balanced against the needs of the adults. Although the events are for the young athletes, it is often the parents or coaches who make the events possible and make decisions as to whether or not their athletes or teams participate. Second, the role of competition can vary greatly across youth sport events. Each event has to address whether the focus is competition, with winning being the ultimate reward, or whether the event is recreational, emphasizing participation over winning. The following is a list of some of the larger youth sport governing bodies:

- Amateur Athletic Union
- American Junior Golf Association
- American Youth Soccer Association
- Babe Ruth Baseball
- Little League Baseball
- Pony Baseball and Softball
- Pop Warner
- U.S. Youth Soccer
- USA Football
- USA Hockey

Events for People With Disabilities

A variety of sporting events exist for persons with either physical or intellectual disabilities. Some are traditional sports adapted for people with physical disabilities (wheelchair basketball and sledge hockey), while others have been created specifically for disabled participants (goalball and torball).

The preeminent event for persons with physical disabilities is the Paralympic Games. The Paralympic Games are a multisport, multicountry event governed by the International Paralympic Committee (IPC) and held in conjunction with the Olympic Games. Originally staged for rehabilitation, the Paralympics have grown into a major international sporting event featuring the top disabled athletes in the world. According to the IPC, 4,237 athletes from 164 countries participated in London in 2012. Athletes compete in 26 different summer and winter sports in six different classifications according to their disability: amputee, cerebral palsy, visual impairment, spinal cord injuries, intellectual disability, and a group that includes all those who do not fit into the aforementioned groups.

Similarly, the Deaflympics is an elite sport competition for people with hearing impairments. Summer and winter games are held every four years, and athletes compete in 25 sports. According to the International Committee of Sports for the Deaf, the 21st Summer Deaflympics in Taipei in 2009 attracted 2,493 athletes from 77 countries competing in 20 sports.

The Extremity Games are an extreme sport competition for people with physical impairments. Organized by the Athletes With Disabilities Network (ADN), the Extremity Games have many of the same sports you would find in other extreme sport events. Extremity Games 4 (eX4) in Michigan included competitions in skateboarding, rock climbing, wakeboarding, kayaking, mountain biking, and motocross.

The most prominent event for people with intellectual disabilities is the Special Olympics. Founded as a series of summer camps by Eunice Kennedy Shriver in 1962, the event grew into an international competition by 1968. Today there are local and national competitions in more than 160 countries, with more than 2.5 million athletes competing in 30 different sports. The events are based on a philosophy that people with intellectual disabilities can learn and benefit from participation in sports.

Senior Events

Numerous senior events exist for older participants. The Summer National Senior Games are the largest multisport event in the world for seniors. The games are organized by the National Senior Games Association, a nonprofit member of the United States Olympic Committee. The 2009 National Senior Games in San Francisco attracted more than 10,000 athletes over the age of 50 to participate in 18 medal and 7 demonstration sports. Organizers estimated 20,000 visitors attended the games, generating $35 million in economic impact (Dremann 2009). The 2007 games in Louisville, Kentucky, attracted approximately 12,000 athletes and 25,000 additional friends and family members. In addition to the national games, the organization supports and sanctions member-state competitions.

According to the Louisville Senior Games organizers, senior events are lucrative because senior athletes tend to have high incomes, eat at upscale restaurants, and take advantage of local attractions (Shafer 2007). Even smaller senior events can have a significant impact on the local economy. The Senior League Softball World Series costs $225,000 to organize and operate, but it delivers an estimated economic impact of $1.2 million (Shortridge 2009).

Family Events

Family events provide families with opportunities to gather and enjoy sport. In these events, family togetherness and educational components often take precedence over competition. An example of an event often designed with family in mind is a fishing derby, where adults and youth spend time together fishing. Many of these events will have games, contests, and educational components on water safety and fishing techniques. Another good example is the All-American Soap Box Derby. Since 1934 children have built and raced nonmotorized cars (All-American Soap Box Derby 2009). Winners of local events can move on to race in the world championship finals. In addition to the races, there are several educational and entertainment programs for families.

Some organizations have added family-friendly elements to their events in order to widen their appeal. The National Soccer Festival, a collegiate soccer event in Fort Wayne, Indiana, draws some of the top collegiate soccer teams in the country. Organizers have turned this into a family event by adding activities attractive to youth soccer participants and their families. To appeal to families, the event features live music, youth soccer clinics, activities for kids, and a variety of food vendors in addition to autograph and photo sessions. This combination of activities has created an event that draws large crowds in addition to quality competition (Bogle 2008).

Extreme Events

In recent years, new extreme sport events have emerged. Some of the more popular extreme sport events are the Dew Tour and the X Games. The Dew Tour hosts five multisport skateboarding, BMX, and motocross events across the United States. The Winter Dew Tour features freeskiing and snowboarding events. The X Games are an Olympic-style extreme sport event hosting annual summer and winter competitions. The focus on emerging extreme sports makes these events attractive to a new generation of sports fans.

More important to event organizers, these events provide a valuable connection between sponsors and young, active consumers. For example, Gatorade recently became naming rights sponsor for an amateur extreme sports tour. Now known as the Gatorade Free Flow Tour, Gatorade has an opportunity to extend its brand beyond traditional sports through 50 summer and 10 winter competitions (Mickle 2009).

SUMMARY

Sport event management has evolved from the early days of athletes celebrating the end of the harvest by traveling from city to city within ancient Greece to the lucrative and specialized industry it is today. As the sport industry continues to grow, so do the number of sport-related event management jobs. Almost every professional sports franchise and collegiate athletic program hires some type of event manager. Today's sport event planner must be able to manage his personal life along with having strong conceptual, interpersonal, technical, and time management skills. The event planner must also be able to negotiate with sport event venues and recognize the importance of sport tourism and the need for collaborating with a wide variety of network organizations.

Sporting events can also be quite diverse, and each type of event presents its own opportunities and challenges for event organizers. Events vary in size from small local events to mega-events such as the Olympics and the FIFA World Cup. Events also vary in the groups they reach, as competitions for young participants, seniors, and disabled spectators each appeal to different demographic groups. The challenge for event organizers is to be flexible to the needs of different groups and different sports.

LEARNING ACTIVITIES

1. Go to one of the free websites listed in this chapter (see the section Career Paths in Sport Event Management). Print out a job description of interest to you and pertinent to event management from one of these sites. Write a paragraph describing how the job description requires the applicant to have one of the following skills: interpersonal and communication skills, time management skills, and technology skills.

2. Quidditch is a sport based on the Harry Potter books and movies and is currently played by many young people. However, most people could not fully describe the sport if you were to ask them. Therefore, to learn more about quidditch, please go to the

website http://magazine.ucla.edu/features/brooms_up and read the article by Wendy Soderburg from *UCLA Magazine*. Also on the site is a YouTube video that you can click to retrieve additional information. After reviewing the information on this site, please answer the following questions:

- List some of the rules and terms used in the game of quidditch.

- Describe the culture of the game of quidditch.
- What is the relationship between sport tourism and a relatively new game such as quidditch?
- Beyond YouTube and Facebook, what are some additional ways to market the game of quidditch?

REFERENCES

All-American Soap Box Derby. 2009. What is the SBD? aasbd.org. Available: www.soapboxracing.com/about.htm.

Allen, J. 2009. *Event planning: The ultimate guide to successful meetings, corporate events, fundraising galas, conferences, conventions, incentives and other special events.* 2nd ed. Mississauga, ON: Wiley.

Allmers, S., and Maennig, W. 2009. Economic impacts of the FIFA Soccer World Cups in France 1998, Germany 2006, and outlook for South Africa 2010. *Eastern Economic Journal* 35:500-519.

Bogle, M.J. 2008. A premier family event: The national soccer festival. *BusinessPeople.* [Online]. March 1. www.highbeam.com/doc/1P3-1458467711.html.

Breen, T.H. 2010. Horses and gentlemen: The cultural significance of gambling among the gentry of Virginia. In *Sport in America: From colonial leisure to celebrity figures and globalization* (vol. 2), ed. D. Wiggins. Champaign, IL: Human Kinetics.

Carbonell, C. 2012. Social media: Six ways to build your brand. *SportsEvents* 9 (1): 12.

Chalip, L. 2004. Beyond impact: A general model for sport event leverage. In *Sport tourism: Interrelationships, impacts and issues*, ed. B.W. Ritchie and D. Adair. Tonawanda, NY: Channel View Publications.

Chavis, S. 2008. Multi-sport festivals: Broader events, bigger returns. *SportsEvents* 5 (May): 69.

Courcoulas, C., and G. Hay. 2009. The smart choice for the Olympic host. *New York Times*, October 2, B2.

Cutter, C. 2009. Youth, high school events may be next sports thrust. *Indianapolis Business Journal* 29 (52): 16.

Destination Marketing Association International. 2012. About the industry. Available: www.destinationmarketing.org/page.asp?pid=21.

Dremann, S. 2009. 2009 Senior Games: Senior Games a winner with local merchants. *Palo Alto Weekly.* [Online]. August 7. Available: www.almanacnews.com/news/show_story.php?id=4591.

Eugenio-Martin, J.L. 2003. Modelling determinants of tourism demand as a five-stage process: A discrete choice methodological approach. *Tourism and Hospitality Research* 4 (4): 341-354.

Fairley, S. 2003. In search of relived social experience: Group-based nostalgia sport tourism. *Journal of Sport Management* 17:284-304.

Fried, G. 2009. *Managing sport facilities.* 2nd ed. Champaign, IL: Human Kinetics.

Gems, R.R., L.J. Borish, and G. Pfister. 2008. *Sports in American history: From colonization to globalization.* Champaign, IL: Human Kinetics.

Getz, D. 2005. *Event management and event tourism.* New York: Cognizant Communication Group.

Gibson, H.J. 1998. Sport tourism: A critical analysis of research. *Sport Management Review* 1 (1): 45-76.

Goldblatt, J. 2011. *Special events: A new generation and the next frontier.* Hoboken, NJ: Wiley.

Graham, S., L.D. Neirotti, and J.J. Goldblatt. 2001. *The ultimate guide to sports marketing.* New York: McGraw-Hill.

Grant, M. 2009. D-II championships boost for Louisville. *Louisville Courier-Journal*, December 4, C4.

Higham, J.E.S., and T.D. Hinch. 2003. Sport, space, and time: Effects of the Otago Highlanders franchise on tourism. *Journal of Sport Management* 17:235-257.

Hiller, H.H. 2000. Mega-events, urban boosterism and growth strategies: An analysis of the objectives and legitimations of the Cape Town 2004 Olympic bid. *International Journal of Urban and Regional Research* 24 (2): 449-458.

Hoyle, L. 2002. *Event marketing.* Hoboken, NJ: Wiley.

Kelly, J. 2000. Looking to sports for development dollars. *American City & County* 115:20-21.

Kurtzman, J., and J. Zauhar. 1998. Sport tourism: A business inherency or an innate compulsion? *Visions in Leisure and Business* 17 (2): 21-30.

Kurtzman, J., and J. Zauhar. 2003. A wave in time: The sports tourism phenomena. *Journal of Sport Tourism* 8 (1): 35-47.

Lizandra, M., and J.M. Gladden. 2005. International sport. In *Principles and practice of sport management* (2nd ed.), ed. L.P. Masteralexis, C.A. Barr, and M.A. Hums, 166-194. Sudbury, MA: Jones and Bartlett.

Martens, R. 2001. *Directing youth sport programs.* Champaign, IL: Human Kinetics.

Masteralexis, L.P., C.A. Barr, and M.A. Hums. 2009. *Principles and practice of sport management*. Sudbury, MA: Jones and Bartlett.

Masterman, G. 2009. *Strategic sports event management*. 2nd ed. Oxford, UK: Butterworth-Heinemann.

Mickle, T. 2009. Gatorade's name on amateur tour. *Street and Smith's SportsBusiness Journal*, March 23, 6.

Miller, R.K., and K. Washington. 2012. *Sports marketing 2012*. Loganville, GA: Richard K. Miller & Associates.

Moutinho, L. 2001. Consumer behaviour in tourism. *European Journal of Marketing* 21 (10): 5-44.

National Association of Sports Commissions. 2011. *Bylaws*. Available: www.sportscommissions.org/Documents/Amended%20NASC%20Bylaws%20(Approved%204-12-2011).pdf.

National Association of Sports Commissions. 2012. About NASC: Who we are. Available: www.sportscommissions.org/About-NASC.

O'Connor, J.T., and M. Martin. 2009. 2009 Market report: Stability & optimism. *SportsEvents* 6 (March): 26-33.

Rader, B.G. 2009. *American sports: From the age of folk games to the age of televised sports*. 6th ed. Upper Saddle River, NJ: Pearson Education.

Reisinger, Y. 2001. Concepts of tourism, hospitality, and leisure services. In *Service quality management in hospitality, tourism, and leisure*, ed. J. Kandampully, C. Mok, and B. Sparks. Binghamton, NY: Haworth Hospitality Press.

Robinson, T., and S. Gammon. 2004. A question of primary and secondary motives: Revisiting and applying the sport tourism framework. *Journal of Sport Tourism* 9 (3): 221-233.

Shafer, S. 2007. Let the games begin. *Louisville Courier Journal*. [Online]. June 22. Available: www.courier-journal.com/apps/pbcs.dll/article?aid=2007706220446.

Sharrow, R. 2009. Not kids play: Youth sports eyed to boost Maryland tourism. *Baltimore Business Journal*. [Online].

July 31. Available: http://baltimore.bizjournals.com/baltimore/stories/2009/08/03/focus2.html.

Shonk, D.J., and G. Bravo. 2010. Interorganizational support and commitment: A framework for sporting event networks. *Journal of Sport Management* 24:272-290.

Shortridge, D. 2009. Delaware set to plunge into youth sports market. *The News Journal*. [Online]. August 17. Available: www.delawareonline.com/article/20090817/BUSINESS/908170329/1006/NEWS

Silvers, J.R. 2004. *Professional event coordination*. Hoboken, NJ: Wiley.

Standeven, J., and P. DeKnop. 1999. *Sport tourism*. Champaign, IL: Human Kinetics.

Struna, N.L. 2009. American sports, 1607-1860. In *Encyclopedia of sports in America: A history from foot races to extreme sports* (vol. 1), ed. M.R. Nelson. Westport, CT: Greenwood Press.

Super Bowl XLVII New Orleans Host Committee. 2012. *Frequently asked questions*. Available: www.nolasuperbowl.com/FAQ.php#Q3.

Supovitz, F. 2005. *The sports event management and marketing playbook*. Hoboken, NJ: Wiley.

Swaddling, J. 1999. *The ancient Olympic Games*. Austin: University of Texas Press.

Swanson, R.A., and B. Spears. 1995. *History of sport and physical education in the United States*. Boston: McGraw-Hill.

Thwaites, D., and S. Chadwick. 2005. Service quality perspectives in sport tourism. *Sport in Society* 8:321-337.

Turco, D.M., R. Riley, and K. Swart. 2002. *Sport tourism*. Morgantown, WV: Fitness Information Technology.

Wann, D.L., B. Allen, and A.R. Rochelle. 2004. Using sport fandom as an escape: Searching for relief from under-stimulation and over-stimulation. *International Sports Journal* 8 (1): 104-113.

Weed, M., and C. Bull. 2004. *Sports tourism: Participants, policy and providers*. Oxford, UK: Elsevier Butterworth-Heinemann.

CHAPTER 2

Event Conceptualization

Chapter Objectives

After completing the chapter, the reader should be able to do the following:

- Understand the process involved in conceptualizing and developing an event.
- Adopt a systematic approach to event planning.
- Identify the various stakeholders in event planning.
- Outline the steps in developing a SWOT analysis.
- Identify a purpose and develop a mission, goals, and objectives.
- Develop timelines, manage logistics, and plan for contingencies.

Michael Belot is director for the 2012 Ryder Cup, golf's most patriotic and prestigious international team competition, matching the top U.S. golf professionals against those of Europe. Before being named Ryder Cup director, he was the operations coordinator for the 2002 and 2004 PGA Championship and the championship director for both the 2006 and 2009 PGA Championship. In addition to his work with the PGA of America, Michael consulted with the NFL on the postgame show for Super Bowl XLV and was on a planning committee for Super Bowl XLVI.

Q: How do you begin planning for an event the size and scope of the Ryder Cup?

A: The first things I really focused on were establishing the local relationships and all the people you need. We also need to make sure that we magnify all the opportunities we can. There is a lot of strategic planning regarding pricing, packaging, and trying to give customers what they are looking for.

Q: How do you work with so many different entities?

A: One of the biggest things in this job is working with so many entities and so many stakeholders. They range from the Medina membership, to the government and county officials, to all our vendors, to my staff, and to the 4,000-plus volunteers that we have working on the event. One of the major aspects of my job is managing personalities and this is one of the things I always reference when people ask what the job encompasses. You always need to know where everything stands, and you always need to keep everything moving forward, because you have an end goal and date. We have the ultimate deadline, as the Ryder Cup dates are not going to change. You need to be ready for that week as opposed to other projects that can be pushed off for a week or two.

Q: What is your approach to leadership?

A: What I have found is that the more responsibility and the more power or authority you give people, the more you are going to get in return, and the more excited they are going to be in the process and engaged in what they are doing. With all these details, there is no time to micromanage everything. You really need to have good people, trust that they're going to do the job, and monitor things from a management level.

Q: With so many people involved, how do you go about making decisions?

A: It's a collaborative process. Although I am the person who makes the most decisions, I want to make sure everyone is on board because you don't do anything in a vacuum. You always need to make sure people are aware of what is going on, that they feel supported and engaged. If people do not feel engaged or that they are part of a process, they tune out. A lot of times it is just letting people know of the decision I made so they are aware of it, they're not surprised, and they are a part of the process. There are multiple decisions made every day, and you try to be as collaborative as possible.

Q: What kind of research do you do when planning an event?

A: I look not just at how other golf entities are planning events, whether it be the U.S. Open or the Masters to see how my competitors and cohorts are doing things, but across all entertainment venues as well. I've gotten ideas about how to do things from going to the Super Bowl, Final Four, and even just NBA regular-season basketball games. Whatever it may be, I am really looking at competitors to see what they are doing. It gives you a great sense of what you are doing well and what you could do better. I read a lot on sport business and trends. Some of the greatest ideas are borrowed from others and made applicable to your own event.

Q: What are you going to do to set this event apart from other events?

A: The biggest thing we have focused on is the spectator experience. There are so many people out on the golf course, but there is so little golf being played. That gives us a great opportunity to engage the spectators and enhance their experience outside of just watching golf. Some of the things we have done is put together an extensive video board and entertainment program. We have really switched things out so that people who are waiting for golf to come through are going to be entertained in a whole new way they have never experienced before in a golf tournament. It's going to be a lot more festive. We are going to have things such as face painters and official Ryder Cup ambassadors to make peoples' experience feel a little more patriotic. We are looking to add all sorts of things to focus on the spectator, because ultimately they're your customer and you want them to keep on coming back. We are hoping this will be one of the greatest spectator experiences people have ever had at a golf tournament.

Q: What are the biggest challenges you face in planning this event?

A: The biggest challenges are keeping everybody informed of what is going on and making sure everyone gets the proper say. There are 900 Medina members and 200 PGA staff members at PGA headquarters, so letting all people know what's going on is a challenge because there are so many different things happening from day to day. Other challenges are related to preparing for the unexpected. A large amount of parking and security planning takes place. You need to have a backup plan for your backup plan. You need to prepare for weather you may not see coming. You need to prepare and make the event as safe and easy for people to get in and out of as absolutely possible while preparing for things you hope never happen. There are so many things that can happen that are out of your hands that you may need to react to.

EVENT PLANNING

Planning for sporting events can be quite complex when you consider the number of decisions that have to be made and the number of people involved in those decisions. Specifically, multiple stakeholders are involved (local organizing committees, participants, sanctioning bodies, facilities, sponsors, and so on), and multiple tasks have to be undertaken (such as logistical planning, marketing, and leadership). Further, events go through multiple stages, and event planning takes on different roles at each stage. Mallen and Adams (2008) outline an event planning model with four different phases: (1) the event development phase; (2) the event operational planning phase; (3) the event implementation, monitoring, and management phase; and (4) the event evaluation and renewal phase (table 2.1).

During the first phase, the event development phase, event organizers envision an event and champion the intention to hold an event (Wanklin 2005). During this phase, the event organization is established to facilitate the planning process.

Table 2.1 Event Planning Model

Event phase	Tasks
Event development phase	Event is envisioned. Event organization is created.
Event operational planning phase	Internal and external environments are analyzed. Goals and objectives are set. Key decisions are made.
Event implementation, monitoring, and management phase	Resources are gathered and allocated. Staff are trained. Activities are managed.
Event evaluation and renewal phase	Results are matched to objectives. Plans are modified based on results.

Supovitz (2005) argues that successful event planning must involve stakeholders such as sponsors, broadcasters, communities, and facilities throughout the event planning process. Large events will frequently utilize a local organizing committee (LOC). These groups are often made up of members from different stakeholder groups and are enlisted with the task of planning and managing an event.

For example, an LOC made up of a variety of stakeholders with a wide range of experience in hosting events was created for the 2010 NCAA Division I Men's Basketball Championship first- and second-round games being played in Buffalo, New York. The group chose former Buffalo mayor Anthony Masiello as chair of the committee (MAAC Sports 2009). The other members of the committee included the following:

- Representatives from the Metro Atlantic Athletic Conference
- Athletic directors from two local universities
- Representatives from the local media
- A representative from the local police department
- Representatives from the Niagara Frontier Transportation Authority
- The director of special events for the City of Buffalo
- Representatives from the Buffalo Niagara Convention & Visitors Bureau
- The director of amateur athletics for the Buffalo Sabres hockey club

During the planning phase, the members of the organizing group undertake activities to turn their vision into reality. After careful situational analysis of the organization and environment, they set goals and objectives for the event. In addition, it is during this phase that details related to what needs to be done to meet those goals and objectives are outlined. Key decision areas at the planning stage include the name and theme of the event, the program or schedule of events, the timing and duration, and the location. These decisions will lead to more decisions about budget and personnel (Mallen and Adams 2008).

Planning continues during the implementation phase. During this phase, event organizers gather resources, train staff, implement management procedures, and coordinate activities (Wanklin 2005). Leadership is important during this phase to make sure all activities come together as they should. Further, event plans need to be flexible because incidents may occur or situations may change, necessitating changes to the plan. Great ideas, if mismanaged, can fail if event organizers do not understand what it takes to effectively implement the event.

During the evaluation phase, results are matched with objectives to ensure the event is going as planned. Event organizers assess various activities throughout the event and after the event to ensure desired results are being achieved. If things are not going as planned during the event, plans may need to be readjusted. If at the end of the event the results do not match the objectives, organizers may need to amend, modify, or completely change plans for the next event. In addition, event planners should always be asking how they can make the event better. This is vital because customers will expect more, better, or different experiences from the next event.

LEADERSHIP AND DECISION MAKING IN EVENT MANAGEMENT

Strong leadership is frequently the key to a successful event. Without good leadership, event planners can be left directionless and unmotivated. Therefore it is important to understand the differences between being a manager and a leader. Goldblatt (2008) explains that managers are people who make decisions, assign tasks, allocate resources, and solve problems. Leaders, on the other hand, motivate and inspire others to achieve the event's goals. A leader will be able to provide a vision of how to achieve the event's outcomes and will be able to collaborate with others to achieve those outcomes.

Some event leaders prefer to be very hands-on, focusing on every task and every decision. Others may prefer a more democratic or collaborative process. The effectiveness of each style often depends on the type of staff and organization. A staff with little experience or direction (e.g., new employees, volunteers) may need more direction, requiring more control from people in leadership positions. Conversely, leaders with staffs of experienced or more qualified people are more likely to cede more control to others in order to utilize their skills and engage them in the planning process. This is especially true of large-scale events where the tasks are too large for one person, or even a small team, to handle on his own. In these cases, the leadership has to be more collaborative, giving more control over decision making to others in the organization.

Given the complexity of the decision-making process and the importance of making good decisions, it is essential to understand what goes into making collaborative decisions. Successful events can be seen as partnerships between stakeholders, athletes, and spectators. Making decisions is much easier when event organizers understand what each party wants from the event. Each stakeholder may have expectations of what the event will generate for them in terms of revenue, goodwill, or experience. Further, each stakeholder is risking something in terms of money, time, or support. Understanding each party's expected benefits and risks will facilitate the decision-making process.

Organizers also need to define levels of authority and determine how both short-term and long-term decisions are made (Supovitz 2005). Organizers have to ask who will have authority in making decisions—the event manager, event staff, committee, or task force. Defining roles and responsibilities for key decision makers allows for a better understanding of the authority each unit possesses (e.g., will this person or committee have the authority to hire personnel, commit to purchases, sign contracts, and so on). Further, event organizers will have to define which stakeholders will have input into decisions (e.g., the sanctioning body, local government, host, or committee).

These questions can often be addressed by developing an organizational chart. An organizational chart is a document that shows how different units are related. In addition, organizational charts define reporting structures by illustrating who reports to whom. Figure 2.1 illustrates a sample organizational chart. Supovitz (2005)

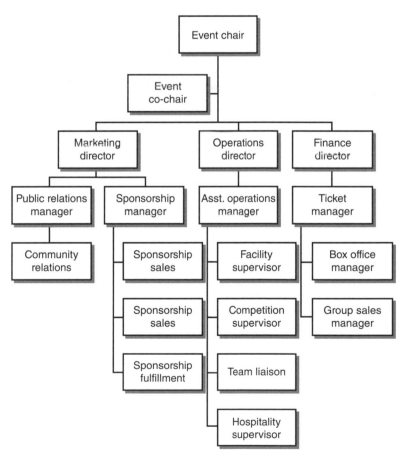

■ **Figure 2.1** Sample event organizational chart.

argues that organizational charts are important because they define areas of responsibility and accountability, streamline decision making, and communicate how functional areas fit into the overall management structure.

BRAINSTORMING IN EVENT MANAGEMENT

Brainstorming is a useful technique for identifying opportunities to make an event unique. In a typical brainstorming session, several members are brought together to discuss and explore concepts for an event. The team effort allows members to encourage and stimulate each other's thinking. For sporting events, brainstorming sessions often incorporate multiple stakeholder groups. For example, a championship golf event may include representatives from the local sports commission and tourism board in addition to the local organizers.

To increase creativity, Osborn (1963) suggests that participants in brainstorming sessions focus on quality, withhold criticism, welcome unusual ideas, and improve ideas. While focusing on the objectives, members should try to say all the positive things that come to their minds. Negatives can be saved for later. At this stage, it is acceptable to ignore restraints and dream big, with the goal of finding the right idea (Bowdin et al. 2006). Sometimes the worst ideas lead to good ideas; therefore it is important to be accepting of all ideas while leaving the feasibility questions for later.

Brainstorming sessions are often the result of an issue or crisis. For example, high school athletic directors faced with tight budgets might get together to brainstorm ideas to cut budgets without cutting sports. Or a new event may bring people together to develop a name and logo for the event. The following is a list of potential issues that could be resolved through brainstorming.

- Creating an event brand
- Planning an effective event program
- Developing a SWOT analysis
- Creating ideas for promotional programs
- Formulating effective pricing programs
- Identifying sponsorship prospects
- Conceiving additional sponsorship benefits
- Finding new target markets
- Categorizing event risks
- Identifying ways to recruit and reward volunteers
- Devising methods of developing community support
- Suggesting ways to maximize revenues
- Locating areas to cut costs
- Recognizing areas for contingency planning
- Generating customer service initiatives

PURPOSE OF THE EVENT

The purpose of the event will drive many decisions related to event design and event planning. Events can serve many purposes; therefore it is important for event organizers to clearly identify what they want to accomplish. Is the purpose of your event to make money, create an image for your community or cause, attract tourists, or provide memorable experiences? Purposes vary widely among events. Beyond competition and revenue, some of the other common purposes include the following:

- Promoting an issue: The San Antonio Stock Show and Rodeo is an annual rodeo event that raises awareness in support of agriculture education.

- Raising funds for a cause: The Maine Shrine Lobster Bowl Classic is a high school senior all-star football game sponsored by the Kora Shrine to raise funds for orthopedic and burn care services.

- Promoting an image for an organization: The U.S. Army All-American Bowl is an all-star game showcasing the top high school football players. Event organizers must create the best possible experience for both players and fans. The broader purpose, however, is to promote the Army's positive brand attributes.

- Driving tourism and promoting economic impact: The Rose Bowl football game in Pasadena annually matches two of college football's top teams; however, the game's original purpose was quite different. The event was started by members of Pasadena's Valley Hunt Club to attract tourism by showcasing the region's great weather.

• Meeting sponsorship objectives: Australian beer brand XXXX Gold created a new sport called beach cricket and sponsors the XXXX Gold Beach Cricket Tri-Nations Series. They developed the event because they wanted to take advantage of Australians' passion for cricket, but other beer companies had existing relationships with the other major competitions.

• Promoting a sport: The World Baseball Classic's purpose is to grow the game internationally. The event features participating teams from 16 different countries, and media coverage reaches more than 200 countries (Fisher 2009).

Further, event organizers should also consider for whom the event is planned because different groups may have different purposes for supporting an event. Therefore, it is imperative to understand your stakeholders and their primary needs. For example, each of the following stakeholders may have different needs:

• Sponsors: Sponsors seek multiple benefits including increasing sales of their products, generating awareness of a brand, building an image for a brand, reaching target markets, and providing hospitality for key customers or employees.

• Broadcast partners: Broadcast partners seek to maximize viewership in order to maximize value for advertisers.

• The local community: Community partners seek to generate economic impact, attract tourists, and create exposure for the location.

• Charitable causes: Given that many events have charitable connections, it is important to understand the charity's needs, which may range from promoting its cause to raising funds for the organization.

• Sport governing bodies: Governing bodies provide a regulatory function by providing oversight, setting rules, and sanctioning events. The mission of these organizations is to provide competitive opportunities or promote the sport.

A few examples of governing bodies include the National Federation of State High School Associations, USA Triathlon, the United States Equestrian Federation, and the United States Youth Soccer Association.

Consider an NCAA championship event. These events have multiple stakeholders including the governing body, the community hosting the event, the host committee, and sponsors. The governing body, the NCAA, may be concerned with providing an elite competitive environment and an excellent experience for participants. The community's primary purpose for supporting the event will most likely be to generate tax dollars and economic impact through tourist spending. Sponsors may be most concerned with product exposure or product sampling. Event organizers have the task of identifying their stakeholders, their stakeholders' objectives, and how to deliver results.

Questions to Ask When Assessing Your Stakeholders

• Who are your key stakeholders? Do you have multiple stakeholders? If so, who are the primary stakeholders?

• Are there conflicts of interest between stakeholders?

• What resources do your stakeholders possess?

• What are your stakeholders' needs? Expectations?

• What can you do to meet stakeholders' expectations?

• How can you positively influence stakeholder outcomes?

• How can you avoid negatively influencing stakeholder outcomes?

CHOOSING THE TYPE OF EVENT

Considering the many purposes for staging events and the many different beneficiaries served by events, it is important to choose an event that will best meet relevant stakeholders' needs. To serve some purposes, a large full-scale event may be necessary, while other purposes may be best served by smaller, local events. There are also several different formats for sporting events. Will it be a tournament or a single-game event? Will it be competitive or recreational? Will it be for young participants? Will it include participants with special needs?

In addition, event managers need to consider whether or not they have the resources (time, money, people, and facilities) necessary to make the event a success. For example, a local high school may need to develop an event to raise funds for a building project. Hosting a high-profile professional golf tournament would have the potential to attract a lot of attention and revenue; however, it would not be feasible considering the limited resources available to the school. Instead, the school would be better off planning an intimate golf scramble to attract local donors; this event would meet their purpose while making use of available resources.

Swart (2005) suggests four additional factors organizers should consider when selecting an event (see table 2.2). First, event organizers need to consider the target market and must design activities that will be appropriate for the target market. Second, they must consider the time required to plan the event because larger events require significantly longer lead times. Third, the timing of the event, including scheduling, setup, and breakdown, should also be considered. Fourth, organizers must take into account the availability and size of the facility and the suitability of the location.

SWOT ANALYSIS

Information may be the most important resource during event planning. A valuable strategic planning tool is a situational analysis, or SWOT analysis. The goal of this type of analysis is to identify factors to exploit (strengths and opportunities) or minimize (weaknesses and threats). A well-developed SWOT analysis helps you analyze the state of your event or organization and prepares you to make better decisions as you plan your event.

Strengths and weaknesses are internal and may include factors such as resources (human or financial), structure, and marketing efforts. Strengths are resources, competencies, and advantages your organization or event possesses. Weaknesses, on the other hand, are often direct opposites of strengths.

Potential Organizational Strengths

- Event characteristics
- Financial capacity
- Staff experience
- Community support
- Brand strength and awareness
- Existing technology
- Available planning time
- Facility and location
- History and tradition
- Leadership skill

Potential Organizational Weaknesses

- Event limitations
- Financial restrictions

Table 2.2 Factors to Consider During Event Planning

Factor	Considerations
Target market	Who is your target market? What will you have to do to appeal to that target market?
Planning	How much time do you need to plan the event? How much time will it take to organize all the activities necessary for this event to meet your expectations?
Execution	How much time will it take to execute the event? How much time will need to be invested in preevent and postevent activities?
Location	Do you have an appropriate facility for what you have planned? Is the location appropriate for what you have planned?

- Untrained staff
- Lack of community support
- Brand image
- Technological competence
- Short planning cycle
- Facility and location
- Lack of history
- Leadership inexperience

Once strengths and weaknesses have been identified and dealt with, the organization is better able to handle opportunities and threats (Graham, Neirotti, and Goldblatt 2001). Opportunities and threats are external to the organization and may include factors related to the economic, social, technical, legal, or competitive environments. Opportunities often represent areas for increased efficiency or new growth. Threats are incidents or entities that may endanger your event's success.

Potential Environmental Opportunities

- Potential sponsors
- Potential partners
- Untapped resources
- Underserved target markets
- Copromotional opportunities
- Economic conditions
- Social trends
- Technological advances
- Political and legal environment
- Industry trends

Potential Environmental Weaknesses

- Competitors
- Weather
- Environmental concerns
- Community dissent
- Labor, supplier, or transportation disputes
- Unfavorable economic conditions
- Political or legal uncertainty

It is not sufficient to merely identify your strengths, weaknesses, opportunities, and threats.

It is important to thoroughly analyze each factor in order to appreciate any potential implications. Figure 2.2 gives a brief example of implications associated with a SWOT analysis for a regional amateur golf tournament.

A SWOT analysis requires an honest assessment of each factor. All too often, event organizers choose to focus on the good and trivialize the bad. This shortsightedness leads to poor planning and, ultimately, poor results. For instance, your area may experience heavy rainfall in the month of May. If you were planning the golf tournament in the previous example, this would be a serious threat. You could choose to ignore this and hope for good weather, or you could take the threat seriously, making contingency plans for bad weather. If event organizers believe weaknesses or threats are minor, they may be ignored. But if these weaknesses or threats are major, appropriate steps should be taken to minimize them. Consider another example. For the 2002 world basketball championships in Indianapolis, organizers set a ticket goal of 244,000 based on ticket sales at previous tournaments in Toronto and Athens. This assumption may have seemed reasonable given Americans' preference for basketball and the fact most of the world's best players would be participating (Moran 2002). However, a closer look would have revealed some troubling weaknesses and threats. For example, American basketball fans do not have a strong affinity for international basketball, and the possibility of the U.S. team not making the final rounds could be catastrophic for ticket sales. Further, the event was held over Labor Day weekend, the traditional end of summer and start of football season. The dilemma in this case is determining which is more important. As it turned out, the weaknesses and threats were serious, and attendance fell well short of organizers' goals.

DEVELOPING A MISSION FOR THE EVENT

The event's mission provides it with direction. Without direction, planning and decision making

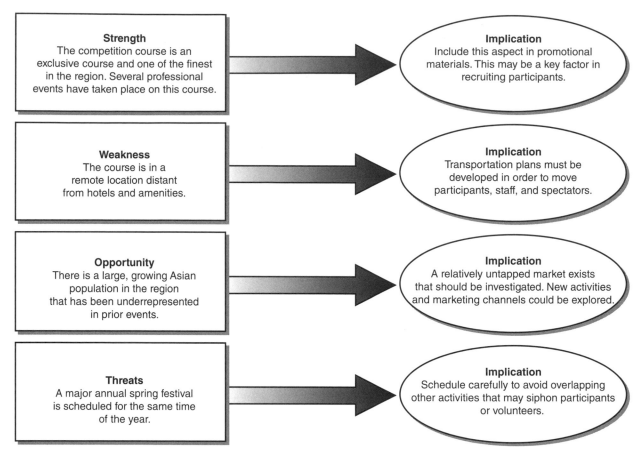

Strength
The competition course is an exclusive course and one of the finest in the region. Several professional events have taken place on this course.

Implication
Include this aspect in promotional materials. This may be a key factor in recruiting participants.

Weakness
The course is in a remote location distant from hotels and amenities.

Implication
Transportation plans must be developed in order to move participants, staff, and spectators.

Opportunity
There is a large, growing Asian population in the region that has been underrepresented in prior events.

Implication
A relatively untapped market exists that should be investigated. New activities and marketing channels could be explored.

Threats
A major annual spring festival is scheduled for the same time of the year.

Implication
Schedule carefully to avoid overlapping other activities that may siphon participants or volunteers.

■ **Figure 2.2** SWOT analysis for a regional golf tournament.

can become difficult and ineffective. Given that events can have many purposes and serve many different stakeholders, it is vitally important for event organizers to identify and communicate their mission to ensure that decisions and activities related to the event serve the purpose of the event. To communicate the event's mission, organizations often develop mission statements. A mission statement is a brief declaration that describes who the organization is; explains what the organization does; and communicates the organization's purpose, philosophy, and values (Hums and MacLean 2009). Good mission statements convey a concise message understandable by everyone in the organization. Every word should have a purpose. That said, mission statements often take a considerable amount of time to write and finalize.

Women's Tri-Fitness is a competition that features female athletes competing in fitness routines, fitness skills, and an obstacle course.

Their mission outlines who they are and what they promote:

To present a women's sporting event with a foundation based on dedication to health, fitness, and the competitive spirit; and an event which embodies a realistically attainable level of athleticism that could be readily identifiable to the general public as well as to the most ardent sports enthusiast.

Sometimes an event's mission can be short while still effectively communicating what the event should be all about. For example, the mission of the Wilmington Grand Prix, a local cycling event, is direct but still communicates enough to guide event planning:

To conduct a sporting event that is respected on the national cycling circuit while creating an urban festival that showcases Downtown Wilmington.

SETTING GOALS AND OBJECTIVES

Goal setting is a very important part of the planning process because goals and objectives provide direction. Without direction, it is possible to waste important resources on activities that do not serve the event's mission or stakeholders. Further, goals and objectives define expectations for the event as well as how the success or failure of an event will be measured. Once defined, strategies and tactics can be developed that will support individual objectives.

At this stage of the process, it is important for event organizers to envision the future of the event, thinking about what needs to be achieved in order to realize the event's mission. Although the terms are often used interchangeably, the following examples define *goals* as broad statements and *objectives* as quantifiable statements that support individual goals.

Goals are broad, qualitative statements that provide direction in support of the event's mission. Goals may be financial or strategic. Examples of goals include the following:

- Maximize attendance or participation.
- Create value for sponsors.
- Create a positive image for the host community.
- Attract tourists to the region.
- Raise money for charity.
- Promote the sport and generate goodwill.
- Increase overall customer service.

Objectives are specific, quantitative statements that serve as measurable indicators of whether or not the organization is meeting its goals. Good objectives are specific, measurable, achievable, realistic, and timely (SMART). The following is an example of some goals and objectives that a high school basketball tournament organizing committee may use.

Goal 1: Increase attendance.

Objective 1: Retain 90 percent of last year's all-tournament package purchasers.

Objective 2: Sell 200 new all-tournament packages.

Objective 3: Sell 1,200 single-session tickets per session.

Goal 2: Attract the highest quality basketball teams in the state.

Objective 1: Recruit at least four teams ranked in the top 20 in the state.

Objective 2: Recruit at least four local teams.

Objective 3: Recruit at least two teams with a recognized star player.

PLANNING LOGISTICS

Several major logistical issues need to be addressed at the planning stage, specifically decisions related to date, time, location, and duration. Remaining logistical issues will be addressed as the planning process proceeds.

- Date: Event organizers should consider major local events, competing sporting events, or important holidays when scheduling. Other events can be either a help or a hindrance. For example, few major events are scheduled around Super Bowl weekend because the game tends to dominate media coverage and attract most Americans' attention. However, the Ultimate Fighting Championship (UFC) routinely schedules major fights in Las Vegas during Super Bowl weekend because that weekend attracts large numbers of affluent sports fans to the city. For outdoor events, time of the year is especially important because weather can be either an advantage or a major deterrent to an event's success (the weather is great on the Gulf Coast, except during hurricane season).

- Time: When setting the time for events, event managers need to consider how long each contest will take. For events with multiple matches (e.g., tournaments), managers need to consider the number of contests, the time necessary to prepare the facility between contests, and the amount of rest competitors need between contests. Similarly, you have to consider constraints your target market may face. Schedule too early in the day and you may make it difficult for some to attend because of work, school, or other commitments.

Schedule too late and some may not be able to attend because of tomorrow's work, school, or other commitments. The media play a role in start times for televised events because broadcasters seek to maximize viewers and fill available time slots.

• Location: Location involves issues with the host city and host facility. The host city is an important factor in determining whether or not people will attend. Organizers need to consider both the attractiveness and convenience of the host city's location. Several issues influence the choice of facility such as size, occupancy, playing surface, participant services, spectator amenities, accessibility, parking and transportation, lease terms, and cost. You may also be faced with the decision to stay in one location, year after year, or to change locations. Each choice has its own set of advantages and disadvantages.

Major Events That Stay in One Place

Kentucky Derby

College World Series

Daytona 500

Little League World Series

The Masters golf tournament

Rose Bowl

Major Events That Change Locations

Breeders' Cup

MLB All-Star Game

NCAA Final Four

Olympics

U.S. Open golf tournament

WrestleMania

Advantages of Staying in One Place

Reputation

Existing fan base

History and tradition

Community support

Event management expertise

Staffing and volunteer base

Client relationships

Vendor relationships

Media relationships

Advantages of Changing Locations

New consumers

New sources of revenue

Healthy competition among sites

Increased media coverage

Community enthusiasm

Larger scope

Event novelty

Flexibility

• Duration: Although many events may last one day, others (NCAA basketball tournament, Olympics, various sports festivals) may last weeks or months. When deciding on duration, event managers need to consider the type of competition, participants' travel needs, facility availability and cost, availability of officials and staff, and flexibility if delays due to weather or unforeseen events occur.

THINKING CREATIVELY AND PLANNING FOR UNIQUENESS

Considering the competition for spectators, participants, and sponsors, sporting event organizers need to be unique to attract attention and separate themselves from the competition. Why is it that some events consistently draw more spectators, participants, and sponsors than others? Quite often, it is because organizers have developed or highlighted special elements that make the events desirable. Here are some examples:

• The Big East men's basketball championship is played in Madison Square Garden each year to take advantage of the unique facility often hailed as "the World's Most Famous Arena." The arena's history with college basketball provides an additional storyline, making the event attractive to media.

• Location and timing contribute to the many holiday basketball tournaments held in

Hawaii or Puerto Rico. Spectators plan vacations around these games regardless of who is playing their favorite team.

- The AT&T Pebble Beach National Pro-Am sets itself apart from other golf events with its celebrity participation.
- The Association of Volleyball Professionals (AVP) tour is unique in that it is played on sand—often created in areas without natural beaches.

Sometimes uniqueness starts with the name, and the Super Bowl is a great example. Although its former name, AFL-NFL World Championship Game, was accurate and descriptive, it did not quite communicate the grandeur of the game. The name *Super Bowl* is consistent with what colleges traditionally call their big games while communicating the size and importance of the event. In recent years, the NFL has continued to add unique elements to their signature event. One initiative has them employing a green philosophy by planting trees in host locations and incorporating renewable energy into the events leading up to the game. Whereas many other events are criticized for the waste they create, the Super Bowl is different in that it incorporates practices likely to have a lasting environmental impact (Muellner 2008).

Another great example of planning for uniqueness is Cincinnati's Flying Pig Marathon. While other marathon names (e.g., New York, Boston, San Diego) all sound alike, the name *Flying Pig* makes the race stand out in the crowded race calendar, indicates the fun nature of the race, and creates multiple branding opportunities (Olberding and Jisha 2005). The name comes from the four bronze flying pigs at the entrance of Cincinnati's Sawyer Park and is appropriate because pork processing had been one of Cincinnati's primary industries. In fact, Cincinnati was once known as "Porkopolis" (Burfoot and Post 1999). In addition to the pig theme, organizers incorporate a variety of events into the weekend such as the Health & Fitness Expo, Family Fun Festival, Diaper Dash (for children five and under), and Flying Piglet Kids' Fun Run.

Sometimes a simple idea can lead to great results. In 2003, the National Hockey League (NHL) decided to hold an outdoor regular-season game featuring the Edmonton Oilers and the Montreal Canadiens. The creativity of putting an indoor sport in an outdoor football stadium generated significant attention and delivered huge results. More than 57,000 fans attended the game (a lottery to allot tickets attracted more than 750,000 entries), and the Canadian television broadcast attracted more than 2.75 million viewers, setting records for a regular-season game. The NHL has continued the idea by creating the NHL Winter Classic, holding games in Ralph Wilson Stadium in Orchard Park, New York, in 2008; Chicago's Wrigley Field in 2009; and Boston's Fenway Park in 2010. These games have generated not only significant ticket sales (71,217 in 2008) but also significant publicity for the NHL (Borzi 2009). The 2011 game between the Washington Capitals and the Pittsburgh Penguins drew an average of 4.5 million viewers, the most for a regular-season game since 1975.

It is not just high-profile or big-budget events that try to stand out; smaller events can benefit from creative planning, too. In recent years, mud runs have emerged as an alternative sporting event. Mud runs are running events where competitors must negotiate hills, obstacles, and mud to test their endurance as well as mental stamina. These events provide a unique challenge that differentiates them from other running events. Another example is snow golf, where golfers compete in the snow using orange golf balls. The "greens" are referred to as "whites." In many tournaments, golfers are encouraged to wear costumes as a way to focus on the fun element of the event.

PLANNING PROMOTIONAL AND ANCILLARY COMPONENTS

In addition to the main event, ancillary events such as fan expos, music festivals, contests, youth clinics, and interactive events are often planned to further organizers' objectives. The type of event and its objectives will dictate the type of ancillary events. An event desiring positive publicity may schedule a preevent clinic for disadvantaged children in order to gain positive preevent news coverage. An event needing to add value for participants may schedule a side trip to a local attraction or other recreational activities.

A great example of an ancillary event designed to promote an organization and its signature event is the World Wrestling Entertainment (WWE) Hall of Fame ceremony. WWE schedules their Hall of Fame ceremony the night before Wrestle-Mania in hopes of increasing the grandeur of their signature event and encouraging a few last-minute pay-per-view buys. Similarly, organizers of the 2008 NHL Winter Classic game between the Detroit Red Wings and Chicago Blackhawks at Wrigley Field created the Winter Classic Spectator Plaza, a free fan festival outside the historic stadium. The event offered fans a variety of interactive activities as a way to promote the event (Tedesco 2008). Sometimes these ancillary events can be used to support a cause. In conjunction with the 2012 Super Bowl, the NFL held the NFL Charities Celebrity Bowling Classic featuring retired players and Pro Football Hall of Famers to benefit NFL Charities.

Many competitions will schedule numerous ancillary events to meet multiple objectives. For the Atlantic Coast Conference football championship, Charlotte scheduled a coaches' luncheon, awards banquet, and football legends dinner in addition to a fan festival, pep rally, and concert. These events were added to make Charlotte a more attractive destination for the conference's signature game (Spanberg 2009).

Another example is the NCAA men's basketball Final Four, which hosts several events in addition to the main event (the championship game). For the 2012 tournament in New Orleans, organizers scheduled a number of ancillary events to reach philanthropy objectives through charitable and educational activities:

- Career in Sports Forum
- USBWA Sports Writing Workshop
- NCAA Final Four Youth Day
- NCAA Youth Clinics
- Four Courts in Four Days (court refurbishment)

- Middle School Madness
- NCAA and Feed the Hungry
- Minority/Women Owned Business Enterprise (MWBE) Access Program

In addition, organizers staged a number of other activities designed to provide additional entertainment for event attendees and the local community:

- Bracket Town
- Block Party at the Big Dance Concert Series
- College All-Star Game
- Final Four Dribble
- College Slam Dunk and Three-Point Championships
- Pep Rally

DEVELOPING AN OPERATIONAL TIMELINE

Small events may require only a few weeks to a few months of planning, but larger events may require years of planning. The key to success is to start early. Solomon (2005) suggests planning should start 18 to 24 months before the event in order to work well with media, sponsors, and sites without being rushed. When developing the operational timeline, it is vital to identify important tasks and logistical needs and budget an appropriate amount for completion. Important tasks left to the last minute add time, costs, and stress. Further, tasks must be scheduled in relation to each other (e.g., promotional materials cannot be printed until the date and site have been confirmed). The following is a sample event timeline. Keep in mind that every event will have different needs, and the length of time to complete tasks will vary according to the event. It is up to the organizers to identify needs and effectively schedule operations.

One to Two Years Out

Determine the purpose of the event.

Investigate the feasibility of the event.

Develop a mission.

Select the date and site.

Six Months to a Year Out

Start event program planning.

Start promotion planning.

Develop contingency plans.

Assess staffing needs.

Three to Six Months Out

Arrange for security, parking, transportation, and vendors.

Order equipment.

Contact printers.

Create a publicity plan, and publicize the event.

One to Three Months Out

Confirm arrangements.

Follow up with teams or participants.

Begin ticket sales and registrations.

Contact officials.

One Week Out

Perform on-site checks.

Install equipment.

Finalize event-day timelines.

Continue staff and volunteer training.

Schedule transportation for VIPs and guests.

Event Day

Perform equipment checks.

Perform preevent briefings.

Conduct event.

Postevent

Conduct postevent review.

Perform aftermarketing.

PLANNING FOR CONTINGENCIES

Odds are that something planned will not go off as expected. Therefore, event managers should identify what could go wrong and develop contingency plans to address any possibilities. The goal of a contingency plan is to create a level of preparation so that you can minimize problems and reduce the inconvenience to participants and spectators.

When developing contingency plans, it is first important to identify areas of concern and develop plans for how you would deal with each instance. Typical situations needing advance preparation may include the following:

- Fire, gas leak, or other emergency
- Bad weather
- Power failure
- Equipment failure
- Scoreboard or scoring system failure
- Larger than expected crowd
- Hostile crowd
- Late-arriving team or official
- Staff shortage
- Ticket irregularities
- Medical emergencies
- Food and beverage issues
- Parking and transportation

Although some occurrences are unlikely, they should be planned for if the severity of the occurrence would have a major impact on the event. Consider a scoreboard failure at a college basketball game. Although this happens rarely, this failure could bring an event to a close, and therefore event managers should be prepared. Even FIFA had a contingency plan in case delays in stadium construction had prevented South Africa from hosting the 2010 World Cup.

Once areas of concern have been identified, managers need to develop action plans detailing what to do in each case. The plan should also define the staff, budget, time, training, and resources needed to deal with each situation. Some plans will be more complex than others according to likelihood and severity of the problem being considered. Depending on the problem, contingency plans may necessitate procedures for emergency access, evacuation plans, communication plans, security procedures, staff responsibilities, and plans for dealing with media.

For example, many events have contingency plans for weather-related issues. For outdoor events, weather is an important concern because rain, wind, and snow (or lack of snow for a winter event) can significantly alter event plans. In 2012, rain delayed both the NHL Winter Classic and Daytona 500 (first postponement in 54 years). Even indoor events are susceptible to weather issues. For example an ice storm could prevent staff or supplies from reaching the facility, or a thunderstorm could keep spectators from exiting a facility. Considering the different types of weather events, managers may need to have plans to provide rain gear for staff, procedures to protect equipment, public address announcements to inform participants and spectators, evacuation plans, and procedures for rescheduling or cancelling.

Contingency planning should be a dynamic process. Continual review and revision are necessary to identify additional risks and alternative ways to deal with those risks. This phase involves reviewing existing plans and developing new plans defined in the project scope. For example, the NFL decided to expand its contingency planning after unexpected levels of ice and snow in North Texas caused considerable transportation problems at the 2011 Super Bowl. Before this event, organizers planned for the most likely worst-case scenarios, but now they plan for a greater scope of circumstances (Kaplan 2011).

SUMMARY

Event planning can be a time-consuming and complex process. Multiple stakeholders need to be involved throughout the process to ensure success. An understanding of each stakeholder's interest in the event assists in decision making. Many of these decisions will be driven by the purpose of the event, such as raising funds for a cause, promoting an image, driving tourism, promoting sponsors, or promoting sports. In addition, decisions will be made according to whom the event is planned for.

A significant part of the planning process is the SWOT analysis. A frank assessment of an event's strengths, weaknesses, opportunities, and threats enables organizers to make informed decisions. The event's mission, goals, and objectives provide direction so that organizers can prepare strategies and plan logistics to efficiently meet the event's purpose. Once the major issues have been identified, logistical issues such as date, time, and place are determined and operational timelines are developed to ensure everything that needs to be done is accomplished at the right time. Considering the number of things that could change or go wrong, contingency plans are developed to deal with deviations from the plan.

LEARNING ACTIVITIES

Assume you have decided to stage a 5K mud run. Mud runs are races through trails, hills, and other assorted obstacles (especially mud). There is no standard course; each event host plans unique and creative obstacles to challenge competitors' stamina and mental discipline. Further, mud run organizers usually add ancillary events such as awards ceremonies and postevent parties to create an exciting event.

1. Who would be the key stakeholders? What would be the primary purpose of the event?

2. Assess the event's strengths, weaknesses, opportunities, and threats (you may have to do some research to complete this task).

3. What would be some appropriate goals and objectives for an event such as this?

4. If you were to host an event like this, what would you call it? What would you do to make it unique?

5. What could go wrong with this event? What contingency plans would you have to make?

REFERENCES

Borzi, P. 2009. Blackhawks take over Wrigley, then fall to Red Wings. *New York Times*, January 2, B12.

Bowdin, G., J. Allen, W. O'Toole, R. Harris, and I. McDonnell, I. 2006. *Events management.* Oxford: Butterworth-Heinemann.

Burfoot, A., and M. Post. 1999. *Runner's World* 34 (March): 18.

Fisher, E. 2009. WBC finds more support second time around. *Street and Smith's SportsBusiness Journal*, February 23, 4.

Goldblatt, J. 2008. *Special events: The roots and wings of celebration.* Hoboken, NJ: Wiley.

Graham, S., L. Delpy Neirotti, and J.J. Goldblatt. 2001. *The ultimate guide to sports marketing.* New York: McGraw-Hill.

Hums, M.A., and J.C. MacLean. 2009. *Governance and policy in sport organizations.* Scottsdale, AZ: Holcomb Hathaway.

Kaplan, D. 2011. NFL changing how it plans Super Bowl. *Street and Smith's SportsBusiness Journal*, April 4, 1.

MAAC Sports. 2009. Masiello to chair the local organizing committee for the 2010 NCAA Men's Division I Basketball Championship first and second rounds in Buffalo. July 16. Available: www.maacsports.com/ViewArticle.dbml?DB_OEM_ID=17400&ATCLID=204762704.

Mallen, C., and L.J. Adams. 2008. *Sport, recreation and tourism event management: Theoretical and practical dimensions.* Oxford: Elsevier.

Moran, M. 2002. Staying home in droves. *USA Today*, September 4, 2C.

Muellner, A. 2008. The Super Bowl isn't stuck in carbon neutral. *Street and Smith's SportsBusiness Journal*, November 10, 26.

Olberding, D.J., and J. Jisha. 2005. The Flying Pig: Building brand equity in a major urban marathon. *Sport Marketing Quarterly* 14:191-196.

Osborn, A.F. 1963. *Applied imagination: Principles and procedures of creative problem solving.* 3rd ed. New York: Scribner's.

Solomon, J. 2002. *An insider's guide to managing sporting events.* Champaign, IL: Human Kinetics.

Spanberg, E. 2009. Countdown to kickoff on for ACC's big game in Charlotte. *Charlotte BusinessJournal.* [Online]. December 4. Available: http://charlotte.bizjournals.com/charlotte/stories/2009/12/07/story1.html?b=1260162000%5e2536561&s=industry&i=sports_business.

Supovitz, F. 2005. *The sports event management and marketing playbook.* Hoboken, NJ: Wiley.

Swart, K. 2005. Event planning. In *Event management: A professional and developmental approach* (2nd ed.), ed. D. Tassiopoulos, 413-438. Lansdowne, MD: Juta Academic.

Tedesco, R. 2008. NHL runs Wrigleyville Fest for Winter Classic. *Promo Magazine.* [Online]. December 31. Available: http://promomagazine.com/eventmarketing/news/nhl-runs-wrigleyville-fest-1231/index.html.

Wanklin, T. 2005. Event planning. In *Event management: A professional and developmental approach* (2nd ed.), ed. D. Tassiopoulos, 96-121. Lansdowne, MD: Juta Academic.

CHAPTER 3

Event Bidding

Chapter Objectives

After completing the chapter, the reader should be able to do the following:

- Appreciate the reasons why host communities would bid on sporting events.
- Outline the steps in the bidding process for sporting events.
- Understand the role of sports commissions and how events work with sports commissions.

Dr. Susan C. Blackwood was named the executive director of San Antonio Sports in 1996. Her connections across the country with businesses, national governing bodies, the NCAA, and the United States Olympic Committee have strengthened San Antonio Sports' efforts to attract events and raise funds. With a mission of transforming the community through the power of sport, San Antonio Sports bids on and hosts major amateur sporting events. Since 1991, the organization has been responsible for attracting events resulting in more than $357 million in direct economic impact and millions of dollars in national and international media exposure. Its youth initiatives touch the lives of more than 160,000 children each year.

Q: How do you decide whether or not to bid on an event?

A: We have a bid committee made up of our staff and board members with the responsibility of looking at the feasibility of an event, what the budget may be like, how we would fund it, and if it is a good fit for San Antonio in terms of the interest it would garner. Does it sell hotel rooms? Is there some component of the event that could result in a legacy for San Antonio? Those are our main considerations.

Q: Once you have decided to bid on an event, how do you ensure your bid is competitive?

A: We like to think we have a lot of experience putting a creative bid together. That is certainly something most of the stakeholders consider important. You put a lot of time and effort in the process and are as thorough as possible. We reach out to our partner groups to make sure they are involved from the standpoint of what kind of collaborations we can demonstrate in putting together a bid.

Q: What do you do to build a reputation to ensure events keep coming back to San Antonio?

A: We don't take anything for granted, and we work really hard putting on an event. Complete attention to detail is extremely important. We do elaborate after-action reports so that we, in the future, can eliminate any problems we might have had. We continue to fine-tune and make the event better if we hold it in successive years. We've got a pretty seasoned staff with a lot of experience. Those things are really important.

Q: What tips would you give to others who are trying to attract and retain sporting events?

A: A lot of the process is relationship building with members of the stakeholder organizations. It is a lot of hard work. People have to recognize the effort that is put in when you are in the event business because it is not a nine-to-five job. Pay attention to detail, go to other events, and learn from your colleagues.

Q: What are the biggest challenges you face?

A: A big challenge concerns funding of events. We are in a city that has a small corporate base and a lot of small businesses that cannot afford to sponsor or support those kinds of initiatives. But we have a unique opportunity to do a lot of community outreach. The other challenge is keeping facilities in tip-top shape and having the kind of venues that are attractive to the stakeholders. We have had a shortage in some sports of the facilities you need to attract major events.

Q: What advice would you give to sport properties when they put their events out for bid?

A: Make sure there is a lot of clarification and specifics in the bids themselves, which should be exact in terms of what you are looking for. Make sure there is an adequate timeline because we do put a lot of time and effort into the bids, and we would like to have as much time as possible to respond to the bids in a thorough fashion.

Q: What advice would you give to sport properties when working with a sports commission?

A: It is important for both our organization and the stakeholder to have great lines of communication. If it is at all possible, appoint one person to be the spokesperson or contact person for that organization so you don't have to work with 14 people on each side on the same project. You can avoid a lot of duplication from that standpoint.

Considering the substantial benefits associated with hosting events, many organizations or event owners will request competing proposals from interested parties. The bid process may be very complicated, as in the case of the Olympics or FIFA World Cup, or very simple for smaller events. The purpose of soliciting bids is to identify the most qualified prospective hosts for the event.

Hosts for sporting events are often local sports commissions, convention and visitors bureaus (CVBs), civic organizations, or colleges and athletic conferences (for many intercollegiate athletic events). For larger mega-events, a city or country may serve as the host. When placing a bid, hosts are looking for events that will do the following:

- Enhance the economy by attracting spectators, participants, and officials who will spend money on hotel rooms, in restaurants, and at local attractions.
- Provide a catalyst for improving the host community's infrastructure and facilities.

- Enhance community image and provide an increased quality of life.
- Showcase the community's attributes and benefits.

Table 3.1 includes examples of some events seeking bids for a host. As you can see, each of these events has the potential to bring a large number of athletes, coaches, and spectators to a community.

BIDDING PROCESS

The event owner will specify bid procedures and timetables for the bid. Much of this will be outlined in a request for proposal (RFP). The RFP outlines the event's minimum requirements. The most often cited requirements for sporting events concern the venue. Organizations may have very specific requirements regarding the venue or venues to be used such as facility specifications, playing surface, spectator capacity, locker rooms, and amenities. Minimum requirements may also relate to dates, event staff and officials, and any fees or revenue guarantees.

Table 3.1 Examples of Events Seeking Bids

Event	Length	Room nights	# of athletes
UPA College Ultimate Championships	3 days	450	600
National AAU Taekwondo Championships	5 days	3,400	2,000
USA Junior Olympic Boys' Volleyball	4.5 days	9,500	14,500
NAIA Baseball National Championship	5 days	750	300
Western States Police and Fire Games	3 days	10,200	6,000
USA Water Polo Junior Olympics	9 days	5,000	8,300

The following is an example of some of the minimums a governing body may require in order to host a tennis championship event:

- Facility with a minimum of 15 hard-surface courts
- Four warm-up courts separate from playing areas
- Locker and shower facilities on or near the site
- Scorecards, water, and singles sticks on each court
- Squeegees available for wet courts
- Local transportation or shuttle service for participants between airport, housing, and tennis facility
- Certified athletic trainers on site for each day of competition
- Administrative personnel available for check-in and court assignment

In addition to checking the minimum requirements, organizations requesting bids will also assess a host location's suitability for an event by evaluating other attributes of the bidders such as their experience in hosting events; financial strength and abilities; level of community support; and support services such as transportation, housing, and meals. For example, the Professional Disc Golf Association (PDGA) requires that each potential host address the following topics:

- The organization proposing to host
- The host course
- Support amenities surrounding the course
- Host hotel
- Event organizational structure
- Budget
- Publicity and marketing plan
- Proposed event schedule

FEASIBILITY STUDIES

Before bidding, host committees usually conduct some sort of feasibility study to ensure the benefits of hosting the event outweigh the costs.

Feasibility studies involve detailed forecasting and careful evaluation of available physical facilities, financial resources, human resources, community support, and political support (Graham, Neirotti, and Goldblatt 2001). Often, the feasibility study will start with a market analysis followed by a financial analysis. Maralak and Lloyd (2005) suggest that the decision to bid should be based on an analysis of several issues including costs of hosting, economic impact, business opportunities stemming from the event, opportunities to boost the host's image, ability to attract visitors, and benefits offered by the host location. If benefits outweigh costs, and the local organizing committee is confident they can deliver what the organization requires, the local organizing committee may proceed to put together a bid.

In 2007, Her Majesty's Treasury completed a feasibility study commissioned by the Secretary of State for Culture, Media and Sport in the United Kingdom (UK) assessing the feasibility of the country's hosting the 2018 World Cup (HM Treasury 2007). HM Treasury is the UK's economics and finance ministry. The final feasibility report suggested the following characteristics of successful bids:

- Behind the detailed planning and work was a professional bid team.
- A reasonable budget was needed to support the bidding phase for a sporting event.
- There was a high level of political support for the event.
- The bid had strong leadership.
- A professional bid document was meticulously planned, with careful attention to detail.
- Proper plans were submitted along with clear and specific government guarantees, where appropriate.

Furthermore, the report suggested that other successful bids of major sporting events to be hosted in the UK addressed key principles such as economic feasibility, technical feasibility, a clear motivation for bidding, early identification of key partners, and a clear process for bidding. Finally, the UK feasibility study suggested that the following factors must be considered when bidding on the World Cup:

• The economic impact of hosting the event. Of those who favored the idea of England's bidding to host the 2018 World Cup, 42 percent did so because they believed it would be good for the economy.

• Affordability and costs. Revenues include ticket sales, commercial rights, and in-kind value along with income from FIFA. Costs for hosting the event include costs related to the following: stadium infrastructure, operations, government, and security.

• Infrastructure such as stadiums and transportation. The World Cup requires 8 to 12 stadiums with certain seating capacities. An analysis of international transport connections and local transport arrangements is also important.

• Security requirements that considered recent football security measures.

• Regional impact such as public opinion, economic benefits, location of existing stadiums, and an assessment of the likely economic and social legacy in the regions.

• A clear legacy. This would need to be planned, such as long-term impact on the tourism industry or boosting of the country's profile.

BID DOCUMENTS

Once the decision to bid has been made, a bid document is produced. Bid documents are thorough accountings of the site's key assets and how they conform to bid requirements. Bid documents typically include detailed information in the following categories:

• Purpose statement: Why is the host committee bidding on the event? What do they hope to achieve through hosting this event?

• Host committee credentials: What experience does the committee have hosting events? What is the relationship between the host committee and the local sports commission or convention and visitors bureau? Who will be the tournament director, and what experience does that person bring to the event?

• Budget and finances: What is the proposed budget for the event? What are the costs associated with the facility, labor, equipment, supplies, printing, and so on? What are the estimated revenues from registrations, ticket sales, sponsorship, media rights, merchandising, concessions, and so on?

• Staff and volunteer support: Is there an experienced staff available to support the event? Is there a sizeable volunteer base available to support the staff? What experiences does the host committee have in recruiting and training volunteers?

• Playing facilities: What facilities will be available for the event? What are the facility specifications (e.g., seating, parking, restrooms, locker facilities)?

• Support facilities: What other facilities can be used to support the event (meeting space, exhibitor space, space for social events)? What are the arrangements for concessions and merchandise sales?

• Transportation: Where is the nearest airport, and how accessible is the event to air travel? What ground transportation is available (e.g., rental cars, bus, train)? How can spectators and participants get around the city when not participating in or watching the event?

• Accommodations: What accommodations are available near the site? How are accommodations priced, and what is the availability during the time of year when the event will take place? What other lodging options exist?

• Emergency services: How will the host committee provide for the health and safety of participants and spectators? How close is the nearest hospital?

• Public relations and media coverage: What are the opportunities for media coverage? Who will be handling public relations for the event?

• Environmental sustainability: How will supplies be properly disposed of?

• Weather-related issues: Will smog or extremely drastic climates factor into the event?

• Health services: Will proper medical teams be available?

In addition to meeting requirements, host committees should include information that highlights the key strengths of their bid and competitive advantages over other bidders. These documents may contain information about the host committee to illustrate their expertise and credentials; information about community and sponsor support; and other facts about the community that make the location attractive such as population, weather, accommodations, media, and attractions.

In 2007, North Texas was awarded the 2011 Super Bowl over bidders from Arizona and Indianapolis. The following is a sample of what organizers promised the NFL in order to win the bid. They were willing to commit to these promises in anticipation that the Super Bowl would generate hundreds of millions of dollars in economic benefit to the region ("Texas Committee" 2007).

- 10,000 trained volunteers
- 750 buses, 500 limousines, 1,000 taxis, 10,000 rental cars
- 90,000 hotel rooms, including 23,887 reserved for the NFL
- 187 hotel suites and 1,416 luxury rooms for NFL owners and other VIPs at top-of-the-line hotels
- 150 luxury suites in the stadium for the exclusive use of the NFL
- Four luxury suites on the 50-yard line: one for Fox, the network televising the game; one for the owner of each participating team; and one for the NFL commissioner
- 300 percent more staff at the stadium on game day than what is normally needed for a game
- 730 concession, souvenir, merchandise, and program stands
- 2.3 million square feet of space at the stadium "to accommodate all of the NFL's needs for Super Bowl XLV—at no cost to the NFL"
- $1 million to be paid to the NFL to cover game-day costs

Considering the bid process is open to multiple suitors, bidders need to make their bids as competitive as possible. Keep in mind that those evaluating bids will be looking to award their bid to the organization that offers the most for the least cost. Westerbeek, Turner, and Ingerson's (2002) survey of managers involved with major events identified eight key success factors in the event-bidding process: accountability, political support, relationship marketing, ability, infrastructure, bid-team composition, communication and exposure, and existing facilities. In a 2011 survey, *SportsEvents* magazine found that availability of sport venues and hotel rooms was the most important factor followed by hotel room rates, number of volunteers, and the host committee's history of organizing successful events (O'Connor 2012).

The financial aspects of a bid cannot be overlooked. Many host communities will extend considerable benefits in order to attract an event that will generate a significant economic impact. For example, host cities do not charge the National Football League rent when they host the Super Bowl. In fact, the NFL gets most of the revenue from the event, while the host city absorbs most of the costs. However, host countries for events such as the FIFA World Cup are entitled to the gross receipts of all ticket sales. Competition is strong because organizers agree the benefit of hosting the event in their communities outweighs the costs (Muret 2004). In 2012, the city of Whistler, British Colombia, increased the amount of public money available to the local organizing committee in an attempt to bring the 2013 Winter X Games to Canada. The amount pledged was two-and-one-half times what previous host, Aspen, had given to X Games organizers ("Public money sweetens X Games bid" 2012). ESPN was in the position to ask for more financial support considering the increased number of sites bidding on the event.

SPORTS COMMISSIONS

The creation of sports commissions is a relatively new idea when you consider that only 30 such organizations existed back in 1993 (Kelly 2000). Today, almost every large city has a sports commission or someone assigned within the convention and visitors bureau to sell to the sport market. In sum, the National Association of Sports Commissions (2012) claims there are more than 300 in existence today. Some are housed within the convention and visitors bureau, while others are completely separate entities. Most sports commissions operate with a relatively small staff (fewer than 10). The sports commission in Indianapolis is one of the largest, with approximately 24 full-time employees.

Sports commissions are normally nonprofit or governmental entities designed to attract and assist sporting events. Here are some examples of mission statements illustrating their role.

The mission of the Louisville Sports Commission (LSC) is to attract, create, and host quality sporting events in the Louisville area that increase economic vitality, enhance the quality of life, promote healthy lifestyles, and brand Louisville as a great sports town.

The mission of the West Michigan Sports Commission is to promote Michigan's West Coast as the premier venue for hosting a diverse level of youth and amateur sporting events, enhancing the economy and quality of life in the region.

The Charlotte Regional Sports Commission promotes the Charlotte region by creating sporting events, recruiting and supporting sporting events and organizations, and encouraging community participation. These efforts are intended to result in a positive economic impact on the region and to improve its quality of life.

The Utah Sports Commission is working to distinguish the State of Utah as a leader in the world of sports marketing, event attraction, sport development, and sport-related tourism. The Sports Commission is continuing to exercise fiduciary responsibility in allocating public and private funding to sporting events as it promotes the State of Utah and generates economic impact through sport.

Sports commissions can play an important role in promoting economic activity. One major event can have a large economic impact on a community. According to the Greater Kansas City Sports Commission and Foundation, the community received an economic benefit of about $18 million by hosting intercollegiate basketball tournaments (Mid-America Intercollegiate Athletic Association men's and women's basketball championships, Big 12 men's and women's basketball championships, NAIA national championship) during a three-week period in March of 2012 (Dornbrook 2012). Denver Sports estimates $20 million was infused into the local economy through the 2012 NCAA women's basketball Final Four through visitors spending money on hotels, restaurants, bars, and transportation. The events don't have to be major to have a major impact. Frisco, Texas, a community of about 100,000 outside Dallas, estimates nearly $7.3 million was pumped into the economy from 10,000 people who attended or participated in the 2009 U.S. Youth Soccer Region III Championships (Brock 2009).

The benefits of having a sports commission are both economic and social. For example, enhanced visitor spending and increased revenues generated by a sports commission in a region help reduce residents' taxes in many cases. The social benefits to the community are also important. For example, without a sports commission or convention and visitors bureau, cities such as Miami, Tampa, and New Orleans would not be attracting major events that provide enhanced social entertainment to residents within the region. The economic impact of events is estimated by calculating expenditures from multiple sources, including the following:

- Visitor spending in local hotels and other lodging
- Visitor spending at food and beverage establishments
- Visitor spending at retail outlets
- Parking expenditures
- Rental car expenditures
- Organizational spending
- Taxes and charges (hotel taxes, car rental taxes, sales taxes, and airport fees)

Sports commissions are adept at promoting the strengths of their respective communities. For example, the Cedar Rapids Area Convention and Visitors Bureau promotes Cedar Rapids as a safe, friendly community that is easy to navigate. The Atlanta Sports Council promotes Atlanta's 90,000 hotel rooms and its world-class entertainment and shopping (Bradford 2008). As these examples illustrate, each community may have something unique to offer; therefore, event organizers need to carefully match the event's needs with the community's strengths. *SportsEvents* magazine (Bradford 2008) provides a list of 10 tips sport event planners should consider when selecting a host site.

1. Learn the host's skill set.
2. Ask for facts and figures.
3. Encourage potential hosts to attend the event before bidding.
4. Look for sites that do it right the first time.
5. Be specific about needs.
6. Learn about problem-solving capabilities.
7. Build a team.
8. Look for win–win opportunities.
9. Request promotional assistance.
10. Find out who rolls out the red carpet

SUMMARY

Sporting events can be catalysts for a variety of positive outcomes, both economic and noneconomic. Sporting events can bring participants, spectators, coaches, and officials who generate revenue through local spending on lodging, food, and entertainment. Communities often create sports commissions to attract and assist sporting events. To ensure the best possible site is chosen, event organizers often put their events up for bid. To win a bid, sports commissions, or other interested parties, must be able to create bid documents showing not only how they meet the needs of event organizers but also how their location or host organization may be more attractive than others.

LEARNING ACTIVITIES

Assume your home community is looking to attract sporting events.

1. What benefits would your community gain by hosting sporting events?
2. What does your community have to offer that would be attractive to events looking for a host location?
3. What information would you include in a bid document to illustrate that your location is competitive with other locations?

Go to a sports commission's website and look at the events they are hosting.

1. What types of events does that community attract?
2. What resources does the sports commission or the community possess that make it attractive to events?

Find and examine an event that is up for bid, and evaluate their bid procedures.

1. What are the key elements of a bid?
2. What do you think would be the key issues the organization would focus on in determining who would win the bid?

REFERENCES

Bradford, M. 2008. Powerful partners: Sports commissions, CVBs critical pieces to sports events success. *SportsEvents* 5 (December): 18-22.

Brock, K.C. 2009. Sports-crazed Frisco scores. *Dallas Business Journal*. [Online]. June 26. Available: http://dallas.bizjournals.com/dallas/stories/2009/06/29/story11.html?b=1246248000%5E1851884.

Dornbrook, J. 2012. Kansas City bounces back into college basketball spotlight. *Kansas City Business Journal*. [Online]. March 1. Available: www.bizjournals.com/kansascity/news/2012/03/01/kansas-city-bounces-back-basketball.html.

Graham, S., L.D. Neirotti, and J.J. Goldblatt. 2001. *The ultimate guide to sports marketing*. 2nd ed. New York: McGraw-Hill.

HM Treasury. 2007. Hosting the World Cup: A feasibility study. London: HMSO Licensing Division. Available: www.hm-treasury.gov.uk/d/world_cup_feasibility.pdf.

Kelly, J. 2000. Looking to sports for development dollars. *American City & County* 115:20-21.

Maralak, N., and N. Lloyd. 2005. Bidding for major events. In *Event management: A professional and developmental approach* (2nd ed.), ed. D. Tassiopoulos, 56-73. Lansdowne, MD: Juta Academic.

Muret, D. 2004. NFL gets free rein at Super Bowl stadiums. *Street and Smith's SportsBusiness Journal*, January 26, 40.

National Association of Sports Commissions. 2012. About us. Available: www.sportscommissions.org/About-NASC.

O'Connor, J.T. 2012. The business of sports: Hitting our stride. *SportsEvents* 9 (March): 24-32.

Public money sweetens X Games bid. 2012. *Pique Newsmagazine*, February 9 Available: www.piquenewsmagazine.com/whistler/public-money-sweetens-x-games-bid/Content?oid=2283897.

Texas committee releases details of 2011 Super Bowl Bid. *Street and Smith's SportsBusiness Daily*, May 24, 2007. Available: www.sportsbusinessdaily.com/Daily/Issues/2007/05/Issue-168/Leagues-Governing-Bodies/Texas-Committee-Releases-Details-Of-2011-Super-Bowl-Bid.aspx.

Westerbeek, H.M., P. Turner, and L. Ingerson. 2002. Key success factors in bidding for hallmark sporting events. *International Marketing Review* 19:303-322.

CHAPTER 4

Event Staffing

Chapter Objectives

After completing the chapter, the reader should be able to do the following:

- Describe organizational structure, and explain the use of an organizational chart in event management.
- Analyze the factors taken into account when staffing a sporting event.
- Explain various tools used in scheduling staff.
- List reasons why organizations might use outsourcing for their events.
- Present and describe a number of motivational theories.
- Provide suggestions for adopting a personal management and leadership style.
- Discuss the stages of meeting management.
- Define communication, and describe various forms of social media.
- Highlight the need for event volunteers.

Jason Aughey is the senior director of the Tampa Bay Sports Commission. Recognized by *Connect Magazine* as a "40 Under 40" honoree in 2013, Jason is responsible for coordinating the commission's direct sales and marketing efforts to attract and organize amateur events of all sizes on behalf of the community. Before joining the Tampa Bay Sports Commission, Jason worked for Central Florida's Polk County Sports Marketing (PCSM) as the sports sales and events representative. In this position, Jason was responsible for assisting with the recruitment, development, management, and implementation of all PCSM special events and served as a liaison to most of PCSM's major clients. He was also the cohost and coproducer of PCSM's weekly sports talk radio show, *Sports Central*, and was a special correspondent for PCSM's weekly television show.

Q: What do you believe are the biggest challenges in terms of staffing a sporting event?

A: One of the biggest challenges I have seen in my years with the sports commission has been the ability to effectively delegate responsibilities in terms of staffing. Often, the initial thought is to take on as much responsibility as possible. At some point you realize that staffing an event requires the input and efforts of a lot of people from various backgrounds. We help put together a local organizing committee (LOC) and assign a point person in charge of each functional area, such as communications and public relations, volunteers, event signage, event operations, accommodations, and facilities. Once you have created an organizational chart identifying these areas, it is then a matter of communicating specific goals for each person running point for each part of the event. We have found it helpful when hosting an event to create a system of checks and balances. In this regard, it is helpful to have regularly scheduled meetings so the responsibilities assigned in each of the functional areas are completed at the appropriate times. We may start by meeting twice a month, then twice a week, and as the event gets closer, the meetings may be held on a daily basis.

Q: How does the Tampa Bay Sports Commission assist an event rights holder with staffing?

A: With our small staff at the sports commission, we are not in the business of staffing the events that come to Tampa. We do a lot of work leading up to the event, but once the group holding the event arrives in Tampa, the expertise of their event organizers comes into play. Almost 99 percent of the time, the event rights holder will provide the staffing and manpower necessary to staff the event, such as officials, timekeepers, and scorekeepers. However, we will help gather volunteers, which is a big component that we are able to offer to the event rights holder. We also serve as an intermediary by connecting the event organizers with local facilities managers, hotel managers, and rental agencies. We do our best to create a consistent message with all stakeholders and to ensure that everything runs smoothly while the event organizers are in Tampa.

Q: How important are volunteers, and how do you keep them coming back to events?

A: Needless to say, volunteers are extremely important not only to the Tampa Bay Sports Commission but to the entire industry as well. Volunteers provide the first impression for a lot of the visitors who are coming to the event. Volunteers play the role of ambassadors of the city, and their smiling faces, knowledge, and helpfulness play a critically important role. Our volunteer database consists of approximately 6,000 people.

In terms of retaining volunteers, it is important to introduce new and exciting events into the community and to allow volunteers to be exposed to a wide variety of sports. One of the primary selling points in Tampa is that volunteers will have the opportunity to see an event and be part of history. For example, consider the excitement of a large-scale event such as the NCAA basketball tournament for a volunteer. The events that we attract to the area give volunteers a sense of pride that they are Tampa natives. Another important key to retaining volunteers is constantly keeping them aware of upcoming events and giving them things to do. We are fortunate to have a number of larger events, but we also host some smaller events that come to Tampa. The larger events help us capture information and build our volunteer database so that when a smaller event comes along, we can pull names from the database. You should always be ready to tell the story about your event, about your organization, and to explain how an effective volunteer program helps the local community.

Q: Provide a list of some of your most recent events, and describe some of your job duties that may relate to staffing.

A: Following is a partial listing of some of the larger events hosted by the Tampa Bay Sports Commission. A more detailed listing can be found by going to www.tampabaysports.org. My primary duties related to staffing consist of coordinating the internship program and assisting with volunteer recruitment.

2007 ACC men's basketball tournament

2008 NCAA men's basketball first and second rounds

2008 NCAA women's Final Four

2008 ACC football championship

2009 SEC men's basketball tournament

2009 ACC football championship

2009 NCAA women's volleyball championship

2011 NCAA men's basketball second and third rounds

2012 NCAA men's Frozen Four

Planning and implementing a sporting event can be a complex process. Consider, for example, the numerous stakeholders involved (e.g., athletes, coaches, venues, hotels, sponsors, rights holders, sports commission), the organizations, and the people within each organization. In many cases, multiple technologies are employed, and for those events that travel from place to place, new cultures are explored. In addition, events must adhere to government and environmental regulations. There are a number of reasons why you need an organizational chart for a sporting event. The organizational chart defines areas of responsibility and accountability, helps streamline decision making, and assists in more clearly communicating to those who work within an organization and to key external contacts (Supovitz 2005). Most important, the organizational chart helps the employees understand levels of authority and responsibility. Although not all organizations involved in developing an event have an organizational chart in document form, the chart is important from the standpoint that employees know to whom they report, who reports to them, and what level of responsibility one has at a certain point in time (Goldblatt 2011).

ORGANIZATIONAL CHART

The organizational chart displays the structure of an organization (i.e., the way an organization arranges its employees and jobs so that work can be performed and organizational goals met). Organizations may be characterized by a tall or a flat organizational structure. For example, the International Olympic Committee has a tall organizational structure. Tall structures have many levels of management, whereby managers have many ranks and a narrow span of control, referring to the number of employees each supervisor is responsible for managing. The advantage of a tall organizational structure is this narrow span of control, which allows for close supervision of employees. Tall organizational structures are often referred to as bureaucratic in nature, which can be very beneficial in terms of the stability of the organization. For example, many large organizations such as governments and educational institutions have such a long history of survival because of their bureaucratic nature. However, as an organization grows and becomes a bureaucratic structure with multiple hierarchical layers, communication begins to break down, and it takes too long to exchange information between levels. Thus, flat organizational structures (an example is USA Field Hockey) can be beneficial because of their flexibility and ability to adapt to change. Flat structures have fewer management levels and a broader span of control. This structure gives employees more autonomy and allows them to be more innovative and flexible in solving problems and making decisions.

Although the traditional organizational chart is helpful for defining relationships within the organization, sporting events are often planned and implemented by networks of multiple organizations. Because of these interorganizational relationships, a good strategy for developing an event organizational chart is to break the event into functions. According to Supovitz (2005), typical functional areas for sport event organizations include the following:

- Operations: facility management (e.g., ticket takers, ushers, security, first aid and EMTs), staff and vendor accreditation, transportation, office services, staff uniforms and attire

- Competition: tournament/competition scheduling, athlete scheduling and communication, playing field preparation and maintenance, competitive equipment acquisition and maintenance, officiating and judging, training facilities, equipment, athlete medical services

- Guest services: ticketing, VIP invitation process and seating, VIP gifts, VIP hospitality, information guides, hotel room and function space management

- Marketing: sponsorship, creative services (e.g., logo development, style manual, printed materials, marketing artwork, and sponsor signage), advertising, promotions, publicity, merchandising

- Presentation: creative services (e.g., rundowns, scripting, music, costumes, and wardrobe), production management (e.g., talent booking of announcers and entertainers; rehearsal scheduling), stage management, scoreboard operations, video production and technical production (e.g., staging and set construction, lighting, sound, and special effects such as lasers and pyrotechnics)

- Other common functional areas: hospitality and social events (e.g., receptions and parties); fan festivals and activities; broadcasting of television, radio, and Internet; business affairs (e.g., accounts payable, accounts receivable, purchasing, and legal)

IDENTIFYING NECESSARY STAFF

Identifying necessary staff members is a key factor to the success of any sporting event. Perhaps no industry is as dependent on the management functions of planning and organizing as the event industry. Planning involves setting organizational goals in order to reach objectives, whereas organizing is the process of allocating your human resources in an effort to accomplish the organization's goals. Thus, numerous factors must be taken into account when a sport event manager analyzes his staffing needs. These factors include the following:

- The type of event being planned (e.g., mega-events, multiple-location events, cross-cultural events, international events, youth events, events for people with disabilities, senior events, family events, extreme events, tournaments, championships, meets): Some events will require specialized staffing needs. For example, international or cross-cultural events may require staff to speak multiple languages. Mega-events may require a very large staff, and events for people with disabilities may require various health-related specialists.

- Destination-specific factors: The geographic location where the event takes place is a very big factor, especially in relation to volunteers. Sporting events being hosted by smaller-market destinations may not have the same access to a large database of volunteers. Another destination-specific factor is the level of support and assistance in securing staffing by the host destination. Some sports commissions and convention and visitors bureaus provide better support than others. A third factor may be the demographics of the destination. Depending on the staffing needs of the particular event, certain destinations may have the ability to staff more effectively. For example, Florida has a large population of elderly citizens who are willing volunteers. A fourth and final destination-specific factor is the current economic environment of the host region. For example, in geographic regions with high levels of unemployment at the time of an event, it seems reasonable to believe that residents would be seeking employment. However, this becomes detrimental when the staffing needs are primarily volunteer jobs, and often these types of depressed regions provide fewer corporate volunteers.

• Duration and time of event: The longer an event lasts, the more staff you will need. A small-scale sporting event such as a three-hour baseball game played on a Tuesday evening is easier to staff than a mega-event such as the Olympic Games or Paralympic Games, which occur over the course of a two-week period and entail multiple events lasting multiple hours each.

• Functional factors: These are factors specific to the functional skills of employees. In the section on organizational charts, we listed a variety of functional areas such as marketing, operations, guest services, competition, and presentation. Certain staffing positions require greater training and skill than others. For example, ticket takers and ushers require less training and specialized skill than do officials. Thus, generally there are significantly more potential employees to fill a ticket taker position than those employees who have been specially trained to officiate.

• Relationship with organizational actors within the sporting event network: As suggested earlier, the planning of a sporting event requires the collaboration of a number of representatives from the multiple organizations that make up a sporting event network. For example, an event may require the staffing of officials from the league office, local government officials, a local hotel, media, sponsors, and many other actors. The relationships that develop between these interorganizational actors are vitally important to the success of the event (Shonk and Bravo 2010). In this respect, a rights holder who has a very strong relationship with an existing sponsor may be able to staff its event with employees who work for the sponsorship organization. For example, since 2005, toymaker Mattel, Inc. has had more than 8,500 employees from 35 countries volunteer at hundreds of local and national sporting events. One of Mattel's strong partnerships is with the Special Olympics, and in 2011 Mattel sent 50 employees to the Special Olympics World Games in Athens, Greece. Mattel employees from 20 countries around the world were selected to serve in the spirit of diversity and inclusion (Business Wire 2011).

SCHEDULING STAFF

Scheduling the appropriate number of staff members who are qualified to carry out the objectives of the event is critically important. Some organizations use a project management system to assist with scheduling full-time, part-time, and volunteer staff. According to Goldblatt (2011), tasks are usually divided into two types of scheduling when using a project management system: parallel scheduling and serial scheduling. *Parallel scheduling* refers to tasks that may be performed at the same time, whereas *serial scheduling* refers to tasks that must be performed in a sequence. An example of parallel scheduling would be the tasks pertaining to merchandising at a baseball game, which may entail operating cash machines at multiple locations or hawking concessions in multiple seating sections. A good example of serial scheduling is the tasks involved in public address announcements at the same baseball game, whereby the script may start with the starting lineup followed by the national anthem and then the first pitch in this particular order for every game. In a similar manner, the grounds crew must complete their field maintenance before the players take to the field for the start of the game. Staff scheduling should take into account tasks before, during, and after the event.

Staffing Before the Event

A number of factors must be taken into account when scheduling staff before an event. Perhaps the most important question facing event planners is what must be completed before the event takes place. Goldblatt (2011) suggests that once the event is clearly defined, the work must be carefully analyzed and broken down into smaller units of work called tasks. Tasks are singular, independent entities that are individually managed, require clearly assigned resources (e.g., labor, finance), and have specific start and finish times. Certain tasks cannot be completed once the event is under way. For example, if the event involves food and beverages, most caterers require that food orders be placed before the event. Print programs cannot be produced while the event is taking place, and tasks such as busing require prior planning in order to meet the requirements necessary for servicing event attendees.

Once a clear list of tasks has been developed, it is then easier to divide the work and schedule staff for specific tasks. Supovitz (2005) recommends using a critical dates calendar, which is distributed to a wide audience. Everyone listed in the responsibility column of the calendar should receive a copy, and confidential or sensitive information should be deleted from widely distributed calendars.

A sample critical dates calendar is provided in table 4.1. The calendar outlines necessary tasks such as calling and scheduling busing, ordering equipment, and securing a title sponsor. Maria is responsible for calling and scheduling the busing; she started on January 2 and needs to complete this task by June 1, 2012. Thomas is responsible for ordering equipment, and he has less than a month to accomplish this task between January 2 and January 30, 2012. Michael and Sara are working on securing a title sponsor for the event, and they have a full year to accomplish this task between January 2 and December 31, 2012.

Staffing During the Event

Ask almost any event planner the key to success and he will tell you it is planning and preparation. As mentioned earlier, once the event begins, the planning is over and event maintenance and operations kick in. Now the goal is to implement the plans that were made before the event. One of the key staffing goals during the event is to have enough workers scheduled so that the event runs smoothly. However, supervisors should monitor staffing issues during the event to ensure that workers are actually needed in various positions. Supovitz (2005) describes a number of tools that can be developed beforehand and used during the event. These tools include the event rundown, scripts, production schedules, and cast lists, and all are very helpful in the scheduling process.

The *event rundown* is an event presentation tool that outlines the precise details of how the event will unfold, including a description of various activities, time and duration of activities, and audiovisual needs. During the event, the host or public address announcer should read from a *script*, which details important components of the event such as player introductions, customer service information, sponsor acknowledgments, game analysis, and introductions of special performers such as the national anthem singer. The *production schedule* highlights all the activities at the event facility and is the primary tool for the actual presentation of the event. Some events may also include a *cast list*, which is a roster identifying the various people or groups and listing their roles or functions as defined in the running order.

A sample production schedule for the Dodge National Circuit Finals Rodeo (DNCFR) in 2011 is provided in table 4.2. For example, on Wednesday, March 30, the stall office opened for contestants at 8:00 a.m. and remained open until 6:00 p.m. The barrel stakes needed to be set for the Women's Professional Rodeo Association at 10:30 a.m. Also you will see times and locations for working and running the timed event cattle and the DNCFR Kick-Off Party from 7:00 to 9:30 p.m. at the Renaissance Hotel.

Table 4.1 Sample Critical Dates Calendar

Task	Start date	End date	Responsibility
Call and schedule busing	1/2/12	6/1/12	Maria
Order equipment	1/2/12	1/30/12	Thomas
Secure title sponsorship	1/2/12	12/31/12	Michael, Sara

Table 4.2 Sample Production Schedule for the Dodge National Circuit Finals Rodeo 2011

Day/Date/Time	Activity	Location
WEDNESDAY, MARCH 30		
8:00 a.m. to 6:00 p.m.	Stall office open for contestants	HP / KI
10:30 a.m.	Set barrel stakes for WPRA	TG / WPRA
1:00 p.m. to 2:00 p.m.	Work and run timed event cattle: SW	Ted / FT / JG / TC
2:00 p.m. to 3:00 p.m.	Work and run timed event cattle: CR	Ted / FT / JG / TC
3:00 p.m. to 4:00 p.m.	Work and run timed event cattle: TR	Ted / FT / JG / TC
7:00 p.m. to 9:30 p.m.	DNCFR Kick-Off Party at Renaissance Hotel	ML / All

Staffing After the Event

An evaluation of the staffing plan should take place at the conclusion of a sporting event. Both supervisors and all staff who worked the event, including volunteers, should be included in the evaluation process. Critical areas of evaluation include identifying tasks or activities that were overstaffed or understaffed. In addition, supervisors should conduct exit interviews with volunteers as well as a brief performance appraisal of staff members. Key staff should also provide feedback concerning the strengths and weaknesses of the event along with identifying additional human and material resource needs that would improve the event.

CONSIDERING OUTSOURCING STAFF

Allen and Chandrashekar (2000) report that more than 90 percent of major corporations in the United States have outsourced some services. Mol (2007) defines outsourcing as the state or process of procuring goods and services from external suppliers. According to Burden and Li (2009), "outsourcing is a means of providing the organization access to highly skilled and knowledgeable personnel often not available in-house and increased flexibility in conducting business" (p. 139). Many examples of outsourcing across multiple segments of the sport industry can be cited. Most notably, athletic programs at colleges and universities throughout North America have focused on outsourcing such items as merchandise; tickets; and advertising, radio, and broadcast rights. Georgia Tech recently hired Aspire Group to handle ticket sales for football and men's basketball, the first case of a university outsourcing its ticket operations (Lombardo and Smith 2009). In addition, Ohio State's recent outsourcing of their marketing and media rights to IMG College for a guaranteed $110 million over 10 years was the richest annual rights fee ever given to a university (Smith 2009).

The reasons companies outsource may vary depending on the circumstances. Burden and Li (2009) suggest that companies generally outsource for one of the following four reasons:

1. Outsourcing helps companies operate in a more efficient manner by focusing in-house resources on core competencies while outsourcing peripheral functions.

2. Outsourcing provides the company with economies of scale because the unit cost charged by the service providers is generally reduced because they are dealing with multiple organizations at one time.

3. Companies that outsource eliminate personnel costs such as recruitment, retention, and employee relations. The company gains access to highly skilled and knowledgeable personnel who may not be available in-house.

4. Companies outsource because they do not have the technical expertise in-house, the resources to invest in new technology, or the ability to train staff.

A wide variety of functional areas are outsourced within the sport industry. For example, concession operations are often outsourced to companies such as Aramark, Levy Restaurants, and Centerplate. These companies operate concessions in major professional leagues, such as the NFL, NBA, and NHL as well as Major League Baseball and Major League Soccer, and in minor league venues, convention centers, and entertainment centers. Ticketing is another functional area that is often outsourced, and Ticketmaster is the largest company in this market, serving thousands of events. According to the Ticketmaster (2012) website, in 2009 it was appointed the official ticketing services provider for the London 2012 Olympic Games and Paralympic Games. The sale of marketing and media rights along with scoreboard operations are often outsourced within the sport industry. In addition, some organizations may choose to outsource the maintenance of their athletic fields. For example, Lakes Community High School located in a Chicago suburb outsources field maintenance requirements such as aeration to Lohmann Sports Fields, a company from Marengo, Illinois, that renovates, constructs, and maintains athletic fields (Phillips 2011).

The practice of outsourcing is becoming a larger part of the industry from a human resource perspective. Because of the transient nature of some sporting events that travel from market to market, staffing is a challenge that is often solved by outsourcing. For these types of events, volunteers play a vital factor in staffing everything from concessions, merchandise booths, ticket booths, registration tables, welcome centers, hospitality tents, and shuttle services for players and coaches along with performing other duties such as officiating, scorekeeping, and timing. In many instances, destination marketing organizations (DMOs) such as the regional convention and visitors bureau or sports commission can be very helpful in assisting event planners with the recruitment of volunteers and other paid part-time employees. As noted by Jason Aughey in the industry profile at the beginning of the chapter, a sports commission will help gather volunteers, which is a big component of what the commission is able to offer to the event rights holder. Upon booking an event, some DMOs will state the number of part-time employees they will provide for the event in the contract. In some cases, the staffing is outsourced to temporary employment agencies such as Manpower or Kelly Services. According to the website for the American Staffing Association (2012), U.S. staffing companies such as these employed 2.8 million temporary or contract workers per day in 2011. Using a temporary employment agency can be an excellent way to ensure that the functional needs of a sporting event are fully staffed. However, some temporary agencies are more reputable than others, and therefore event planners should do some research before hiring a particular company.

MANAGING AND MOTIVATING STAFF

Managing and motivating an event staff can be a challenge at times, but these tasks are vitally important to the success of the event. The primary challenge may be that the event planner is managing a staff of both full-time and part-time employees and volunteers. In cases where an event planner is managing a one-off event, the event may occur in such a short period that it leaves little time for not only training employees but also building any type of cohesion among them. Job performance is considered a function of one's ability multiplied by motivation multiplied by resources (Lussier and Kimball 2009). Although many management scholars agree on the importance of hiring talented people who are highly skilled and knowledgeable, there is no consensus as to how to motivate employees. Thus, a number of theories have emerged throughout the years regarding employee motivation, including those offered by Taylor, Mayo, Maslow, and Herzberg.

Frederick Taylor's Scientific Theory

In the late 1800s, Frederick Taylor argued that employees are primarily motivated by pay. Taylor's scientific theory of management suggests that employees do not naturally like work and therefore need close supervision. Scientific management theorized that how tasks were performed could be optimized by simplifying the jobs in order to train workers to perform a specialized sequence of motions in the one "best" way. Thus, workers were focused on one set task and encouraged to work hard in an effort to maximize productivity. However, the routine nature of these tasks soon became boring for many employees, and it became apparent that this approach to motivation treated employees more like machines than human beings.

Elton Mayo's Human Relation School

Between 1927 and 1932, Elton Mayo conducted a series of experiments at the Hawthorne factory of the Western Electric Company in Chicago, Illinois. Coming from the Taylor school, Mayo soon learned that workers were motivated not only by money but also by having their social needs met. In essence, Mayo found that scientific management was unable to explain certain aspects of employee behavior within the workplace. Workers were best motivated under the following circumstances: when managers and employees had better communication; when there was greater management involvement with the employees; and when employees worked in teams. Mayo's research suggested that recognition, a sense of belonging, and job security were important factors for employees.

Maslow's Hierarchy of Needs Theory

In the 1940 and 1950s, Abraham Maslow developed his hierarchy of needs theory, which highlighted the responsibility of employers to provide an environment that encourages their employees to reach self-actualization. The thrust of Maslow's theory is that human beings are motivated by unsatisfied needs and that certain lower-level needs must be addressed before a person can meet the next level of needs. The first level is physiological needs such as hunger and thirst. Safety needs such as security and protection are the second level of needs. Third, people need to be loved and feel a sense of belonging, which Maslow referred

to as social needs. Only when these lower-level needs are met can a person progress to higher-level needs such as esteem and self-actualization. Esteem includes such needs as self-esteem, recognition, and status. Self-actualization is the summit of Maslow's needs and can never be fully satisfied.

Herzberg's Two-Factor Theory

Frederick Herzberg was closely linked to Maslow, and he developed a two-factor theory made up of hygiene and motivational factors. Hygiene factors are those that surround the job rather than the job itself. They are essential for the existence of motivation in the workplace and when absent lead to dissatisfaction in the workplace. Hygiene factors may include pay, safe working conditions, company policies, fringe benefits, job security, status in the workplace, and interpersonal relationships. Motivational factors are more concerned with the job itself, yield positive satisfaction, and motivate employees to strive for superior performance. Herzberg referred to motivational factors as satisfiers, and employees are intrinsically motivated by these factors. Motivational factors may include recognition, job enlargement, job enrichment, sense of achievement, responsibility, and meaningfulness of an employee's work.

Other Studies on Motivation

Some studies suggest that various motivational tactics can lead to desirable behaviors by employees and thus greater performance. For example, Perry, Mesch, and Paarlberg (2006) suggest that financial incentives and challenging and specific goals improve an employee's task performance. Numerous studies have shown that employees become more loyal when they receive praise and recognition from supervisors. Nelson (1999) provides the following low-cost "I" suggestions for developing a loyal and committed group of employees:

• Interesting work: The duties for employees working in the event industry may change on a daily basis. For example, one day an employee may need to travel to conduct a site visit, while the next day she may be on the computer developing a proposal for a client. Although the work for an event planner never gets boring, this may not be true for part-time and volunteer employees involved in game-day operations such as ticket takers or parking attendants. The key to keeping these types of employees motivated may revolve around providing training for multiple jobs and rotating them between jobs.

• Information: Employees want and need to be empowered with the information required to do their jobs in an effective manner. Volunteer and part-time labor forces often believe they are not provided with adequate information. A study by Taylor and colleagues (2006) found that volunteers expect to be consulted by management regarding their positions and tasks, but rarely did this happen. The other source of information employees desire is feedback about how they are doing in their jobs. *Inc.* magazine suggests that employers open the channels of communication, thus allowing employees to be informed, ask questions, and share information.

• Involvement: Employees appreciate being involved in decision making, and as you involve others, you increase their commitment and facilitate the implementation of new ideas. There are a number of ways to get employees involved in various aspects of an event. You can assign them various leadership roles, ask for feedback, empower them to make various decisions, and generally let them know you value their involvement on a regular basis.

• Independence: Most employees appreciate the flexibility of not having someone looking over their shoulders and being able to do their jobs as they see fit. With any job, but especially with volunteers and short-term labor, it is always a good idea to set guidelines and highlight your expectations. However, once you have done so, it is best not to micromanage your employees.

• Increased visibility: Most people need a pat on the back or a compliment every once in a while. Managers who do this and provide their employees with new opportunities to learn and grow as a form of recognition are highly prized.

PERSONAL MANAGEMENT STYLE AND EFFECTIVE LEADERSHIP

Leadership is critically important to the success of a sporting event. Although early leadership studies focused on the individual leader, today the study of leadership also focuses on additional factors such as followers, peers, work setting, supervisors, and culture (Avolio, Walumbwa, and Weber 2009). Scholars have set forth numerous definitions of leadership. Chelladurai (2005) suggests that most definitions of leadership contain the following three significant elements: (1) Leadership is a behavioral process; (2) leadership is interpersonal in nature; and (3) leadership is aimed at influencing and motivating members toward group or organizational goals. Bass (1990) defined leadership as an "interaction between two or more members of a group that often involves a structuring or restructuring of the situation and the perceptions and expectations of the members" (p. 19). Tosi and Mero (2003) defined leadership as a "form of organizationally based problem-solving that attempts to achieve organizational goals by influencing the action of others" (p. 248).

The successful planning and implementation of a sporting event is critically dependent on strong leadership. A leader in the sport event industry must be capable of influencing people within multiple organizations and representatives of various stakeholder groups to achieve common goals for the advancement and successful implementation of the event. Regardless of your job title, if you work in the sport event industry, you will be asked to take on a leadership role. Some questions to consider include the following: What leadership traits do I possess? What steps can I take to become a more effective leader? What is my role in the leadership process? What style of leadership describes me?

According to Chelladurai (2005), leadership theories fall into three categories: trait theories, behavioral theories, and situational theories:

1. Trait theories: This approach assumes that people inherit certain traits that make them better

suited for leadership. The early research on leadership tried to identify specific traits such as height, weight, age, intelligence, personality, dominance, aggression, self-esteem, and achievement.

2. Behavioral theories: Contrary to the trait approach, the behavioral approach to leadership assumes that leaders are made and not just born. Research studies at Ohio State University and the University of Michigan supported the thought that leader behavior was a significant factor.

- The Ohio State studies indicated that nine behaviors were indicative of leader activity. Later research condensed these nine behaviors into two broad categories: consideration and initiating structure. *Consideration* is defined as the leader's concern for member well-being and warm and friendly relations within the group. *Initiating structure* is defined as the leader's concern for the effective performance of the group's tasks.

- The Michigan studies also identified two styles of leadership behavior, employee orientation and production orientation. *Employee orientation* is defined as the degree to which a leader is concerned about human relations on the job, whereas *production orientation* highlights the degree to which the leader is concerned about the technical aspects of the job and productivity.

3. Situational theories: Different styles of leadership may be most appropriate for making decisions; thus leaders must take situational variables into account. Three common situational theories include Fiedler's (1967) contingency model of leadership, House's (1971) path–goal theory, and Osborn and Hunt's (1975) adaptive–reactive theory of leadership.

- Fiedler's (1967) contingency model of leadership: Fiedler sought to determine the orientation of the leader (relationship or task); the elements of the situation (leader–member relations, task structure, and the leader's position power); and the leader orientation found to be most effective as the situation changed from low to moderate to high control. Fiedler found task-oriented leaders to be more effective in low- and moderate-control situations and relationship-oriented managers more effective in moderate-control situations.

- House's (1971) path–goal theory of leadership: The path–goal theory focuses on members' personal goals, their perception of organizational goals, and the most effective paths to these goals. This theory suggests that a leader should motivate subordinates by emphasizing the relationship between subordinates' own needs and the organizational goals as well as clarifying and facilitating the path subordinates must take to fulfill their needs and the organization's needs.

- Osborn and Hunt's (1975) adaptive–reactive theory: Osborn and Hunt conceptualized leader behavior as a dichotomy consisting of adaptive and reactive behavior. Adaptive behavior is concerned with how much the leader adapts to the requirements of the organizational system. Reactive behavior considers the leader's behavior in reaction to member preferences and the various differences among the tasks performed by members.

Environmental factors and the changing and evolving nature of organizations have had an impact on leadership. An environmental factor such as the economy can impact leadership and how a leader allocates resources. The complexity of planning and implementing a sporting event is evident when considering that multiple organizations, people, and stakeholder groups are attempting to deliver a carefully crafted experience that is so polished that the mechanics are imperceptible to the consumer. This goal becomes increasingly complex when you consider that each of these organizations, people, and stakeholder groups has diverse goals and objectives. However, a strong leader can take these diverse goals and focus on the primary goals of the event. The changing climate of business requires leaders who can also transform organizations. Transactional and transformational leadership are two popular styles of leading.

Transactional Leadership Style

According to Yukl (1981), transactional leadership involves exchanges whereby both the leader and the subordinate influence one another reciprocally, and thus each derives something of value. Both the leader and follower receive something they want (Kuhnert and Lewis 1987). Chelladurai (2005) suggests that transactional leadership is a very fruitful approach when the environment of the work group is stable and when both the leader and followers are satisfied with the work group's purposes and processes. However, effective transactional leaders must regularly meet the expectations of their followers; thus effective transactional leadership is dependent on the leader's ability to meet and respond to the reactions and changing expectations of their followers. Because most sporting events are planned between representatives from multiple organizations, leadership is often transactional because of the expectation that various organizations will exchange resources in an effort to create a successful event.

Transformational Leadership

The critical focus of transformational leadership is the vision and a general discontent with the status quo. Transformational leaders are often described as charismatic. Transformational leadership originates in personal values and beliefs and can be defined as "the process of influencing major changes in the attitudes and assumptions of organization members (organizational culture) and building commitment for major changes in the organization's objectives and strategies" (Yukl and Van Fleet 1992, p. 174). According to this definition, Chelladurai (2005) suggests that transformation occurs at three levels: (1) an organization's objectives and strategies; (2) a member's commitment to goals and strategies; and (3) a member's assumptions and attitudes. Through their personal values and beliefs, transformational leaders are able to both change follower goals and beliefs and unite them (Kuhnert and Lewis 1987). The end result of transformational leadership is higher levels of performance by followers (Bass 1985).

MANAGEMENT MEETINGS

In the event industry, it is not unusual for an event planner's entire day to be consumed by meetings. Endless meetings can be both boring and tiring. However, meetings do not have to be this way. Because they may be required to attend so many meetings, it is important for event planners to become proficient at meeting management. Depending on your role within the organization and in planning the event, you may be required to call meetings or attend them. Meeting attendees may include employees within your organization and representatives of network organizations involved in planning the event. Each of these network organizations probably has a stake in the event. Thus, numerous stakeholders may attend the meeting, including government officials, sponsors, governing and sanctioning bodies, sport venue personnel, representatives from the organization that owns the rights to the events, local businesses, sports commissions, convention and visitors bureaus, chambers of commerce, local hoteliers, representatives from local attractions and rental car companies, and security personnel.

Poorly planned meetings can influence a sporting event. Streibel (2007) suggests that bad meetings waste time, talent, and resources and can negatively affect the climate, culture, and image of an organization, whereas good meetings help answer questions, assist in the discovery of new questions, and allow for discussing important issues and reaching decisions as a group. Francisco (2007) provides guidance for planning and running a successful meeting using crucial checklists. She claims that creating and facilitating effective meetings requires (1) preparation; (2) conducting and documenting the meeting; and (3) following up after the meeting. This section discusses each of these stages.

Stage 1: Preparing for the Meeting

One of the first questions to consider is whether or not you actually need to call a meeting. Francisco suggests that meetings are needed for the following reasons:

- To present information that is better delivered in person
- To get input from others
- To gain buy-in on an issue
- To motivate and energize a team or individuals
- To solve problems

When considering whether you should meet, Francisco suggests taking the following important questions into account:

- Can you state the purpose of the meeting?
- Is the purpose of the meeting worth the participants' time?
- Would an e-mail or phone call produce a more efficient result than calling a meeting?
- Do you truly want or need participant input?
- Will you truly act on participant input?
- Do you have all the information you need to meet productively?
- Have you given yourself and the participants enough time to prepare for the meeting?
- Are the participants able to work together on the issues necessitating the meeting?

If you do call a meeting, it is important to set a purpose for the meeting and develop objectives that will be accomplished during the meeting. You will also need to develop and distribute an agenda; secure a meeting location; and inform attendees of the meeting date, purpose, and location.

Stage 2: Conducting and Documenting the Meeting

Because everyone is so busy, some staff will enter a meeting without adequately preparing for it. Thus, Francisco suggests that meeting facilitators attempt to get everyone on the same page by leading an exercise that highlights the purpose and objectives of the meeting and by having the group identify norms for behavior. During the meeting,

the facilitator needs to strike a balance in how the group approaches critical and creative thinking. The group can become overwhelmed with too much creative thinking; alternatively, excessive critical thinking can lead to situations where ideas are not given enough time to come to life. Another component of this stage is documenting the discussion, decisions, and actions that take place in the meeting. Facilitators should delegate the responsibility of taking meeting minutes to another staff member involved in the meeting.

Stage 3: Following Up After the Meeting

The real work begins at the conclusion of a meeting, especially in the sport event industry. Follow-up and follow-through are critical components of the successful implementation of an event. Meeting minutes will need to be distributed, and action items from the meeting will need to be carried out. In particular, specific action items in the minutes should be documented for further follow-up along with listing the staff member responsible for each item.

COMMUNICATING WITH STAFF

Communication is defined as "the process of transmitting or interchanging information thoughts, or ideas through speech, writing, images or signs" (Irwin, Sutton, and McCarthy 2008). Communicating with staff members is vital for success, especially before and during the implementation of a sporting event. Staff communication can take place in a number of ways, including direct interpersonal communication, social media, and on-site event communications.

Direct Interpersonal Communication

Although we live in a society where direct human interactions have been replaced by the newest and trendiest forms of technology, employees still need and want strong interpersonal relationships with their coworkers. Direct interpersonal communication involves face-to-face interactions between a sender and a receiver of a message. Interpersonal communication is so important because it provides that human link we all need.

The key to effective communication is listening to staff and conveying a sense that you understand their issues and concerns (deLisle 2009). But it also involves clear and consistent communication with employees. Employees develop a sense of direction and focus and exhibit a higher level of satisfaction when communication is clear and simple (Green 2009). Providing feedback is also an important element of building a relationship because it closes the circle of communication that links the listener and speaker. The people involved in the communication are either speakers or listeners until feedback is provided. Once the speaker receives feedback, the roles switch and both parties are equally involved in the conversation (Axzo Press 2002).

Social Media

Social media is becoming a vital part of the sport event management industry, especially when event planning involves a wide variety of stakeholders. At a rapidly increasing pace, organizations are using social media as a way to communicate with each other. Some of the types of social media used in the planning and implementation of sporting events are listed here.

• Social networks: Websites that connect people. Facebook (facebook.com) is the most popular social networking site that allows users to connect with friends, share photos, and send messages. It allows users to create a profile and timeline that chronicle their lives. Event planners use this site to cultivate relationships with attendees, families, friends, colleagues, and clients.

• Blogs: Websites that allow authors and readers to engage in conversation. Authors write and record their information in the format of a diary. When writing a blog, authors should do the following:

• Use plain language.

• Organize content so it is easy to read.

• Include bullets, bold letters, and key words.

• Develop connections with the reader by sharing how work and personal life connect.

• Use audio, video, photos, and images to enhance interest.

• Provide links to supporting information.

• Show readers where to find additional information (HowTo.gov 2012).

Many websites provide free blogs; one of the most popular is Wordpress.com. For example, *SportsEvents* magazine hosts its blog on Wordpress. You can find the blog by going to http://sportseventsmagazine.wordpress.com.

• Microblogs: Similar to a text message, microblogs allow the writer to post short messages. With more than 175 million users, Twitter is the most popular microblog. Twitter allows users and senders to receive and send photos, videos, and text-based posts of up to 140 characters. Event planners use Twitter to send out photos and videos along with short messages to announce, promote, or provide information about an event or to provide recognition to an organization or person.

• Videos: Videos can communicate a variety of types of information. A common website for videos is YouTube (youtube.com), which allows people to upload and watch originally created videos. Destination marketers use YouTube as a tool for selling a destination. For example, you can learn about the city of Louisville, Kentucky, if you type in "Louisville, It's Possible Here." In addition, event planners use YouTube to promote and chronicle events. By typing in the name of the organization, you can learn more about the National Senior Games Association by watching its promotional video.

• Discussion forums: Also known as discussion boards, these are online communities that allow for discussions by groups with a common interest. Posts to the site are organized into related threads around questions and answers or by community discussions. Rivals.com is a popular website that provides discussion forums for high school and college sports. According to its website, Rivals (2012) drives what it calls the "ultimate fan experience" by integrating exclusive expert content into a network of team-based sites with message boards and various community tools.

• Photo sharing: Sites such as Flickr (flickr.com) allow users to share their photos to a large audience via the Internet. Event planners may use photo sharing as a customer service and relationship marketing tool by posting event photos after the conclusion of the event. These photos can then be used by multiple parties for various purposes.

On-Site Event Communications

In many cases, the social media forms just described are used predominantly before and after a sporting event. However, on-site communication during the event is also critically important. Key staff personnel should be readily available during the course of an event. There are a number of ways that staff members communicate with each other and other key stakeholders during the course of a sporting event. One way is via handheld two-way radio devices often referred to as walkie-talkies. Perhaps used most often is mobile technology, including cell phones, texting, and various mobile applications. Another popular form of communication is Foursquare (foursquare.com), a location-based social networking site that allows users to check in at venues using a mobile website, a text message, or an application specific to a certain device. This is important to event planners because sporting events may be dispersed over a wide geographic region, and Foursquare allows staff to communicate their current location to others.

VOLUNTEERS

Volunteers are the lifeblood of most sporting events, especially for youth and amateur events that travel between markets. According to the Bureau of Labor Statistics of the United States Department of Labor (2011), approximately 64.3 million people volunteered between September 2010 and September 2011. Volunteering is "an activity which takes place through not for profit organizations or projects and is undertaken to be of benefit to the community and the volunteer; of the volunteer's own free will and without coercion; for no financial payment; and in designated volunteer positions only" (Cuskelly, Hoye, and Auld 2006, p. 5). The Canadian National Survey of Giving, Volunteering and Participating (2000) estimated that 1.17 million (5 percent) of Canadians volunteered in organized sport (Cuskelly, Hoye, and Auld 2006). In 2002, 14.8 percent of adults in England volunteered in sport programs (Sport England 2012).

Finding Volunteers

The quality of volunteers for a sporting event is directly related to the efforts by event planners to attract people who will make a positive contribution to the success of the event (deLisle 2009). According to Kim and Bang (2012), several factors are important when recruiting and hiring volunteers. First, it is important that managers understand the demographics and motivations of volunteers. For example, the demographic makeup of volunteers for a marathon may be middle-aged males, while another event involving extreme sports may consist of younger volunteers. People's motivations may also differ. A volunteer may be motivated for egoistic, humanitarian, leisure, or career-related reasons. However, most people volunteer because they want to be involved with something worthwhile, make the event a success, contribute to a better society, and give back to the community. Second, event managers should seek to identify individual fans and participants who may have an interest in volunteering. For example, avid golf fans may be willing to volunteer for an event such as the U.S. Open because they are rewarded with free tickets in exchange for their work. Third, it is important that event planners place volunteers in those positions that match their skill and aptitudes.

Working With Volunteers

Although the event industry is highly dependent on volunteers, utilizing them properly is one of the biggest weaknesses of many organizations. There are many reasons why volunteers are not effectively utilized, and deLisle (2009) offers a number of strategies for enhancing the volunteer experience.

Organizations should interview volunteers and be prepared to answer questions related to the job such as the necessary responsibilities and qualifications. The sport organization should gain an understanding of the motivation of each volunteer and try to satisfy the volunteer's needs in terms of her motivations. As suggested by deLisle, some volunteers simply want to feel important as they carry around a two-way radio, and others simply want a free T-shirt. The interview should provide a volunteer with information about the organization and should start the process of developing a positive rapport with the candidate. The interview should also assist with placing the volunteer in a position in which he will succeed because of his qualifications and motivations.

Volunteer training is critically important to the success of the event. Organizations spend months and years planning for a successful event that will be delivered to both participants and spectators. However, many of these same organizations do not train those persons who will be interacting with the event participants and spectators. Volunteer training should not happen on the job; rather, an orientation meeting should occur before the start of the event. According to deLisle, the orientation meeting should cover the following topics:

- Introduction to the organization and staff
- Goals and objectives of the event
- Rights and responsibilities of volunteers
- Discussion and distribution of the volunteer manual
- Accident procedures
- Scheduling, attendance, and absenteeism
- Dress code
- Performance evaluation procedures
- Progressive discipline policies
- Parking and access to the site

TEAM BUILDING

A team is a group of people who unite to accomplish a common mission or objective. Organizations develop teams in an effort to empower employees to more fully contribute and to increase productivity (Shonk 1992). In the case of a sporting event, a number of teams may be involved. For example, in a basketball game you have two teams contesting against each other, with the common objective of winning the game. However, event planners have no control over the outcome of the actual contest and, therefore, must take a much wider and holistic perspective on the sporting event. Healthy teams that regularly contribute and are committed to planning and resource funding are vital to the success of any sporting event.

According to Shonk (1982), teams function more effectively when they are able to meet regularly because they are in close physical proximity and have both the appropriate skills and levels of organizational authority present on the team. In contrast, poorly functioning teams are often characterized by a physical separation preventing them from meeting regularly. In addition, poorly functioning teams are often not given adequate resources to do the job, there is no recognition of team effort, and often leadership does not even recognize that a team exists. One of the most important elements of a team is the trust between members. To build trust on the team, Lees (2011) provides the following suggestions:

- When a team is new or changing, get everyone together to agree on how you will work together.
- Encourage and model honest and direct communication.
- Clearly support team members when they raise contentious and challenging issues.
- Be willing to admit weaknesses and mistakes and ask for help.
- Give others the benefit of the doubt before arriving at a negative conclusion.

- Focus time and energy on important issues, not politics.
- Offer and accept apologies without hesitation.

SUMMARY

The planning and implementation of a sporting event can be a complex process because of the numerous stakeholders involved. Staffing the event is a key component of the planning process, and a number of tools such as organizational charts, event rundowns, scripts, production schedules, and cast lists can be helpful to event planners. Understanding the functional areas of event management such as operations, competition, guest services, marketing, and presentation is also a key component of effectively staffing the event. In addition to full-time staff, key personnel for a sporting event often include volunteers and part-time workers. One of the key components of an effective staffing plan is to align the qualifications, motivations, and abilities of these personnel with your needs in terms of the job descriptions.

Event planners have a wide variety of responsibilities in relation to staffing an event. In some cases the event planner must go outside of his own organization to outsource staffing. Components of the sporting event such as concessions, merchandising, scoreboard operation, and hospitality are often outsourced to various companies. Event planners are often required to attend meetings and must serve in leadership roles. During these times, the event planner may assume a transactional or transformational leadership style. In addition, event planners are always working toward developing a highly functional team that will effectively plan and implement the event. Communication with staff during the process may entail direct interpersonal communications along with the use of social media and on-site communications such as two-way radios. As you can see, meeting all these roles within the context of staffing a sporting event is a challenging proposition for an event planner. Therefore, she must be willing and able to adapt to change and to work with a wide variety of people, groups, and organizations in an effort to staff the event.

LEARNING ACTIVITIES

1. Go to the following YouTube video titled "National Senior Games Association (NSGA)" at www.youtube.com/watch?v=aytfWYT1-yQ&feature=youtu.be. Watch the promotional video about the National Senior Games, and describe the types of activities that would need to be staffed.

2. Consult the section in this chapter on meeting management, and recount your last meeting. Did the meeting meet any of the requirements that Francisco suggests for calling a meeting? Describe which requirements were met and which were not met in a paragraph.

3. Have you volunteered with a nonprofit organization within the last year? If not, before the semester ends, please volunteer with one

nonprofit organization (preferably a sport organization) for at least a portion of one day. What did you learn from volunteering? Beyond completing this assignment, what other factors motivated you to volunteer? Finally, list this volunteer experience on your resume. It will be helpful moving forward in your career.

4. Consult the section about social media in this chapter, and describe which forms of social media you currently use. Write a paragraph describing how your use of social media can effectively help a sport organization for which you would like to work.

5. Create a fictitious sporting event, and list 10 tasks that would need to be completed to implement the event.

REFERENCES

Allen, S., and A. Chandrashekar. 2000. Outsourcing services: The contract is just the beginning. *Business Horizons* 43 (2): 25-34.

American Staffing Association. 2012. Staffing employment grew 8% in 2011. Available: www.americanstaffing.net/index.cfm.

Avolio, B.J., F.O. Walumbwa, and T.J. Weber. 2009. Leadership: Current theories, research, and future directions. *Annual Review of Psychology* 60:421-449.

Axzo Press. 2002. Advanced interpersonal communication. Available: http://proquestcombo.safaribooksonline.com/book/communications/0619075996/firstchapter.

Bass, B.M. 1985. *Leadership and performance beyond expectations.* New York: Free Press.

Bass, B.M. 1990. *Bass & Stogdill's handbook of leadership: Theory, research, and managerial applications.* 3rd ed. New York: Free Press.

Burden, W., and M. Li. 2009. Minor league baseball: Exploring the growing interest in outsourced sport marketing. *Sport Marketing Quarterly* 18 (3): 139-149.

Business Wire. 2011. Mattel takes power of play to Special Olympics World Games with largest global team of corporate volunteers: Team Mattel heads for Athens with 50 employee volunteers from more than 20 countries. June 23. Available: www.businesswire.com/news/home/20110623006564/en/Mattel-Takes-Power-Play-Special-Olympics-World.

Chelladurai, P. 2005. *Managing organizations for sport and physical activity: A systems perspective.* 2nd ed. Scottsdale, AZ: Holcomb Hathaway.

Cuskelly, G., R. Hoye, and C. Auld. 2006. *Working with volunteers in sport: Theory and practice.* New York: Routledge.

deLisle, L.J. 2009. *Creating special events.* Champaign, Illinois: Sagamore.

Fiedler, F.E. 1967. *A theory of leadership effectiveness.* New York: McGraw-Hill.

Francisco, J.M. 2007. How to create and facilitate meetings that matter: Learn how to plan and run a successful meeting using crucial checklists. *Information Management Journal* 41 (6): 54-57.

Goldblatt, J. 2011. *Special events: A new generation and the next frontier.* Hoboken, NJ: Wiley.

Green, H.G. 2009. *More than a minute: How to be an effective leader and manager in today's changing world.* Franklin Lakes, NJ: Career Press.

House, R.J. 1971. A path–goal theory of leader effectiveness. *Administrative Science Quarterly* 16:321-338.

HowTo.gov. 2012. How to blog. Available: www.howto.gov/social-media/blogs/writing.

Irwin, R.L., W.A. Sutton, and L.M. McCarthy. 2008. *Sport promotion and sales management.* 2nd ed. Champaign, IL: Human Kinetics.

Kim, M., and H. Bang. 2012. Volunteer management in sport. In *Handbook of Sport Management*, ed. L. Robinson, P. Chelladurai, and P. Downward. New York: Routledge.

Kuhnert, K.W., and P. Lewis. 1987. Transactional and transformational leadership: A constructive/developmental analysis. *Academy of Management Review* 12: (4): 648-657.

Lees, I. 2011. Building teams for performance. *Keeping Good Companies* 63 (9): 562-565.

Lombardo, J., and M. Smith. 2009. Ga. Tech hands ticket sales to Aspire Group. *Street and Smith's SportsBusiness Journal*, May 25.

Lussier, R.N., and D.C. Kimball. 2009. *Applied sport management skills.* Human Kinetics: Champaign, Illinois.

Mol, M.J. 2007. *Outsourcing: Design, process and performance.* Cambridge, UK: Cambridge University Press.

Nelson, B. 1999. Low-cost ways to build employee commitment. *Inc.* [Online]. December 1. Available: www.inc.com/articles/1999/12/16412.html.

Osborn, R.N., and J.G. Hunt. 1975. An adaptive–reactive theory of leadership. The role of macro variables in leadership research. In *Leadership frontiers*, ed. J.G. Hunit and L.L. Larson. Kent, OH: Kent State University.

Perry, J.L., D. Mesch, and L. Paarlberg. 2006. Motivating employees in a new governance era: The performance paradigm revisited. *Public Administration Review* (July/August): 505-514.

Phillips, H. 2011. Will outsourcing become the new normal? *SportsTurf* 27 (7): 32-35.

Rivals. 2012. About us. Available: http://highschool.rivals.com/content.asp?CID=36178.

Shonk, D.J., and G. Bravo. 2010. Interorganizational support, commitment, cooperation and the desire to maintain a partnership: A framework for sporting event networks. *Journal of Sport Management* 24 (3): 272-290.

Shonk, J.H. 1982. *Working in teams: A practical manual for improving work groups.* Ridgefield, CT: Third Printing.

Shonk, J.H. 1992. *Team-based organizations: Developing a successful team environment.* Homewood, IL: Business One Irwin.

Smith, M. 2009. Ohio State lands $110M deal. *Street and Smith's SportsBusiness Journal*, March 30.

Sport England. 2012. The scale of sports volunteering in England in 2002. Summary report of the findings of the Sports Volunteering Study commissioned by Sport England from the Leisure Industries Research Centre, Sheffield, October 2003. Available: www.sportengland.org.

Streibel, B.J. 2007. *Plan and conduct effective meetings: 24 steps to generate meaningful results: The employee handbook for enhancing corporate performance.* New York: McGraw-Hill.

Supovitz, F. 2005. *The sports event management and marketing playbook.* Hoboken, NJ: Wiley.

Taylor, T., S. Darcy, R. Hoye, and G. Cuskelly. 2006. Using psychological contract theory to explore issues in effective volunteer management. *European Sport Management Quarterly* 2 (6): 123-147.

Ticketmaster. 2012. Our history. Available: www.ticketmaster.com/history/index.html?tm_link=abouttm_history.

Tosi, H.L., and N.P. Mero. 2003. *The fundamentals of organizational behavior: What managers need to know.* 1st ed. Oxford: Blackwell Publishing.

U.S. Department of Labor Bureau of Labor Statistics. 2011. Volunteering in the United States—2011. News release. February 22.

Yukl, G.A. 1981. *Leadership in organizations.* Englewood Cliffs, NJ: Prentice-Hall.

Yukl, G., and D.D. Van Fleet. 1992. Theory and research on leadership in organizations. In *Handbook of industrial and organizational psychology* (vol. 3), ed. M.D. Dunnette and L.M. Hough, 147-197. Palo Alto, GA: Consulting Psychologists Press.

CHAPTER 5

Event Budgeting

Chapter Objectives

After completing the chapter, the reader should be able to do the following:

- Understand the budgeting process and develop event budgets.
- Identify appropriate revenue streams.
- Identify appropriate expense categories.
- Understand how to control costs and manage cash flows.

Phil Milliner was appointed vice president of finance at Churchill Downs in December 2010. In that post, he oversees the financial planning and analysis for the home of the Kentucky Derby. Additionally, he assists in ensuring that the company is in compliance with local, state, and federal regulations. Having joined Churchill Downs in December 2004, he previously served as the company's controller, where he was responsible for the periodic financial close of the consolidated group as well as ensuring that the company fulfilled its quarterly and annual public reporting responsibilities.

Q: What is the process you go through to develop a budget for an event such as the Kentucky Derby?

A: The interesting thing about the Kentucky Derby itself, because of the size of the event and just how huge it is, is that all our expenses have to be locked down very early on with a lot of our vendors. So we end up with a lot of multiyear deals that allow us to, from a financial standpoint, really get pretty comfortable in establishing those costs pretty firmly. There is not a ton of variability except for the attendance-based costs that we have. A lot of the corporate hospitality we sell and a lot of the base setup costs we have are set in stone. Now the attendance-based stuff is just a matter of looking at history. With the Derby itself we are so dependent on the weather those days and that week that you really never know. The wagering, admission, and walk-up general admission revenues that we have and the associated costs with those can really change based on the weather, so we use historic trends.

Q: What are some areas where you have to estimate costs?

A: We factor in assumptions around our current strategy. What types of new thing are we doing in areas like the infield to increase our brand, for example? The last several years the red carpet has been new for us. Another area is what we are doing around Oaks Day, really marketing around a lifestyle theme, partnering with some of our community relations initiatives as we have in the past like with Komen. Those charitable purposes have really started to strengthen and have allowed us to make some more aggressive assumptions around the attendance.

Q: With such a big event, what are some things you do to try to control costs?

A: A lot of the costs related to things such as corporate hospitality, our sales strategy, and decorating the facility, we will know what those are. With labor costs, because we know we are going to be at capacity, we are assuming we are going to be all hands on deck, and all the costs associated with that we can count on. Our operations team does a great job of really holding our vendors accountable on that day and making sure our prices don't grow too much from year to year.

Q: What are some of the challenges you face in putting a budget together?

A: One of the things that is interesting about the Derby is that it is such a huge facility. There are probably 50 to 75 various venues throughout the facility, and it is a different experience and a different product for our consumers. Balancing all of those initiatives is definitely a challenge.

Q: What tips would you give to people who are developing budgets for events?

A: Your budgets are only as good as the information you get from your team. What we try to do is keep open lines of communication with the different members of our team and our different department heads. We try to realign department heads' goals with our budgetary goals. So we will tie their compensation to their individual budgets. The good thing about our team is that many members have been doing the Derby in some cases for 25 to 30 years, so they know what to do. Because of that factor, you have to challenge the team. It is easy to get into the habit of doing things the way we did them in the past. As an analyst, I have to challenge them to get creative and think outside the box a little bit. For example, on the sales side of corporate hospitality, we'll challenge them to mitigate potential weaknesses in that area by not relying so much on the same customers to come back every year. Let's open up our prospect book a little bit, expand a little bit more regionally, and create a little more diversification with that group. If a customer is unable to buy for budgetary reasons or some other reason, we have the flexibility to step in and call someone else to make that sale.

Q: **What is the appeal of working in sport finance?**

A: In the sport arena, not only do you get a chance to be at the table when you are closing various deals, which is exciting within itself, but you get to challenge the team to do better and continue to grow. You are in a business that is pretty exciting. Being a part of that and being in something you are interested in can be quite exciting.

A budget provides event organizers with realistic estimates of upcoming revenues and expenses associated with the event. Good budgeting requires managers to project all potential revenues and anticipate relevant expenses, and the budgeting process requires significant information gathering and planning. Planning is beneficial in that it helps event organizers recognize revenue streams that can be maximized as well as reduce waste by identifying and scrutinizing expense categories. Budgeting also communicates financial limitations to management and employees while at the same time empowering management to make good decisions with their available funds.

STAGES OF THE BUDGETING PROCESS

The budgeting process is an in-depth and necessary exercise that typically involves five detailed steps: (1) Gather information, (2) forecast sales, (3) project profits and losses, (4) compare industry norms, and (5) determine capital needs (Fried, Shapiro, and DeSchriver 2007).

Gather Information

Event organizers need to first gather information as they begin the budgeting process. This initial step will help them make more informed and insightful estimates and projections as they begin constructing a budget. Information gathering typically involves the collection of both internal and external information. Internal information is found within the company and specifically addresses organizational activities. The information may include organizational financial statements and details about marketing, research, and other activities. Event organizers can also use information external to the company. External information in the form of trade publications and industry benchmarks may give insights about activities taking place beyond the organization in the wider community and industry. Event organizers may use this information to learn about what their competitors and other organizations are doing within the industry. Economic indicators and other external information help provide perspective about the larger economy and its potential impact on the event's projected financial success.

Forecast Sales

After completing the first step, event organizers can use the information gathered to forecast future sales associated with the event. Organizers should examine internal documents such as financial statements, which provide details about the organization or event's past performances and historical sales information. Event organizers should take time to review this information and address the question of where previous events generated sales: from the sales of tickets, merchandise, sponsorships, concessions, or other activities? Historical sales information may be found within a series of historical financial statements, particularly more recent ones from the previous three to five years. This information can provide insights into the latest financial trends and seasonal patterns, will give organizers perspective regarding the types of sales generated from past events, and will help them make estimates about potential sales associated with the newest events.

Organizers can also look beyond historical organizational performances to understand industry and community activities discussed in external information gathered during the first step. This information may help organizers identify potential opportunities and threats that could directly affect future sales. Opportunities include new customers, products, channels, and price increases, which could have a positive effect on sales. Threats include competitors and accompanying price wars, government regulations, and challenging economic conditions, which could have a negative effect on sales. Have new competitors or events arisen since the last time the organizers hosted the event? What is the current economic climate—do economic indicators show evidence of spending by spectators and participants on sporting events similar to this one?

Coupling internal information with external information, event organizers should attempt to forecast sales and make projections about how much the event will generate. As part of these projections, organizers should consider using scenario analysis—estimating a best-case, worst-case, and most likely scenario. These scenarios allow event organizers to see the range of projected sales figures and make decisions based on several potential outcomes.

Project Profits and Losses

After forecasting sales, event organizers should develop an event budget, which includes revenues (the event's sales projections) and expenses (the costs associated with hosting the event). Revenues can derive from a variety of sources: tickets, merchandise, concessions, and parking. Event costs can also come from numerous places.

Event organizers may handle expenses associated with game-day operations, securing participants and sponsors, and renting or managing the event facilities. Organizers should spend time examining the information gathered earlier to forecast potential expenses, similar to the process of projecting revenue streams.

Event organizers can calculate expense line items by employing the same process used for forecasting sales. You should review historical data, examining how much was spent on similar events in the past. Have costs increased over time? What costs have other event organizers incurred related to operating or hosting the same or similar events? Do opportunities exist to minimize or reduce costs with the upcoming event? What other information can be gleaned from organizational financial information or external trade journals and economic indicators that may factor into expense projections? The opportunities and threats identified during the sales forecasting process may also provide insights into related expenses. For example, marketing and promotion expenses may increase with an influx of new competitors or waning economic conditions.

Event organizers can use this complete pool of information to develop an expense-related scenario analysis, projecting best-case, worst-case, and most likely scenarios that now incorporate sales and expenses. The planning process should focus on getting the most out of every dollar spent. Every expense dollar represents a cost to the event and organization and reduces the event's profit potential. Yet the adage "it takes money to make money" remains true. Event organizers must spend money on a variety of expenses, from paying staff and other personnel to preparing the site for the event to promoting and marketing the event. These expenses may reduce the event's overall profit potential. The goal is to ensure the event generates the "biggest bang for its buck," meaning each dollar spent leads to an accompanying increase in sales and profit generation.

Compare Industry Norms

After projecting profits and losses, event organizers should examine industry data where possible. You should use this information in conjunction with your projections. Comparing internal estimates and forecasts to industry data helps you determine whether your event estimates are in line with, or similar to, the competition. Did other events incur similar expenses related to this event's marketing and operating expenses? Did other organizers bring in similar sales on the number of forecasted athletes and spectators for this event? Event organizers should feel greater comfort with their budgets when the estimates are similar to those of other events. Yet, in some cases, event projections may not reflect the numbers of similar events. This may require a thorough review to determine where differences lie and what justifications may exist for those differences.

For example, revenue numbers may differ based on expected changes in revenue streams. Event organizers may expect higher revenues related to charging more for people attending or participating in the event. The organizers may have identified additional sponsorship opportunities or expect higher attendance rates as a result of an improving economy. From an expense perspective, the event organizers may expect reduced costs. They may have negotiated more favorable contracts with vendors, or they can reuse equipment from a previous event—eliminating expense items. Additionally, event organizers may plan to rely more on volunteers, which could lower their expected personnel costs. Differences from industry norms are not necessarily negative. Instead, they simply merit a second look, whereby event organizers can provide adequate support or rationale for the variances.

Determine Capital Needs

Finally, event organizers need to assess whether they can meet their revenue and expense projections with their existing assets. For instance, you may expect an increase in the number of people attending the event. When higher sales are projected, you need to determine whether more inventory is needed or if an investment in additional assets is required. You may need to purchase more seating to provide adequate space for your customers. Equipment and infrastructure used previously may face obsolescence or deterioration over time, and event organizers may need to invest in new purchases as a result. If so, you may consider pursuing additional funding through increased revenue streams or borrowings to make these capital investments.

Several capital financing options exist for event organizers. Large capital investments are frequently funded through bonds, which are financial instruments that require repayment of the principal (i.e., the original amount of the investment) plus interest. Bonds are typically issued to corporations and governments with excellent credit records and financial histories. The financial obligations can give event organizers access to millions or even billions of dollars for their events and related investments. In turn, event organizers must demonstrate that their projects are financially viable and that they ultimately can repay the bond.

Two major bond options exist for qualifying parties: general obligation bonds and revenue bonds. Governments can take advantage of general obligation bonds, which are repaid through new and existing tax revenues. Governments receive tax revenues from income, sales, and property taxes. The revenues are placed into a general fund, which governments can use for a variety of projects (Brown et al. 2010). For example, Olympic Games host cities and their government officials may rely on general obligation bonds. Beijing organizers used $2.5 billion of government bonds to fund the $70 billion event ("Beijing Olympics" 2011). Event organizers also have the opportunity to secure revenue bonds, which are repaid via revenue sources generated specifically by the project. Events can receive revenues from ticket sales, concessions, and merchandise. Event organizers must designate in advance which revenue streams they will use to repay the revenue bonds (Brown et al. 2010). The KFC Yum! Center in Louisville, Kentucky, cost $238 million and was partially funded through revenue bonds. Revenues originating from premium seat revenues, advertising and sponsorships, and naming rights were designated for the bond repayment (Green 2010).

Bonds are an appealing option for event organizers. However, not every event needs or can take advantage of this sizeable financial option. Other financial opportunities exist, including private funding via corporations and individual donors. Through capital funding campaigns, organizers can attract donors who express an affiliation with the organization and a willingness to contribute. The donors may reside in the same community where the organization is located and witness firsthand the event's or organizer's impact. Donors also may share similar interests with the event or support the event's activities and feel excited to contribute to its longevity.

Sponsorships are another viable funding opportunity. Sponsor corporations provide financial support or in-kind goods and services in exchange for access to the event's participants and spectators. Event organizers can receive sponsorship money ranging from thousands of dollars for small events to millions or even billions of dollars for mega-events such as the World Cup and Olympic Games. FIFA and Anheuser-Busch InBev signed a contract extension to sponsor the 2018 and 2022 World Cup events, where Budweiser would continue to serve as the official beer sponsor. The beverage company paid $1.1 billion for the rights (Panja 2011).

Beyond donations and sponsorships, sports commissions and foundations can offer funding to sporting events and organizers. These organizations operate as nonprofit entities and may raise money to attract sports and other events to their local communities. For example, Denver Sports is a 501(c)(3) nonprofit organization, and its mission is to develop "a legacy of economic and social vitality through sport." The organization actively seeks to bring sporting events to its community, including most recently the 2012 NCAA basketball women's Final Four and 2014 Federation of International Lacrosse (FIL) Men's Lacrosse World Championships. Foundations can raise funds for and host sporting events. The Adaptive Sports Foundation (ASF) works with athletes with disabilities, offers a variety of events such as winter and summer programs, and generates funding for athletes and events. Through their financial contributions, these organizations can raise money and help athletes participate in a range of activities. Event organizers can partner with groups that share similar values and missions to fund their events.

How do you derive budgetary figures?

• Past trends: The first step of the budgeting process asks event organizers to gather information from internal and external sources. Using information collected during this first step will provide more insights about past trends related to hosting and operating events. Examine revenues and expenses from previous events. Notice where estimates varied from actual charges, and identify potential reasons for those variations. Incorporate those variations where appropriate in the estimates for the upcoming event.

• Competition: Speak with other event organizers to understand their revenues and expenses. Some competitors may prove hesitant to provide this information, while others may willingly offer advice and insights about their events. Competitors may have insights about overlooked or unexpected areas. Organizers may also find this information by looking at trade publications and online sources for similar events and examining their reported numbers. Learning from other competitors may help event organizers avoid the potential mishaps and account for previously unexpected occurrences.

• Professional associations: Ask members of professional associations who have hosted similar events for their advice. What events have they hosted? What costs did they incur versus revenues generated? What challenges did they face? What differences did they see in projected versus actual numbers? Attending trade shows or professional association meetings gives event organizers an opportunity to network with others in the field and gather this critical information. Information may also be gleaned from any publications produced by the professional association, whether in the form of trade publications or other official reports and white papers. Gaining valuable perspective from other industry members will help event organizers capture a more complete listing of the revenues and expenses associated with their events. These industry personnel may also provide ideas or insights that the event organizers had not considered previously.

• Suppliers and buyers: Speak with vendors regarding the products needed for the event. Event organizers can use online sources before shopping around for multiple price estimates. How much do the requested goods and services cost? What credit terms and payment processes will the vendors provide? What discounts exist? This information can prove helpful when negotiating with vendors. Ask for discounts or price reductions where appropriate. Receiving more favorable contracts can help rein in costs and boost the event's profitability. Additionally, speaking to multiple vendors can ensure an opportunity to work with top-quality people who can deliver needed products on time and at the quoted prices. Working with reliable vendors may help manage the overall costs of the event—and help event organizers avoid unnecessary headaches.

BUDGET COMPONENTS

The budget consists of three primary elements: revenues, expenses, and net income or loss. Revenues represent money coming into the event or organization through an exchange of money for goods or services. For an event, revenues may come from the organizers selling tickets, merchandise, or concessions to spectators. Organizers may also generate revenues by selling advertising and sponsorship space to corporations and other organizations. Expenses, on the other hand, represent money flowing out of the event or organization and are the costs associated with generating revenues. Organizers will incur expenses as they attempt to generate revenues. For example, the event may create sales through parking. Organizers will hire or contract employees to manage those parking transactions—collecting parking fees, directing traffic, and helpings fans get to the event quickly and safely. The third element of the budget is net income (or net loss), which is the difference between revenues and expenses. Net income occurs when revenues exceed expenses, while net loss occurs when revenues do not cover the incurred expenses. Obviously, event organizers will certainly hope that every event creates net income rather than net losses. Careful tracking of revenue streams and associated expenses will help event organizers as they attempt to achieve financial successes.

The revenue, expense, and net income (net loss) numbers are forecasted or identified by completing the five steps in the budget process outlined in the previous section. Gathering information helps determine potential revenues and expenses. Steps two and three ask event organizers to forecast sales, expenses, and related profits and losses. These steps require event organizers to spend time thinking about their sales or revenue opportunities along with the associated costs of generating revenue. Consideration of industry trends and capital needs may also have an effect on forecasting revenues, expenses, and the resulting net income.

TYPES OF BUDGETS

The budgeting process involves five steps, and event organizers should create two budgets during the budgeting process: (1) a preliminary budget and (2) a working budget.

Preliminary Budget

As the name suggests, preliminary budgets are constructed during the earliest phases of the event planning process. Event organizers spend time gathering information about projected revenues and expenses as they plan for the event. Preliminary budgets reflect this information gathering, whereby the event organizers continually make modifications to their estimates and the budget over time as they receive information from multiple sources. For example, you may talk to several potential sponsors and offer them a range of sponsorship opportunities. From these discussions, you may attempt to project or forecast which potential sponsors will agree to sponsor the event and how much they are willing to pay for the opportunity. The preliminary budget represents a work in progress; event organizers continue to gather additional information and modify the event budget over time.

Working Budget

Event organizers will continue to gather information and refine the budget. Doing so helps ensure they have the most accurate information and have considered multiple scenarios. At some point, however, they will believe the numbers presented in the preliminary budget reflect their most informed and accurate estimates. The preliminary budget then becomes a working budget, which occurs when the estimating process is complete and actual numbers are included. These numbers will guide the event organizers as they begin to organize and then host the event. The budget numbers should include specific and expected revenues. For example, sponsors may have signed contracts detailing that they will receive specified sponsorship benefits and pay a specified amount in return. Participants may have paid registration fees, and spectators may have purchased tickets. Similarly, event organizers may have signed contracts with vendors, agreeing to pay the suppliers a certain amount in exchange for the requested products.

These contractual numbers become part of the working budget. As organizers receive revenues and incur expenses, they will compare them to the working budget. This document will help them track how their actual financial performances compare to their detailed estimates and will help them make changes as needed. For instance, if you see that your incoming revenues are lower than expected, you may attempt to identify ways to increase the number of paying participants or spectators. If staffing costs are too high, you may look for ways to supplement your staff through the use of volunteers. Having a working budget helps organizers maximize every dollar spent in their pursuit of revenue and profit generation.

TYPES OF REVENUES

Revenues represent money coming into an organization, resulting from an exchange of goods or services. On an income statement, revenues are referred to as the top line because of their location on the income statement—typically on the statement's first line. They are a key determinant of an event's potential financial success. Although high revenues do not necessarily guarantee financial success, they represent the cornerstone or the pathway toward a more profitable event.

Event organizers should understand their available revenue streams and determine where they will focus their revenue generation efforts for upcoming events. This section provides a listing of common revenue streams with examples from various sporting events.

Tickets, Registrations, and Memberships

Tickets, registrations, and memberships from attendance at or participation in an event generate revenue. Sporting events such as the Olympic Games and NCAA championships generate revenues from spectators purchasing tickets to attend the event. Participatory events such as the Chicago Marathon and Ford Ironman generate revenue through participants paying registration fees. Other organizations such as USA Triathlon and the U.S. Tennis Association receive revenues when sporting event participants pay membership dues as part of their entry into the events. This revenue category is an important revenue stream; therefore, event organizers should work to identify multiple ways to facilitate purchase of tickets, registrations, and related membership fees.

Sponsorships

Spectator and participatory sporting events often generate revenues through sponsorship rights by partnering with corporations and other organizations. Event organizers may agree to create signage, booths, or other displays promoting the sponsorship. In exchange for a sponsorship fee, the sponsor has the opportunity to reach a desired target market attending or participating in the event. Selected USA Triathlon Collegiate National Championship host cities receive $50,000 for promotions and advertising, and this benefit includes advertising in *USA Triathlon Life* and other triathlon-related publications. Additionally, corporate sponsors are featured on related websites, including the event's promotional web page and the governing body's national and regional websites (USA Triathlon 2012).

Sport organizations such as the International Olympic Committee (IOC) pride themselves on their offered sponsorship opportunities and have established programs to generate sponsorship revenues. The IOC's The Olympic Partner (TOP) program gives corporate sponsors the opportunity to feature their products on a global stage at the Summer, Winter, and Youth Olympic Games. Participating TOP program companies include McDonald's, General Electric Company, and VISA (Olympic.org 2012). Former TOP sponsor Johnson & Johnson paid an estimated $100 million over four years for the opportunity to sponsor the Olympic Games and reach athletes and spectators watching the events in person or on television and the Internet (Mickle 2008).

Chapter 6 provides more information about the potential benefits sponsors could receive as a result of their sponsorship participation and shows the specific language used by event organizers as they search for potential sponsorships.

Merchandising and Licensing

Sport organizations view sales of merchandise and licensing rights as another revenue opportunity. These products satisfy fans looking for ways to commemorate their attendance at various sporting events and to show their affiliation with a specific athlete, team, league, or sport. Spectators and participants alike appreciate the opportunity to purchase related merchandise. Event organizers can benefit financially from this revenue stream by offering a range of licensed products and merchandise to interested consumers. For example, in 2011 the Big Ten Conference partnered with MainGate to produce and sell the conference's merchandise at the football championship game. Fans attending the event made an estimated $1 million in purchases (Muret 2011).

When budgeting for merchandise sales, organizers need to estimate per capita spending (per cap) and the type of rights agreement (Lawrence and Wells 2009). Per capita spending reflects the amount of spending, per person, on merchandise at the event. For example, if $9,500 in sales is generated for an event attracting 1,000 spectators, per cap spending was $9.50. The type of agreement will also affect what you budget for merchandise sales. A flat fee may be exchanged for the rights to sell merchandise at the event, or event organizers and the facility will agree to a split of gross sales.

Events may also generate revenue by licensing their marks. The All England Lawn Tennis Club (2012), which hosts Wimbledon, created a licensing program with approximately 30 companies and sells products on an international level, partnering with tennis sporting goods providers Prince and Fila. Ralph Lauren, an additional partner, produces apparel and footwear for event personnel, including umpires, ball girls and boys, and other staff members. Spectators and tennis fans can purchase these licensed products at the facility kiosks, in retail stores, and online.

Food and Beverage Sales

Spectators may purchase concessions while attending an event, creating another revenue stream for sport organizations. Budgeting for food and beverage sales is very similar to budgeting for merchandise sales in that you have to consider per cap sales and the type of agreement you enter with your facility or concessionaire.

Food and beverage sales can also be a lucrative revenue stream if managed right. The demand has risen for specialty concessions beyond the ordinary fare of hot dogs and soft drinks, and event organizers have found ways to meet those needs. Stadiums and arenas now regularly offer upscale fare such as sushi, crab cakes, and short ribs accompanied by specialty beers and other beverages (Thomas 2010). Additionally, more event organizers have incorporated technology to better serve consumers interested in purchasing concessions. Fans can place food and drink orders from their seats, using smartphone applications where they input their seat locations and orders. The added convenience is a benefit to fans, who no longer have to leave the action in order to enjoy a range of concessions (Walker 2011). This option may also represent a new revenue opportunity for event organizers, as the added convenience may encourage fans to purchase and consume more—while paying premium prices to do so.

Souvenir Program Sales

Many events will derive revenue from the sales of souvenir or commemorative programs. For example, Churchill Downs creates special programs for its annual Kentucky Oaks and Derby events (Kentucky Derby 2011). These programs sell for a premium over the usual price on a non-Oaks or non-Derby day. These programs provide customers with memorabilia that may appreciate in value over time. Keeping in mind that not everyone will be interested in purchasing a program, some events choose to give away programs in order to put the materials in the hands of more consumers and to provide more value for sponsors.

Corporate Hospitality

Corporations and other large organizations may express interest in corporate hospitality, whereby sport organizations or event organizers set aside seats and space for a group of company employees plus their families, friends, and customers. These corporate hospitality packages provide benefits for event organizers and the corporations purchasing them. Event organizers can work with a larger group of confirmed ticketholders, ensuring a large block of tickets sold. They have the opportunity to upsell the event by offering additional amenities not always offered to individual ticketholders, such as dedicated support staff catering to the guests. In turn, corporations can use these offerings to provide incentives to productive employees, thank current customers for their support, or attract new customers.

Media Rights

Fans who cannot attend the events in person may choose to watch on television or online. As such, event organizers may negotiate with various media outlets, exchanging the right to broadcast their events for contracted revenues. For example, the U.S. Open organizers renegotiated a television contract with CBS. In the previous contract, CBS paid the U.S. Tennis Association (USTA) approximately $20 to $25 million each year. The new contract represented a "slight increase" in dollars and extended the terms through 2014 (Sandomir 2011). *SportsBusiness Daily* noted a significant surge in media rights fees at the collegiate and professional sports levels and questioned whether this growth reflects a sustainable revenue stream or simply a market bubble (Ourand 2011). Media rights exist for a variety of channels, including television, terrestrial and satellite radio, and the Internet.

Television

The biggest sporting events typically negotiate media rights. NBC paid $4.4 billion for media rights to the Olympic Games from 2014 to 2020. The contract extended NBC's rights, as the broadcast company paid $2.2 billion for the 2010 and 2012 Olympic Games (McCarthy 2011).

Terrestrial Radio

Radio is the oldest of the media offerings discussed here. Television and the Internet typically capture more media attention, yet radio still plays a sizeable role in broadcasting sporting events. In October 2011, the Los Angeles Dodgers signed a contract with Clear Channel Communications to broadcast its games for the 2012 through 2014 seasons plus postgame shows, several Spring Training games, and any postseason play (Los Angeles Dodgers 2011). Sport organizations and event organizers continue to use radio to reach fans, whether at home, in the office, or on the road.

Satellite Radio

Coupled with terrestrial radio, satellite radio is another way sports fans access information about and tune into various sporting events. Providers such as SiriusXM continue to negotiate with powerhouse conferences and sporting events, providing sizeable benefits for radio subscribers. In August 2011, SiriusXM signed a contract to broadcast football and basketball games plus coaches shows for the ACC, Big East, Big Ten, Big 12, Conference USA, Pac-12, SEC, and WAC (SiriusXM 2011).

Internet

The Internet continues to expand its reach as a medium by which fans can access sports. In addition to its television contract, the USTA negotiated with ESPN and Tennis Channel to broadcast the U.S. Open event via its USOpen.org website. The USTA also developed iPhone and Android smartphone applications, where fans could access additional content. In 2011, the Atlantic Coast Conference launched an advertising-supported digital network, theACC.com, to expand the amount of content they broadcast and expand their reach to more potential consumers. In addition to news and highlight shows, the network broadcasts numerous live events not available on traditional television outlets (Smith 2011, October 10).

These media channels and the accompanying media rights provide a significant revenue opportunity for event organizers. The largest and most popular events such as the Olympic Games, Super Bowl, and World Cup tend to command the largest media rights contracts. However, event organizers of regional and local levels may also have the opportunity to reach broadcasters and provide their events to a smaller but more targeted audience. The Internet especially has given smaller events a chance to showcase their offerings to dedicated and potentially curious audiences alike.

Although the list of revenue opportunities is long, event organizers should exercise caution in their pursuit and estimates of future revenue streams, as obtaining some revenues may be more challenging than others. Hurdles include shifting economic conditions and contractual conflicts of interest. The U.S. economy has witnessed ups and downs in recent years, and changing economic times can have a pronounced effect on consumer spending. Sports fans may feel reluctant to purchase tickets and related items during an economic downturn. Likewise, corporations and other organizations may want to invest in sponsorships but feel the heat from employees, stockholders, and industry watchdogs, who may frown upon sport-related investments even in the best of times. This reluctance to spend can affect event organizers who rely on sales of sponsorships, tickets, concessions, merchandise, and other items to support their events. In a recessionary period, event organizers must find creative ways to attract spectators and participants, whether through pro-

motions, discounted pricing, or other marketing tactics. They also must employ savvy marketing strategies to justify these spending opportunities and convince potential corporate consumers and sponsors of their value.

In addition to economic conditions, event organizers may face challenges with negotiating contracts, particularly when existing contracts potentially conflict. For example, an event may take place in a stadium or arena that has preexisting signage located in and outside the facility. The facility's management team may have contracted pouring and other concessions rights with vendors, and the contracts can limit the event organizer's ability to secure revenues in these areas. Event organizers should take note of these potential conflicts as they select facilities. When conflicts do occur, organizers must be prepared to adjust their budgets to reflect and offset potential reductions in their various revenue opportunities.

TYPES OF AGREEMENTS

Event organizers can choose from a variety of agreement types and associated fees. These decisions are largely contingent on the size, scope, and popularity of their events.

Rights Fee

A rights fee is an agreement where a broadcaster pays for the rights to broadcast an event and its associated content. The broadcaster is gambling it can sell enough advertising or generate other revenues to offset the cost of the rights fee. Organizers for a hugely popular and global event such as World Cup can pick and choose from numerous suitors and demand large rights fees. Following is a list of major media rights deals from 2011 as reported by *Street & Smith's SportsBusiness Journal* (Ourand 2011):

- The National Hockey League signed a TV rights deal with NBC and NBC Sports Net worth $2 billion over 10 years.
- The Pac-12 Conference signed a media rights deal with ESPN and Fox worth $3 billion over 12 years.

- NBC acquired the rights to four future Olympic Games for $4.38 billion.
- Fox and the Ultimate Fighting Championship agreed to a broadcast deal.
- ESPN extended its deal with the National Football League for eight additional years for $1.9 billion per year.
- FIFA sold the United States broadcast rights for two future World Cups to Fox, Telemundo, and Futbol de Primera Radio for an estimated $1.2 billion.

Although large events with national or global reaches can demand large rights fees, events that are smaller or more regional in nature would typically have more limited negotiating power and would receive fewer media rights dollars. Having said that, event organizers are still encouraged to pursue this valuable opportunity as a way to increase awareness about and interest in the sporting events and to generate important revenues for the event organizers.

Event organizers should use explicit language describing the media rights for media providers and the associated charges these providers will incur. For example, the NAIA championship broadcast rights fees for the spring 2012 season were as follows: Radio and video streaming ranged from $100 to $150 per game, with extra charges for each additional radio station. Television rights fees ranged from $250 to $500 per game, and web blogging fees ranged from $50 to $75 per game (NAIA 2011).

Time Buy

A time buy is somewhat the opposite of a rights fee agreement. For this type of agreement, the event property buys the airtime and broadcasts the event itself. In this situation, the event assumes the risk of selling advertising and sponsorship, keeping the revenue. Many smaller organizations will choose this option when they need the exposure to promote their sport or provide value for their sponsors. Before World Wrestling Entertainment went national, numerous regional wresting organizations would buy airtime on local television stations to promote ticket sales to their live events. Even though most lost money on the broadcasts, they were able to generate revenue through ticket sales that would not exist without the exposure.

Barter

Barter agreements, or partnerships, involve some sort of a split in advertising revenues between the event property and the broadcaster. This type of agreement reduces the risk for each party. In 2011, the National Lacrosse League (NLL) entered into partnership to put Saturday games on CBS Sports Network. Under the agreement, both parties would sell advertising and split the revenues. The NLL had never had a prime-time television slot before; therefore this arrangement was valuable in giving the league airtime to promote the sport and its athletes (Lefton 2011).

Syndication

Event organizers can sell media rights to have their events broadcast simultaneously on multiple television and radio stations. This opportunity expands an event organizer's reach beyond a single channel or station, and it meets consumer sport consumption demands beyond a local market. For example, ESPN provides syndicated content through ESPN Regional Television (SEC Network, Big East, WAC, Big 12, Mid-American) and ESPN International Radio (broadcast in 11 countries) (SEC Sports 2011). The Atlantic Coast Conference has also taken advantage of syndication, expanding its reach to markets in California and Colorado through Raycom Sports. The latest contract between the ACC and Raycom stipulates that the media provider will sublicense games from ESPN and offer them for syndication while paying $1.86 billion over 12 years for the right to do so (Smith 2011, September 19).

The NCAA (2010) also recognizes the popularity of its championship events and includes language on its website regarding syndication. The organization's policy follows.

If Turner/CBS and/or ESPN do not activate their television rights to any round of an NCAA championship, the NCAA may elect *to sell these rights for local syndication in exchange for a rights fee. Local campus and/or non-commercial television stations may have the rights fee waived. Any station selling commercials, selling or airing billboards, sponsors, in-game graphic sponsors, underwriters or phone pledges must pay the NCAA a minimum of $1,000 (One Thousand Dollars) per game rights fee. Rights fees may vary from championship to championship.*

Pay-Per-View

Pay-per-view is an agreement where cable or satellite television providers offer the event, and viewers pay the provider a fee for the right to access the event. Pay-per-view is typically used for events that may attract a smaller but more passionate audience willing to pay a premium for access to the event. Although mixed martial arts, boxing, and professional wrestling have made efficient use of pay-per-view, other events have also found a use for this method. The University of Missouri offered nonconference football games for fans in a pay-per-view format, and viewers paid $29.95 for each game. FSN produced the events and received a guaranteed $50,000 to cover production expenses. Of the remaining amount, 50 percent went to the cable and satellite providers, and FSN and Missouri received the other half (Matter 2009). At the 2011 World Congress of Sports, Fox Sports Television Group chairman David Hill predicted more events would be on pay-per-view in the future as a way of increasing revenues.

TYPES OF EXPENSES

Expenses represent money flowing out of an organization, or the costs incurred to generate revenue. Revenues reflect the event's top line, while net income or profits represent the event's bottom line and result from subtracting the event's expenses from revenues. The old adage that "it takes money to make money" best summarizes the concept of expenses. Event organizers need to incur expenses such as hiring staff or promoting the event in order to provide superior service and encourage potential attendees to purchase tickets. Having said that, event organizers should proceed with caution because expenses can quickly erode the event's bottom line.

Organizers may face sizeable expenses, which can turn a potentially profitable event into a financial quagmire. As such, organizers should carefully consider their expenses—looking for ways to manage and mitigate costs while still hosting a high-quality and successful event. For example, the process of orchestrating and hosting the National Wheelchair Basketball Association National Championship Tournament "involves a substantial financial commitment by the NWBA. The 2011 Tournament incurred nearly $150,000 in costs. These costs are subsidized by funds generated from local and national efforts through sponsorships, contributions, and in-kind donations" (NWBA 2011). Looking for offsetting revenues is one way to ensure profitability. Carefully planning and tracking expenses will also help ensure the revenues generated lead to a more financially successful and viable event. But first event organizers must consider the types of expenses they will incur.

Expenses typically fall into two categories: variable costs and fixed costs. Variable costs change with the organization's activities, while fixed costs remain the same despite the organization's activities. For example, a local YMCA decides to host a youth soccer tournament. The organization has estimated that it needs to purchase T-shirts for participants, and each shirt costs $5. The T-shirts represent a variable cost. The YMCA will pay $500 to a T-shirt supplier if 100 children participate, whereas the organization will pay $250 if only 50 children participate. The YMCA has also hired a tournament director for the event, and she will receive $1,000 for her assistance. This cost is a fixed cost because the tournament director will receive the same amount whether 50 children or 100 children participate in the event.

This section provides a comprehensive listing of the various expenses event organizers should expect when planning for and putting on events. Event organizers should consider these expense items and take a strategic approach in terms of determining which of these expenses and how much to incur in their efforts to generate revenues for the event. The expenses include those directly associated with hosting the competitive events such as facility costs and capital investments. Organizers are also responsible for managing expenses associated with ancillary activities such as sponsorship fulfillment, guest management and hospitality, and marketing and promotions. These expense line items are necessary and often critical components of operating an event. However, they should be managed closely to ensure cost overruns do not limit the event's potential financial successes.

Event Operations

Event organizers have to budget for the expenses directly related to the event itself. Costs such as staff, production, equipment, and officials will be different for each event. Some events may have costs related to talent and entertainment, while others may require additional medical services or security. Your challenge in developing the budget is to identify what it will require to successfully run the event. In addition to the direct costs of running the event, organizers should consider ancillary expenses such as insurance. The World Flying Disc Federation (WFDF) requires the tournament organizing committee (TOC) to offer medical insurance to athletes participating in the event. The federation stipulates that the TOC should provide at least $1 million in insurance coverage for each possible occurrence and a minimum of $2 million for the aggregate event (WFDF n.d.).

Facility or Venue Costs

Estimating facility expenses will present different challenges based on the type of rental agreement. In a straight rental agreement, the event property typically pays a flat fee for the use of the facility. Depending on the facility or type of event, rental agreements may include a percentage of ticket sales or registrations in lieu of or in addition to a guaranteed rental fee. For example, an organization renting a golf course for a fund-raiser may pay the course a $1,000 guarantee plus $45 for each golfer registered to participate. In cases such as this, event organizers have to consider both fixed and variable costs.

In addition to facility rental fees, event organizers may have to budget operation expenses required by the facility. Following is a list of fees you may incur in addition to rental fees:

- Taxes
- Liability insurance
- Setup and teardown
- Security or police
- Ushers and guest services
- Ticket takers and box office
- EMS
- Traffic and parking
- Maintenance and janitorial services
- Electrical and HVAC services
- Utilities
- Physical plant and labor
- Concession and merchandise fees
- Administrative fees
- Use of concession or kitchen areas
- Use of auxiliary facilities (e.g., practice room, driving range)

Player-Related Costs

Player costs will vary by event and may include items such as appearance fees, prize money, transportation and accommodations, equipment and supplies, and player services. Often, these fees are designed to attract the top players. In addition to prize money, many professional tennis tournaments will offer sizeable appearance fees to ensure their events have enough star power. Even amateur events can incur player-related expenses. For example, host cities bidding on the SEC women's basketball tournament are asked to provide a per diem for each player and a travel allowance for each team.

Capital Investment

Event organizers may purchase physical assets for use over multiple events. Large-scale sporting events such as the Olympic Games and World Cup make major capital investments in their host cities and countries, including improvements to transportation and other community-wide infrastructure, in conjunction with investments directly associated with their events. For example, the Qatar World Cup organizers have outlined financial plans to build a team base-camp village and stadiums around the country (FIFA 2010).

Traveling or tour sporting events also make major capital investments, which may be used numerous times across multiple locations during the tour. The Dew Tour worked with a design and engineering company to build a portable concrete bowl for its skating events. The bowl weighed 220,000 pounds (100,000 kg) and could be disassembled and moved from one location to the next (Spohn Ranch 2011). Likewise, Tour de France organizers have starts and finishes at numerous locations across the country during their three-week event. The logistics organizers move a total of 22 tons of equipment and other assets per day, with capital investments including race clocks, cameras, computers, and closed-circuit televisions as well as staging and seating for spectators and participants before and after each day of racing ("Norbert rides on" 2009). Event organizers who operate traveling events should consider the logistical costs associated with transporting these capital investments and include the projected expenses in the budgeting process.

Marketing and Promotion

Event organizers often have to incur significant costs to market their events. Sport organizations and events large and small regularly incur these expenses to generate interest and excitement. The NCAA provides advice on its website for marketing sporting events. Organizers need to consider costs associated with these marketing activities, and these expenses may include the personnel needed to develop the promotions, market the events, and distribute any promotional materials; the promotional materials, giveaways, and souvenirs; and associated advertising expenses, such as print advertisements and radio and television commercials.

Sponsor Fulfillment

Event organizers must ensure they deliver on the terms of their sponsorships, fulfilling what they promised to sponsors. This fulfillment comes with associated costs. Organizers may have to work with a printing company to develop signage, rent or build booth space, or ensure part of the advertising spots are allocated to the sponsor. Corporate sponsors may have also negotiated to receive free or discounted tickets to attend the event plus special access and hospitality while in attendance. Event organizers may need to hire or designate someone on the staff to escort the corporate sponsors during the event and attend to their special requests or needs. Organizers may also provide a special postevent report, outlining what the sponsors received in exchange for their monetary or product commitments. The report may provide detailed information about event viewership and attendance, the time and duration of their commercials, and the estimated number of potential consumers who saw or responded to the corporate sponsorship.

Providing this level of service can be costly in terms of manpower, tickets, media, data, and other amenities. However, sponsorship fulfillment is a critical element. Costs associated with sponsorship fulfillment will involve everything promised to the sponsor, and these expenses should be included in the budget and tracked as they are incurred.

Guest Management and Hospitality

Event organizers work with a variety of stakeholders to organize and host their events. These stakeholders may include participants, spectators, corporate sponsors and other corporations, staff and volunteers, and VIP guests. To keep this varied group happy, you may consider providing special amenities and services as part of your guest management and hospitality offerings. For example, the Olympic Games organizers traditionally have an athlete village for participants, where they can access a variety of services from housing to medical assistance to food and beverages.

Guest management may also come in the form of corporate hospitality, where the event organizers make special arrangements for corporate sponsors and other corporate guests. These groups may use the hospitality offerings to reward employees and current customers plus meet and attract potential customers. Similarly, the Dubai World Championship offers numerous hospitality opportunities, such as a hospitality pavilion located on the golf course. The event organizers will charge guests a premium price to watch golf in close range (PGA European Tour 2011). Although this feature offers a viable revenue source for the event, organizers will also incur related costs such as providing food and drink to guests during the event; personnel dedicated to working exclusively with these guests; and special dining areas with covered viewing areas, tables, and seating. Event organizers will often provide hospitality for coaches, volunteers, and officials to thank them for their assistance. These services also come at a cost, and organizers should consider the number of people required to staff the hospitality area and what items will be provided (e.g., food, beverages, seating).

Event Presentation

One of the largest financial considerations is presenting the actual event from the opening ceremonies to the competition itself to the closing ceremonies. The opening and closing ceremonies are extensive events in and of themselves and require a detailed level of planning and budget forecasting. For example, the WFDF outlines cost considerations for its awards, ceremonies, and social events. These expenses include securing venue space and accounting for associated rental expenses, security and other personnel, tables and chairs, catering food and beverage costs, trash collection and disposal, lighting, entertainment, and a players lounge. Additional expenses required for the closing ceremonies include medals and trophies awarded to players and teams (WFDF n.d.). Event organizers should consider the complete costs associated with these activities. These activities will

leave a lasting impression on the event stakeholders, who include participants, spectators, sponsors, staff, volunteers, and other guests.

Miscellaneous Expenses

Miscellaneous expenses are those costs typically too small to need their own category. Event organizers should include a line for miscellaneous expenses to cover these costs. Miscellaneous expenses may include, but are not limited to, items such as the following:

- Office supplies
- Phone service
- Mileage and travel
- Storage
- Printing
- Taxes
- Postage
- Internet fees
- Gifts and awards
- Communications
- Accounting and legal services

Contingency Allowances

Contingency allowances are funds reserved for emergencies or cost overruns. With most every event, there will be additional or unanticipated costs. For example, you may incur additional costs because of bad weather or price increases from suppliers. Plan to have a contingency amount of 5 to 10 percent of your overall expenses.

Tips on Developing Good Budgets

- Do your research. The more information you have, the better chance you have to make good estimates. Look at similar events, contact suppliers, and involve employees in the process to make sure you have the most realistic and accurate information.

- Maximize revenue and control costs. Identify all areas where income can be generated. Look for ways to reduce costs and limit cost overruns.

• Be conservative in your revenue estimates and liberal in your expense estimates. It is easy to balance a budget by nudging your revenue estimates up and underestimating expenses, but you are setting yourself up for failure.

• Be prepared for the unexpected. Budget for emergencies and contingencies. Anticipate additional costs and be prepared to cover those costs.

CONTROLLING COSTS

The process of controlling costs is an important facet of the event management process. Event organizers may spend significant time making meticulous budgetary estimates and forecasts. However, it becomes equally important to control costs throughout the event to ensure those estimates become a reality. Cost overruns can quickly turn a potentially successful event into a financial nightmare. A great example comes from the National Hot Rod Association (NHRA), who lost a significant amount of money on their racing events in 2011 because of decreases in ticket sales and sponsorship revenue. To reduce their losses, the organization scrutinized every expense, cut spending, and reduced executive salaries (Mickle 2012).

Organizers are encouraged to follow a few recommendations to keep costs under control. Event organizers should take advantage of cost procurement procedures by finding low-cost goods and services through auctions, bids, or negotiations. Organizers can use their working budget in conjunction with a spreadsheet-based tracking system to monitor their expenses. A spreadsheet may take some time to create; however, once a suitable template is created, event organizers can more readily make changes in one section of the budget and have those changes update across the spreadsheet. You can find examples of event budget spreadsheets online, and you can utilize previously created templates when deemed suitable for your purposes.

Spreadsheets can also be used to estimate expected costs. Adding additional columns to the spreadsheet allows organizers to input actual costs and calculate the variances between forecasted and actual expenditures. Updating the spreadsheet throughout the event allows for tracking revenues and expenses in real time. This exercise will help organizers quickly see where cost overruns exist and determine ways to rein costs in for future expenditures. Spreadsheets also create a paper trail and critical documentation for future events.

Controls should be put in place to determine who can make spending decisions. Event organizers should limit who makes these decisions and the spending amounts they can authorize. Restricting spending authorizations and amounts to relatively few people will help ensure spending is monitored and will leave fewer chances for spending to spiral out of control. Similarly, controls should be established for who can use the organization's credit card or submit purchase orders. These spending options typically have higher authorization limits and allow users to make larger purchases. Organizers should have proper knowledge about products and be authorized to purchase them to ensure that spending remains in control.

In conjunction with limited use, event organizers should create spending checks and balances with proper controls and oversight. For example, if one person uses the event or organization credit card or submits a purchase order, someone else in the organization should examine this cost to determine whether this was a necessary and approved expense. Once purchases have been made, organizers should ensure adequate documentation of this spending through credit card receipts and bank statements. This documentation creates a paper trail from the original approval of the expense to evidence of its occurrence. Additionally, event organizers should retain this documentation, inputting the appropriate numbers into the spreadsheet, so others can easily see what has been spent thus far and determine whether spending is on track.

Finally, organizers may utilize a petty cash fund (typically $100 or less in loose currency) to make small purchases. A tracking mechanism should exist for these funds as well. People using the petty cash account should submit receipts, and this spending should be documented in the tracking spreadsheet. Guidelines for spending—who can use petty cash and for what items—should be determined in advance and carefully monitored throughout the event. Proper tracking and documentation of spending will help organizers keep costs under control and may help with related cash flow and cash management considerations.

USING SPREADSHEETS

Spreadsheets are a vital tool for the development and management of event budgets. Event organizers can use spreadsheets to examine historical data, looking for trends in the numbers from one event to the next. Creating a spreadsheet with complete details and formulas may take considerable time to set up on the front end. However, this template will save more time during the budgeting process because you can make changes across the spreadsheet by simply updating a cell or two. You can use spreadsheets to conduct scenario analyses—developing best-case, worst-case, and most likely scenarios—by copying the budget template across several pages or tabs. Spreadsheets allow event organizers to quickly make changes to various line items or to examine the effects of adjusted estimates. Finally, you can use spreadsheets to track your actual expenses, comparing them to estimates and determining where variances exist and why. This information may prove useful during the postevent process as you assess the successes of your events and highlight best practices and improvement opportunities for future events.

CASH FLOW AND CASH MANAGEMENT

Cash flow and cash management address the timing of revenues and expenses. Event organizers often incur expenses before they receive adequate revenues to cover them, especially early in the event planning process. For example, a 5K organizer may need to purchase fliers and other promotional materials to market the upcoming event. However, athletes may not register to participate until they learn about the event through these marketing activities. A delay now exists between when the organizers incurred expenses to market the events and when they received revenues in the form of registration fees to offset the marketing expenditures. As such, event organizers may face a cash flow problem, where they need to pay their vendors but wonder where they will get the funds to do so. As mentioned already with capital investments, organizers can seek out government agencies, sponsors, private sources, and financial institutions to help defray the costs. Providing evidence of a clear budget, cost controls, or previous event and organizational financial statements may help in the effort to secure funds if organizers can show a clear connection between these expenditures and subsequent revenue opportunities.

SUMMARY

Event organizers should consider related revenues and expenses as they plan their events. This examination of revenues and expenses is part of the budgeting process and requires organizers to spend considerable time and deliberation as they work through the financial aspects of their events. Doing so will help them unearth potential revenue opportunities while considering the event's related costs. Thinking about these aspects in advance of the event will help organizers get the most from their expenditures and maximize their revenue opportunities.

In conjunction with putting together the budget, organizers are encouraged to compare the estimated to the actual numbers after the events take place. This exercise will give organizers the chance to see where their estimates were correct and where variances existed. Taking time to examine these variances will provide a valuable reference when planning future events.

LEARNING ACTIVITIES

Assume you are in charge of presenting a three-on-three basketball tournament. Table 5.1 provides a detailed breakdown of the event's projected revenues, expenses, and net income. Considering the financial information found in the table, please address the following questions.

1. What are your major revenue categories? Are you missing any potential revenues?

2. What are your major expense categories? Are you missing any potential expenses?

3. What will be your profit goal?

4. Based on your numbers, does it make sense to host this event? If not, what can you do to make this event work?

Bardstown Basketball Association Three-on-Three Tournament

The Bardstown Basketball Association (BBA) and local community leaders have discussed hosting a regional outdoor three-on-three basketball tournament in July. Community leaders believe this represents a chance to generate revenues and positive economic impact. However, BBA leaders have expressed some concerns about hosting the event. A neighboring community hosted a similar event several years ago and lost $5,000.

The BBA committee has requested your help. The committee members would like you to develop a budget, exploring the potential revenues and expenses associated with the event. They have asked you to present your findings at the next committee meeting. Your research reveals the following findings.

• Venue costs: A local high school has volunteered its parking lot. The school has 1,500 students and plenty of spaces for the two-day weekend event. The tournament will take place from 9:00 a.m. to 5:00 p.m. Saturday (8 hours) and 1:00 p.m. to 5:00 p.m. Sunday (4 hours). Therefore, the tournament will not require additional lighting.

The organizers will need a sound system to announce the event activities and provide musical entertainment during the games. The plan is to hire an MC/DJ, who will bring the sound system, handle the sound and music, and announce each

day's events. The MC/DJ will charge a flat rate of $750 per day.

• Equipment costs: The organizers plan to rent portable basketball goals and balls. You estimate that they will need 15 goals, which cost $50 each for a four-hour rental. The price includes delivery, setup, and removal. The rental company will also provide basketballs plus a rolling cart for an additional $100 per day.

• Officials: The event will require 15 referees for each day. The event will use local high school officials, sanctioned by the state's high school athletic association, who receive $15 per hour. The officials will receive a per diem of $50 per day, which includes transportation to and from the event plus food, which can be purchased from on-site vendors.

• Trophies: The tournament will provide trophies for first, second, and third places. As this is a three-on-three tournament, three trophies will be required for each place—a total of nine trophies. The trophies will cost $50 for first place, $30 for second place, and $20 for third place.

• Promotions: The event organizers will promote the event via the local media (newspaper, radio, and television advertisements plus social media sites). These promotional efforts will cost approximately $1,000.

• Entry fees: The event organizers expect 60 teams to participate in the tournament. Each team will pay $150 for their two-day participation.

• Concessions: The event will partner with a food truck, which travels to events around the city. The food truck owner has agreed to pay $500 for the opportunity to remain on site over the two-day period, and the vendor receives any resulting profits from the two days of sales.

Tables 5.2 and 5.3 offer contrasting views of possible revenues and expenses associated with sporting events, in this case a larger-scale international event and a smaller local event, respectively. Table 5.2 is from the World Flying Disc Federation (WFDF). The governing body provides the template to potential tournament organizing committees

(TOCs) interested in hosting the WFDF world championship. TOCs must forecast revenues from their participants, event services, and marketing activities. The template lists a variety of revenue opportunities, some of which may have application to the BBA tournament. Table 5.3 is from organizers of the Harvest Festival 5K, a local road race. The event organizers created this working budget by forecasting revenues as well as expenses and the resulting net profit. The information may provide insights about revenues and expenses for smaller-scale events, including the use of in-kind sponsorships to help offset costs.

World Flying Disc Federation (WFDF) Bid for Proposal Budget

The WFDF gives tournament organizing committees (TOCs) an opportunity to submit bids for proposal to host its sanctioned events, the World Ultimate Championship and World Guts Championship. As part of the proposal process, TOCs should develop a tournament budget. The WFDF provides guidance in terms of the tournament's expected revenues and expenses via the budget template in table 5.2. The template outlines potential revenue streams, which include participant fees, event services, and marketing.

The Harvest Festival 5K Budget

Organizers of a smaller local event, the Harvest Festival 5K, created the following working budget to outline the revenues and expenses associated with their event. A significant percentage of the event's expenses were offset by in-kind services received from various sponsors. Revenues consisted of participant entry fees.

Table 5.1 Bardstown Basketball Three-on-Three Tournament: Projected Net Profit

	Qty	CPU	Saturday	Sunday	Total
VENUE COSTS					
Event space	1	0	—	—	0
MC / DJ	1	$750	$750	$750	$1,500
EQUIPMENT COSTS					
Basketball goals	15	$50	$750	$750	$1,500
Basketballs plus cart	1	$100	$100	$100	$200
OFFICIALS					
Hourly rate	15	$15	$1,800	$900	$2,700
Per diem	15	$50	$750	$750	$1,500
TROPHIES					
1st place	3	$50	—	—	$150
2nd place	3	$30	—	—	$90
3rd place	3	$20	—	—	$60
PROMOTIONS					
	1	$1,000	—	—	$1,000
Total expenses					$8,700
REVENUES					
Participation fees	60	$150	—	0	$9,000
Concessions	1	$500	—	0	$500
Total revenues					$9,500
Net profit (loss)					$800

Table 5.2 WFDF Template for Projected Revenues

	Per person	Budget
PARTICIPANT FEES		
Team fees (ultimate)		$0
-Open	$0	
-Women	$0	
-Mixed	$0	
-Masters	$0	
-Junior open	$0	
-Junior women's	$0	
Total ultimate team fees	$0	
Team fees (guts)		$0
-Open	$0	
-Women's	$0	
Total guts team fees	$0	
Players' fees		$0
Ultimate		
-Open	$0	
-Women	$0	
-Mixed	$0	
-Masters	$0	
-Junior open	$0	
-Junior women's	$0	
Guts		
-Open	$0	
-Women	$0	
Total players' fees	$0	
Guests		
Total guests' fees	$0	$0
Participants' fees total	$0	$0
EVENT SERVICES		
Player accommodations fees		
Player meal fees		
Guest meal fees		
Accommodations booking commissions		
Event services total	$0	$0
MARKETING		
Sponsorship		
Broadcast rights fees		
Government grants		
Advertising sales		
Concessions		
DVD sales		
Other vendor sales		
Donations		
Spectator event ticket sales		
Marketing total	$0	$0
TOTAL REVENUE		
	$0	$0

Adapted from World Flying Disc Federation. Available: http://www.wfdf.org/events/event-hosting/71-iii-bidproposal-format

Table 5.3 Harvest Festival 5K Projected Revenues and Expenses

	Expense	In-kind service
PROMOTION		
Run and See Georgia series		$250
Printing of fliers (2000)		$200
Mailing/stamps		$300
Website		$0
Domain registration		$10
COURSE LOGISTICS		
Timing services		$250.00
Race numbers	$19.99	
Race pins (400)	$10.85	
WATER STATIONS		
Water stations		$62.04
Water cups (404)	$6.08	
Bottled water (192)	$23.76	
Food		$0.00
Sales tax	$1.90	
Trash cans and bags		$0.00
AWARDS		
11 oz. mugs (90)	$540.00	
15 oz. mugs (4)	$32.00	
Sales tax	$44.04	
Participation awards	$22.47	
T-SHIRTS		
Runners (155)	$775.00	
Volunteers (10)	$50.00	
Sales tax	$57.75	
Packet pickup bags		$0
TOTAL PROJECTED EXPENSES		
	$1,583.84	$1,072.04
REVENUES		
Entrant fees ($20)	$2,020.00	
Student rate ($10)	$170.00	
Late registration ($23)	$184.00	
Total entry fees	$2,374.00	

REFERENCES

All England Lawn Tennis Club. 2012. Wimbledon merchandising. Available: www.wimbledon.com/en_GB/about_aeltc/201205091336578155663.html.

Beijing Olympics bill surges with $2.5 billion of bonds due: China credit. 2011. Bloomberg. August 25. Available: www.bloomberg.com/news/2011-08-24/beijing-olympics-bill-surges-with-2-5-billion-of-bonds-due-china-credit.html.

Brown, M.T., D.A. Rascher, M.S. Nagel, and C.D. McEvoy. 2010. *Financial management in the sport industry*. Scottsdale, AZ: Holcomb Hathaway.

FIFA. 2010. 2022 FIFA World Cup bid evaluation report: Qatar. Available: www.fifa.com/worldcup/qatar2022/index.html.

Fried, G., S. Shapiro, and T. Deschriver, T. 2007. *Sport finance*. 2nd ed. Champaign, IL: Human Kinetics.

Green, M. 2010. Yum! to pay $13.5 million to name downtown arena KFC Yum! Center. *Courier-Journal*. [Online]. April 19. Available: www.courier-journal.com/article/20100419/SPORTS02/4190326/1028/rss0702.

Kentucky Derby. 2011. Kentucky Derby collectibles. Available: www.kentuckyderby.org/2011/12/25/kentucky-derby-collectibles.

Lawrence, H., and M. Wells. 2009. *Event management blueprint*. Dubuque, IA: Kendall/Hunt.

Lefton, T. 2011. CBS Sports Network to put NLL games in prime time. *Street and Smith's SportsBusiness Journal*, November 14, 26.

Los Angeles Dodgers. 2011. Dodgers sign multi-year broadcast deal with Clear Channel. MLB Advanced Media. October 3. Available: http://losangeles.dodgers.mlb.com/news/press_releases/press_release.jsp?ymd=20111003&content_id=25463656&vkey=pr_la&fext=.jsp&c_id=la.

Matter, D. 2009. Big 12 TV contract frustrates Missouri. *Columbia Daily Tribune*. [Online]. September 18. Available: www.columbiatribune.com/news/2009/sep/18/big-12-tv-contract-frustrates-missouri.

McCarthy, M. 2011. NBC wins rights to Olympics through 2020; promises more live coverage. *USA Today*. [Online]. June 7. Available: http://content.usatoday.com/communities/gameon/post/2011/06/olympic-tv-decision-between-nbc-espn-and-fox-could-come-down-today/1#.T2ZHH-BFDAk.

Mickle, T. 2008. J&J won't renew TOP deal with IOC. *Street and Smith's SportsBusiness Journal*. [Online]. November 17. Available: www.sportsbusinessdaily.com/Journal/Issues/2008/11/20081117/This-Weeks-News/JJ-Wont-Renew-TOP-Deal-With-IOC.aspx.

Mickle T. 2012. NHRA expects to sell out race title sponsorships after hits from economy, weather in 2011. *Street and Smith's SportsBusiness Journal*, January 9, 6.

Muret, D. 2011. MainGate signed to sell Big Ten title game gear. *Street and Smith's SportsBusiness Journal*, August 22, 32.

NAIA. 2011. Broadcast fees 2011-2012. Available: www.naia.org/ViewArticle.dbml?DB_OEM_ID=27900&ATCLID=205333227.

NCAA. 2010. Quick reference guide to broadcast rights. Available: www.ncaa.org/wps/wcm/connect/broadcast/media/broadcasting/broadcasting+manual/quickref.

Norbert rides on with the Tour de France. 2009. LogisticsManager.com. July 9. Available: www.logisticsmanager.com/Articles/11874/Norbert+rides+on+with+the+Tour+de+France.html.

NWBA. 2011. Request for proposals to host the National Wheelchair Basketball Association National Championship Tournament. Available: www.nwba.org

Olympic.org. 2012. Sponsorship. Available: www.olympic.org/sponsorship?tab=The-Olympic-Partner-TOP-Programme.

Ourand, J. 2011. How high can rights fees go? *Street and Smith's SportsBusiness Journal*, June 6, 1.

Panja, T. 2011. Budweiser extends soccer World Cup sponsorship as FIFA fights graft. Bloomberg. October 25. Available: www.bloomberg.com/news/2011-10-25/budweiser-extends-world-cup-sponsorship-as-fifa-fights-graft-in-soccer.html.

PGA European Tour. 2011. Hospitality pavilion. Dubai World Championship. Available: www.dubaiworldchampionship.com/tickets/hospitality-pavilion-3.

Sandomir, R. 2011. U.S. Open to stay on CBS through 2014. *New York Times*. [Online]. January 14. Available: www.nytimes.com/2011/01/15/sports/tennis/15open.html?_r=1.

SEC Sports. 2011. The SEC on ESPN. Available: www.sec-digitalnetwork.com/NEWS/tabid/473/Article/132060/unprecedented-espn-agreement.aspx.

SiriusXM. 2011. SiriusXM inks agreement to continue as leader in college sports audio. Available: http://investor.sirius.com/releasedetail.cfm?ReleaseID=601578.

Smith, M. 2011. ACC launching digital network. *Street and Smith's SportsBusiness Journal*, October 10, 8.

Smith, M. 2011. Deal helps Raycom expand ACC's syndication territory. *Street and Smith's SportsBusiness Journal*, September 19, 3.

Spohn Ranch. 2011. The design is finalized. June 18. Available: http://portableconcretebowl.wordpress.com/2011/06/18/the-design-is-finalized.

Thomas, E. 2010. The NFL stadium food power rankings. *Esquire*. [Online]. September 24. Available: www.esquire.com/blogs/food-for-men/stadium-food-ratings-nfl.

USA Triathlon. 2012. Host site request for proposal. TeamUSA.org. Available: http://triathlon.teamusa.org/resources/about-events/host-site-request-for-proposal.

Walker, D. 2011. Need a Miller Park beer and hot dog? Order via smartphone. *Journal Sentinel*. [Online]. March 24. Available: www.jsonline.com/blogs/sports/118579729.html.

WFDF. n.d. Bid proposal format. Available: www.wfdf.org/events/event-hosting/71-iii-bid-proposal-format.

Event Sponsorship

Chapter Objectives

After completing the chapter, the reader should be able to do the following:

- Define sponsorship and comprehend the relevance of the event triangle.
- Identify the various components of sport sponsorship.
- Recognize and relate the benefits of sponsorship.
- Develop a sponsorship proposal.
- Identify sponsorship implementation strategies and evaluation techniques.

Industry Profile ▶ Chris Ulm, Ball State University, Assistant Director of Corporate Sales

Chris Ulm is in his 10th season of working in the corporate sales field at Ball State University. For five years Chris worked for Nelligan Sports Marketing, a professional selling organization that handles the rights at approximately 20 different universities across the country, to whom BSU outsourced the athletic department's corporate sales. He served as director of sales for the Ball State property until the contract with Nelligan Sports Marketing was dissolved and the corporate sales were brought back in-house.

Q: What was the attraction for you to work in the area of sponsorships?

A: Throughout elementary and high school, I was involved in several organizations, and you always had to sell something to raise money for the club. I took an early liking to sales and found it to be a natural fit. Whether it was helping raise money for band uniforms or selling fruit and flowers for the FFA, I enjoyed the entire sales process, from the challenge of getting the commitment to the delivery and fulfillment of the order. The challenge of selling fruit for the FFA was my first experience with cold calling as I literally started with the As in my town phone book and worked my way through the alphabet. I went to high school in a small town and was involved with managing and announcing football and basketball. People in town knew me through my association with sports. When I would call on them to sell something (whether it was fruit, flowers, or candles), it was as if I had a head start with most people. Fast forward to the present, this is why I believe being the on-field and on-court emcee at Ball State football and men's basketball games is a tremendous asset: Most clients know me before I sit in their office.

Q: What is a typical day like for someone in sponsorship and sales for an athletic department?

A: It really depends on the time of year to determine how a typical day goes. From the end of basketball season to the start of football season, that is considered our selling season. That is all preparation for the upcoming year. We start with meeting with each client and presenting a fulfillment summary of all elements they received during the previous year. That leads us to the renewal process. The fulfillment summary is a key asset to our renewal success. Once we have reviewed and renewed all clients, the focus is then on new business. Also during that time, we are starting to assemble all needs for the upcoming year: signage, program ads, radio spots, logos, and so on. Our goal is to always be at 90 percent of our sales goal by kickoff. That gives us basically another month and a half to achieve and exceed our goal before basketball season starts. Once we are in season, we can work 12- to 15-hour days if it's a game night.

Q: How do you determine what type of sponsorship to pitch to a potential client?

A: I never show up to a client's office with a proposal without speaking to the client first. After I have met with someone and have a better understanding of what we can offer them and what they need, I go back with a proposal.

Q: How much time would you say you spend researching? Developing a sponsorship package? Soliciting sponsors?

A: I'm not sure I can put an actual time down to the second, but I think once you've sold corporate sponsorships, you are always selling. Whether I'm watching sports on television or at actual events, I notice the sponsorship elements more now than the actual game. I'm always looking for ideas that we can incorporate here at Ball State. The process of developing the sponsorship package starts with the cold call or the hot lead. My focus on phone calls is to not spend a lot of time going into what I'm going to talk about at the meeting. I like making a brief introduction, getting a meeting time, and leaving it at that. Then at the first meeting, that's where the heavy research happens, asking questions and getting a feel for the business.

Once I think I have enough information, I set a time to come back in the next week to present a proposal. During that time, I develop an actual proposal based on our conversation with the elements I believe have the best chance to achieve the goal.

Q: We know companies are looking for a return on their investment when they sponsor. How often do you utilize trades or bartering in college athletics?

A: When I worked with NSM, I did very little when it came to trade, mostly because NSM didn't receive credit from the university on trade deals. When I was hired as a BSU employee, trades became an option if they helped eliminate an expense, either on the corporate sales budget or the athletic department's overall budget. When we deal in trade with clients, it's just as important as cash deals, and we make that a point with the client. Just because they are paying with trade doesn't mean they get the lesser inventory or that their deal isn't important. Now to make sure that the corporate sales model stays profitable, when another area of the department uses trade brought in through one of our deals, their budget is charged an agreed-upon rate, and the chargeback goes back into the corporate sales budget.

Q: Are there specific skills or knowledge you believe have helped you be successful as a professional?

A: I'm not sure all of these are prerequisites to be in corporate sales, but I believe they can be applied to any profession. (a) Have a sense of being professional. I don't know if I can explain it, you just know. (b) Look the part. They say dress for success, and it's true. (c) Stand by your word. Your word is your bond. Not doing what you say you will do is a good way to fail in sales. (d) Be organized. You won't have just one client, so you have to make sure you fulfill everything you say you are going to do for not just one or two clients, but all of them! (e) Be positive. It's easy to be negative—that's why a lot of people do it. Smile and laugh. You'll enjoy each day. (f) Be passionate. I'm a Ball State grad, so it's easy to have passion for selling Ball State Athletics, but whether that was the case or not, it is important to be passionate about what I do. (g) Find a job you love because you won't have to work a day in your life. I know that's not mine, but I sure follow it. I absolutely love what I do and make sure I always let people know, by my actions and my words, how much fun I'm having.

Q: What advice would you offer to a student who is interested in this field as a career?

A: Learn to accept the word "No." I'm only partially kidding. In sales, no one bats a thousand, so you must be prepared to hear rejection and keep your head up.

Have you ever considered the abundance of messages you are exposed to on a daily basis? Or how much social media have invaded our lives with the exchange of information? The technology and methods may be new, but the concept of communicating a message is not. Magazines, billboards, newspapers, direct mail, television, radio, the Internet, phone apps, and virtual placement are all viable mediums to convey a message to a specific audience. It is estimated that from the time we wake up to the time we call it a night, we are bombarded with between 3,000 and 5,000 communicated messages per day (Johnson 2009; Cowan 1988).

For more than 250 years the "clutter" from advertising has been addressed in the media. According to an essay in *The Idler*, Johnson (1759) proclaimed that "newspapers have become so crammed with adverts that advertisers must use more and more extravagant ploys to get noticed . . . it has therefore become necessary to gain attention by magnificence of promises, and by eloquence sometimes sublime and sometimes pathetic" (para. 3). Not much has changed, in terms of the intent of advertisers, since the late 18th century!

Advertising and sponsorship are kindred spirits, but their intent is very different. To fully understand the role of sponsorship, we must first identify its place in the promotional mix and define various terminologies associated with the traditional marketing mix and promotional mix. The traditional marketing mix consists of the four Ps: product, price, place, and promotion (McCarthy 1960).

Advertising is the action of calling something to the attention of the public, especially by paid announcements. According to Mullin, Hardy, and Sutton (2007), advertising is "any paid, nonpersonal (not directed to individuals), clearly sponsored message conveyed through the media" (p. 237). Whereas, Mullin, Hardy, and Sutton define sponsorship as the "acquisition of rights to affiliate or directly associate with a product or event for the purpose of deriving benefits related to that affiliation or association" (p. 315), Solomon (2002) simplified his definition to state that sponsorship is one company paying a fee to a promoter to endorse the event and promote its products. The 2012 Plunkett Research report on industry statistics and trends asserts the sport industry weighs in at a healthy $435 billion. According to Ukman (2012), sponsorship spending in the United States should top out just below $19 million for 2012. Ukman's International Events Group (IEG) (2012), an expert in sponsorships, estimates that global spending on sponsorship in 2012 will top $51 billion.

Despite market turmoil, growth in sponsorship held steady at 5.2 percent from IEG's 2010 findings, the same growth it saw from 2009 to 2010. What is the lure of sponsorship? Why sport sponsorship? And why are we seeing growth in a down market? Much of the growth can be attributed to the growing desire and need of corporations to be affiliated with sport entities to achieve their strategic goals. Sport is consuming, sport is exciting, and sport provides an avenue for businesses, large and small, to reach their target demographics and to grow and maintain relationships with customers through mutually beneficial interactions. Sport and sport-related properties (fitness centers; apparel and shoes) are a constant

for most people; daily interactions are almost a given. These interactions come in many different shapes, sizes, and methods, but one thing that is common is the idea of partnering with a sport entity to gain exposure through sponsorship.

Keep in mind that sponsorship is a triad, a dynamic connection of the event, the fans, and the sponsors. As Ammon, Southall, and Nagel (2010) presented, this relationship is like a triangle, and "each side represents important stakeholders who must be satisfied for the event to be a success" (p. 14). SponsorMap (2008), a marketing research firm, describes the event triangle as "the emotional connection" between an event and the fans that turns emotion into a reaction that ultimately benefits the sponsor. In essence, the relationship the event has with the sponsor encourages fans to take action, purchasing either the product or service offered by the sponsor. The relationships within the event triangle can be described in three distinct but related parts. First, the event provides the opportunity to attract fans and provide exposure for potential sponsors. Second, fans seek entertainment from the event and are exposed to the various promotional activities during an event. And third, sponsors exploit the opportunity to leverage fans through what we call borrowed equity, the use of a sporting event to market.

These connections and actions allow a sponsor to achieve its anticipated return on investment (ROI) or return on objectives (ROO). The National Association for Stock Car Auto Racing (NASCAR) provides great examples of how the event triangle is utilized to a sponsor's advantage. Having great success with fan loyalty, NASCAR has been the subject of many marketing studies. One such national study by Performance Research, an analytical sport and event marketing firm, revealed that "71 percent elected to purchase products that were involved in NASCAR over one that is not" (Performance Research n.d.).

SPONSORSHIP

Sponsorship has been defined as "a wide array of activities associated with a communications process that is designed to use sport and lifestyle marketing to send messages to a targeted audience" (Mullin, Hardy, and Sutton 2007, p. 315). Ukman (2012) asserted that sponsorship is an exchange of money or products for the purpose of "exploiting commercial potential" on the part of both parties. Shank (2009) defined sponsorship as investing in sports to achieve an organization's goals. And Cornwell (1995) described sponsorship as "the orchestration and implementation of marketing activities for the purpose of building and communicating an association to a sponsorship" (p. 15).

Irrespective of the definition you choose to endorse, one thing remains constant for sponsorship: It is firmly entrenched in sport, and sport clearly has benefited from the relationship. Sponsorship opportunities within the sport industry have attempted to bridge the gap between needs and wants, preying on the sports fan through enticing promotional campaigns, direct selling strategies, and emotions. Ultimately, businesses associate with sport to achieve sales goals, while sport organizations view the relationship as necessary to support the escalating costs of fielding a team (Stotlar 2005).

For event managers, sponsorship is a means to an end, if you will, generating the necessary funds to create a memorable event, thus satisfying customers. Sponsoring an event can range from a simple advertisement in the program to full-blown naming rights and various levels in between. As event planners map out their plans for creating, planning, and executing a successful event, they create manageable components that become targeted sales pitches to businesses and organizations.

Companies seek unique ways to engage potential customers. Traditional methods such as advertising, public relations, and promotions are still utilized, but adding sponsorship to that mix provides a myriad of opportunities to communicate a message. Integrated marketing communications creates a symphony of promotional efforts that work in concert, linking all promotional pieces. This unified effort increases the likelihood that marketing will be successful, leading to consumer action. This process aligns with Lavidge and Steiner's (1961) hierarchy of effects model, which suggests there is a force that guides people

through the six-step (stages) model. The six stages of consumer evolvement range from thinking to feeling to "I must have" (VanDen Heuvel 2009). (See table 6.1.)

As event manager, you can use this information to your benefit, presenting the various marketing opportunities you can offer to sponsors. Realize that you may be the guide on the journey that will take a potential sponsor through the hierarchy of effects process to become your partner.

SPONSORSHIP COMPONENTS

As you begin to weigh the idea of soliciting sponsors for your event, you must first determine your marketing goals and objectives to ensure that potential sponsors know, understand, and relate to them. Consider sponsorship a three-step process of identifying (research), securing (selling), and maintaining (servicing) (Skildum-Reid and Grey 2008).

Once you have your event planned and goals established, you can then turn your attention to developing the components of your sponsorship program. These components allow you (or your sales team) to give companies various opportunities to be associated with your event. Kim Harrison, author, consultant, and founder of CuttingEdgePR.com, asserts that it is up to event managers to identify what a company needs and to package event sponsorship opportunities in a way that will provide the company "with value for money" ("Think of what" n.d.). More information is provided on sponsorship proposals later in this chapter.

Costs of Sponsorship to a Corporation

When considering affiliating with an event, sponsors have two options, in-kind donations or monetary support. In-kind sponsorships are non-monetary partnerships that provide a service or product to an event in exchange for sponsorship recognition. Examples of in-kind contributions include gift bags, basket giveaways, prizes for

Table 6.1 Applying the Hierarchy of Effects Model

Stage	Application
Awareness	If your target market is unaware of your product or service, then the first order of marketing priority is to achieve awareness within your target market. To test awareness, you might ask: Have you heard of our firm?
Knowledge	Awareness can answer the question of whether or not a prospect knows of your firm; however, she may not know the context in which she heard your name and thus cannot accurately describe what you do or what you sell, nor can she determine whether or not she would ever do business with you. To test for knowledge, you might ask: "Do you know what our company does for organizations like yours?"
Liking	When a prospect knows what your firm does and what you might do for him, he begins to form opinions about your firm. Perhaps, because of his heightened awareness, he now seems to notice you in the newspaper and in trade journals, and he now receives your newsletter. He's forming an opinion of whether or not he likes you. Perhaps you provide valuable thought-leading wisdom in the industry, and he likes you for that fact. To test for liking, you might ask: "What is your overall perception of our firm?" (ranging from favorable to unfavorable)
Preference	The preference stage is where we begin to see the real value of the hierarchy of effects. A prospect in the preference stage has a clear definition of why she would want to do business with your firm or purchase a product or service in the category you serve. To test for preference, you might ask: "What criteria will you use to make your decision about XYZ?" Marketers also gauge interest through trials, surveys, and other means to better understand the customer at this stage of the buying cycle.
Conviction	At the stage of conviction, the prospect is in a state of already being convinced that you are the right choice for whatever problem he needs you to solve. He believes, through your credible demonstration of capability, that you're the right fit and you've done everything right to this point. Testing for conviction is now a matter of moving the conversation to purchase. However, in long sales cycles, maintaining conviction is also important. Any lead-nurturing activities you have in progress should not cease once you believe you've reached the conviction stage.
Purchase	Ultimately, the work to move the prospect through the hierarchy will result in her purchasing your offering. However, beware of the purchase or signal to purchase from a customer who has not gone through the various stages. Nor should you try to induce a customer purchase without recognizing the aforementioned stages. A customer purchase without the rigor of traversing the hierarchy of effects can lead to postpurchase dissonance.

Reprinted, by permission, from D. VanDen Heusel, *The hierarchy of effects* (Green Bay, WI: Marketing Savant), 3-4.

raffles, entertainment services, volunteers, food and beverages, photography services, and T-shirts.

It is necessary to secure funding to host an event. The financial needs are identified during the planning phase, presented in the proposal, and secured during active selling. This monetary involvement entails the exchange of cash for the right to associate with an event. The various types of support are outlined in your sponsorship levels, which are discussed next.

Sponsorship Levels

Keep in mind that what you are creating with your sponsorship opportunities is value. The value varies for each potential sponsor, and sponsorship packages neatly represent the various monetary levels that can be purchased. Most classic spon-

sorship values are presented as gradual levels (packages) of involvement ranging from minimal investment to full-blown rights of ownership. These levels allow you to address your needs and potential sponsors' needs at a level that is comfortable for both. For years the standard levels for many events were gold, silver, and bronze, following the ever-popular Olympic medal model. But the increased desire by corporations to be associated with sport has driven event managers to cast aside cookie-cutter models and creatively construct unique levels for their events. In spite of this, some distinctive categories have emerged, such as the following:

- Contributing
- Corporate
- Hospitality/Food

- Major
- Media
- Naming rights
- National
- Presenting
- Supporting
- Title

Depending on the event, event planners will develop specialized categories that represent the available opportunities. For example, a golf tournament may have tee, hole-in-one, or hydration station levels, while Little League organizations would offer levels such as uniforms and fields. The differentiation of these levels from greatest involvement down to minimal involvement allows potential partners to see what level they can afford and helps them identify the best fit (Ukman 2012). Table 6.2 is an example of sponsorship levels for a local Little League organization.

Event managers are limited only by their creative energies as to the types of levels they can create. But take note: You don't want to overwhelm the client with your offerings; your goal is to create interesting opportunities that will provide the potential sponsor with the greatest ROI. How do you know what is right for a company, what will provide that ROI? It's necessary to do your homework, researching potential sponsors and identifying which level will be most beneficial for them and then suggesting that level in your sales pitch.

Naming Rights

As one of the fastest-growing segments of sponsorship, naming rights have truly come into their own as of late. Burton (2008) identified three distinct naming rights options:

1. Rights to a legacy gift
2. Rights for a title sponsor of an event
3. Rights for a long-term partnership

Legacy gifts are best exemplified by names such as Rockefeller and Kennedy and the many buildings that bear these names (Burton 2008). Since many of the events in the sporting world do not require such grandiose names or funding, of particular importance to you is what to name your

Table 6.2 Example of Sponsorship Levels for a Little League Association

Package	Annual value	Details
Teamwork (fall only)	$175	Company banner on fence, team sponsorship, listed on seasonal sponsor-recognition banners throughout park and fall-season team plaque
Single (spring only)	$350	Company banner on fence, team sponsorship, listed on seasonal sponsor-recognition banners throughout park and spring-season team plaque
Double play (spring & fall combo)	$500	Company banner on fence, team sponsorship, listed on both seasons' sponsor-recognition banners throughout park and spring- & fall-season team plaques
Manager	$600 each, $1,200 all	One garage door signage at barn for both seasons (painted artwork, min. 2 years); up to three garage door sponsorships available
Triple play	$750	Signage on all three storage sheds around the park for entire year
On deck	$750 each, $1,500 all	Signage on any batting cage for entire year; up to three batting cage sponsorships available
Power play	$900	Signage on all three golf carts for both seasons (metallic sign on front of each cart)
Cracker Jack	$1,000	Signage on both concession stands at the park for entire year
Clubhouse	$1,250	Walkway naming rights for entire year
MVP	$1,500-$3,000 each	Official naming rights for entire year; field uses sponsor name in all league documents

Reprinted, by permission, from Oaklandon Youth Organization (Indianapolis, Indiana).

event. The extent of the financial undertaking to produce an event has become so great, why not explore new opportunities to augment out-of-pocket costs for your event?

Golf tournaments have had a long tradition of using naming rights for their events. Some tournaments have gone so far as to utilize a legacy right, an event sponsor, and a course name (Bissell 2011). A cursory glance at the PGA Tour schedule is evidence enough that events do draw large sponsors. Names such as AT&T, FedEx, Honda, Sony, Waste Management, and Wells Fargo stand out (PGAtour.com 2012). BB&T, a leading financial services holding company, has truly bought into sport sponsorships, leaving an imprint on collegiate sport (official bank of the Atlantic Coast Conference and 10-year naming rights to the Wake Forest University Football Stadium), motorsports (official sponsor of NASCAR driver number 31, Jeff Burton), and its latest acquisition, the Atlanta Tennis Championships (Limpert 2012; USTA.com 2012).

Don't underestimate the power your event may hold for a potential sponsor. Reach for the stars, and you just might get what you want. You must be willing to accept whatever response you get. Sometimes that response is yes, we would welcome the opportunity to partner with your event; other times, it will be no. But perseverance and belief in your event will ultimately pay off.

Cost of Sponsorship for Event Organizers

Harrison ("How you can" n.d.) maintains that the investment you seek from potential sponsors is a uniquely crafted formula of identifying the cost to fulfill the sponsorship times two. In simplistic form, Harrison presents the formula this way: Total investment asked = cost of providing the benefits offered. Admin staff costs + sales costs + servicing costs = total cost to deliver the package + 100% margin = sponsorship fee.

To illustrate this, let's refer to the Little League levels outlined in table 6.2. Oaklandon Youth Organization (OYO) is seeking a teamwork-level sponsor for the fall. The costs break down as follows:

Company banner	$18
Team sponsorship	$12
Sponsor-recognition banner	$30
Plaque and administration fees	$17
Sales fees	$10
Total OYO cost	$87 + 100% margin = $175 (rounded)

Harrison adds the need to include both direct and indirect costs associated with staff, noting their involvement from conception to fruition of sponsorships. She concludes that event planners should not just think selfishly about what it will take to run the event but rather must consider what is most valuable to the potential sponsor. It is also important to consider the competition (i.e., what they are offering and charging) to ensure you are operating within the boundaries of what the local market will support.

SPONSORSHIP BENEFITS

Inevitably, when a potential sponsor is approached, the company or organization will want to know the proverbial "what's in it for me?" details. To have that conversation, you need to understand what you have to offer. Ukman (2012) contends you must take inventory of your assets before moving forward. She interprets your potential offerings as follows:

- An audience
- Database information
- Hospitality opportunities
- Marks and logos
- Media coverage
- Merchandise
- Possible broadcast package
- Printed materials
- Signage
- Talent
- Venue
- Website and social media outlets

You need to familiarize yourself with the benefits that sponsorship—or maybe a better term is *partnership*—offers to each potential sponsor. Various authors have outlined the benefits of sport sponsorship (Ukman 2012; Lawrence and Wells 2009; Shank 2009; IEG 2008; Mullin, Hardy, and Sutton 2007; Logh, Irwin, and Short 2000; Schmader and Jackson 1997). Following is the consensus of these authors:

- Award presentation (perpetual trophy naming)
- Change in or reinforcement of image
- Community engagement
- Differentiation
- Exclusivity
- Fresh, nontraditional promotional strategies
- Increased brand awareness and loyalty
- Increased sales and achievement of sales goals
- Merchandising opportunities
- Naming rights
- Narrowcasting (targeting a niche market)
- Philanthropy
- Product promotion
- Publicity
- Showcasing of products through samples or displays

Remember you are not the only horse in the race. Your ability to understand these elements, package them to fit your potential sponsors, and then deliver on your promises will not only reduce the clutter of traditional marketing mechanisms but also generate greater opportunities for you, your sponsors, and the fans (event triangle) (Ukman 2012). Your success, according to deLisle (2009) is based on two principles: first, understanding your product and, second, understanding your audience. Understanding your product (event) requires that you grasp the appeal it will have and how it is unique compared with alternatives. This allows you to differentiate your offering, creating that necessary appeal. To understand your audiences, deLisle suggests that you consider marketing to be like "dating" (p. 135). Growing the relationship requires nurturing and effort. This also requires that you do your homework, researching and preparing for that initial experience in hopes that it leads to a "long term and mutually beneficial relationship" (deLisle 2009, p. 135). As with any other relationship, it needs close monitoring to ensure that you are both providing the necessary elements initially prescribed in the arrangement. Shank (2009) concluded that sponsorship provides benefits to all involved and produces the proverbial "win–win partnership" (p. 333).

COMPONENTS OF A SPONSORSHIP PROPOSAL

You have planned your event's mission, goals, and objectives; defined your sponsorship levels; and identified potential companies to approach for sponsorship. The process of selecting companies is a carefully crafted plan of attack based on market research and acumen. With these elements in place, you are now ready to construct your proposal—a carefully crafted and tailored packet that will address all the questions necessary for a company to decide whether to participate or not. Skildum-Reid (2010) boldly stated that "sponsorship is not about your need; it's about achieving the sponsor's objective" (p. 2).

There isn't a magic formula for a proposal, but certain elements are necessary in order to properly ask for sponsorship. According to Singh (2009), event managers should keep these questions in mind when writing the proposal:

- Why should I sponsor this event? (benefit)
- Who is going to come for the event? (audience)
- Why will they come?
- How do I target the audience?
- What is the credential of the organizer?
- Who else is sponsoring the event?
- What is the cost? Does it justify the benefit?

These questions will help you construct a proposal that will garner attention. It has been stated that potential sponsors look at two segments first:

what you are offering and how much it will cost them.

Your first step is not to just put together and mail the proposal. You must first perform due diligence in securing the name of the person responsible for making sponsorship decisions. With technology, you may be able to acquire this information on the company's website. If not, a simple phone call will do the trick. It is imperative that your proposal reach the right person for full consideration. In her blog, Skildum-Reid (2010) professed that most sponsorship proposals are "total crap" because someone failed to adequately research.

Constructing your proposal in a sensible order, professionally presenting your case, and employing the KISS principle while keeping it as brief as possible is a great strategy (Skildum-Reid 2011). Various authors suggest that the following information be included:

- Provide a concise overview of your organization, including your location, main activities, and goals and a brief history.

- Include the benefits your organization can offer a sponsor, and demonstrate how these benefits relate to the sponsor.

- List the credentials of your organization and key personnel. Sponsors need to know they will be dealing with experienced and reputable people.

- Supply a list of current and past sponsors (if applicable). This allows potential sponsors to check for competition.

- Outline any benefits you are prepared to offer the sponsor.

- Explain the nature and extent of potential media coverage.

- Supply a realistic estimate of the number of people who could participate in the event.

- Demonstrate the current level of community support and awareness for your project. Sponsors have a strong interest in supporting projects that have wide community support.

According to Stotlar (2005) the sponsorship submission should include the following elements:

- Cover letter—address it to the appropriate person; focus on tailored benefits for specific partners; be specific; let them know when to expect a follow-up

- Description of the event and program—location, duration, size, media plan, promotional elements, and demographic profile

- Sponsor's benefits—signage, hospitality, preevent and postevent activities, on-site opportunities, cross-promotions, rationale for partnering, evaluation methods, and VIP opportunities

- Sponsorship investment amount—including levels or categories of sponsors, parameters, and a list of former sponsors

- Deadline for decision—critical for keeping the event on schedule

Sponsors are looking to determine the viable benefits of this relationship. Stotlar contends that sponsorship bridges the gap between how people want to be reached and how marketers want to reach them. Keeping these things in mind will help you craft a proposal that will land you the partnership.

ACTIVATION AND EVALUATION TECHNIQUES

The old adage "what's in it for me?" absolutely rings true in sponsorship. Each partner is looking for the win–win scenario that satisfies the needs of each in terms of exposure, recognition, ROI, and ROO (Stotlar 2005). Activation of a sponsorship relates to the process of actively marketing and managing the sponsor's partnership with an event. Technology has greatly changed the way sponsorships are being activated. Twitter, Facebook, and YouTube have "virtually" enhanced the way marketers interact with target markets. With the advent of quick response (QR) codes, the speed at which a fan can connect to a sponsor is fractional. Butcher (2010) reported that Swiss watch manufacturer Tissot added a QR code to the hood of NASCAR driver Danica Patrick's racecar.

Activation closely aligns with advertising—creating public awareness of a product and its association with an event. This process requires more than simply putting a logo on a sign at your event; it requires action. As the term implies, activation refers to stimulation, stimulation translates into action, and action is what the sponsor desires. The relationship you build with the sponsor will help identify the methods of activation you select for your event. Coca-Cola, a longtime supporter of the Olympics and one of 11 companies designated as part of The Olympic Partners (TOP) program, continually shines in the area of activation. Most recently, the Youth Olympic Winter Games saw Coca-Cola sponsoring the Youth Olympic Torch Relay and utilizing red London-style double-decker buses in Innsbruck's city center to provide music and giveaways in conjunction with the Coca-Cola Happiness Truck that traveled the city handing out Coca-Cola products (Mickle 2012).

Concepts such as cross-promotions and cause-related sponsorships are exciting activation techniques. Cross-promotion, according to Donnor (2012), has fast-tracked related business platforms, specifically fan bases, and delivers a measurable return. For instance, he uses the recent cross-promotion of the Dodgers Pride Night tickets on sale at an L.A. Kings game. Donnor contends that the leader in cross-promotion is MSG Holdings; the organization that operates Madison Square Garden utilizes cross-promotions for the seven professional teams it services.

Cause-related sponsorship, better known as cause-related marketing (CRM), is relatively young in comparison to other forms of marketing. Essentially, CRM brings together not-for-profit and for-profit entities that share mutually beneficial goals in an effort to increase attention and facilitate action. American Express was the first company to enter into such an arrangement when it offered to donate a portion of each of its transactions to the fund to restore the Statue of Liberty in 1983 (Grant Space 2012). Some may call this double-dipping—promotion of products or services while raising money—but for event planners, it ultimately comes down to the show must go on, in any way and by any means possible. Regardless of how you spin it, activation is critical to a sponsorship opportunity.

After you have implemented your marketing plan, you must have a means of evaluating the success of your efforts. For an event, it can be as simple as did you sell all the tickets? But evaluating sponsorship can be accomplished in various other ways such as on-site distribution of products; website traffic before, during, and after the event; and an increase in sales after activation. How you establish the success of your event relies heavily on what you are offering and how you will track it. IEG (2012), a leader in sponsorship research, asserts that event managers must consider both the tangible and intangible benefits of sponsorship when determining value and success. Tangible benefits are easily noticed elements such as the use of a logo on goods. The intangible benefits are more elusive such as name awareness, loyalty, and the collection of names for a contact database.

At the close of your event, you should generate and distribute a report encompassing the various components of each sponsor's package. This report, according to Spoelstra (1997), should contain samples of all materials that utilized the sponsor's name and logo. This will aid in determining ROI and ROO. Return on investment relates to the idea of tangible benefits because it asks patrons to recall the sponsors. Built-in expectations can be quantified through data gathering to allow sponsors to determine if their investments were profitable. But what about the qualitative aspect of sponsorship, those intangible benefits discussed earlier. In terms of return on objectives, the qualitative information that can be gathered from interviewing patrons or conducting focus groups can better answer whether objectives were met through sponsorship affiliations. Both ROI and ROO are effective in valuing and evaluating sponsorship success. These data also justify the relationship between the sponsor and the event (Stotlar 2005).

SUMMARY

Sport is big business thanks in part to the immense sponsorship deals that are carved out by major corporations. The billions of dollars spent annually on sponsoring sport entities is somewhat astounding. You may be wondering why anyone would want to sponsor your event. Do not get caught up in the idea that your event may seem small or insignificant compared with others. There are companies and organizations out there that are seeking an event just like yours to sponsor.

Events are created with the goal of at least breaking even financially. In today's tough economic environment, it is becoming increasingly more difficult to pull that off. To help defray the cost of planning and implementing an event, event managers turn to sponsorship as a lucrative and viable option to raise the necessary capital. Knowledge of the sponsorship process and the event triangle will help ground your efforts. Do your research, identify those entities that will benefit the most from an association with your event, and go out there and clinch the deal!

LEARNING ACTIVITIES

Assume you work for an athletic department at a local high school. Because of recent budget cuts that have plagued interscholastic sport, you are looking to raise money for the department. Golf tournaments are a great way to secure funding from various sources, including sponsors. The local golf course has donated the use of the course for your event. You must now solicit your sponsors.

1. You begin the process with goal setting. What are your goals for this event?

2. How would you begin to identify potential sponsors? Are there any sponsors you should be leery of approaching? (Remember your product.)

3. Identify the parties of the event triangle. What are the investments of each?

4. Categorize the levels of sponsorship you will utilize. (This may require you to research similar golf tournaments for ideas.)

5. What benefits will you provide to sponsors (i.e., what differentiates the levels you have established)?

6. How will you present the ROI and ROO to the potential customer? How will you evaluate?

REFERENCES

Ammon, R., R. Southall, and M. Nagel. 2010. *Sport facility management: Organization events and mitigating risks.* 2nd ed. Morgantown, WV: Fitness Information Technology.

Bissell, K. 2011. Most ridiculous PGA tour tournament names in history. Bleacher Report. November 14. Available: http://bleacherreport.com/articles/940985-most-unwieldy-pga-tour-tournament-names-in-history.

Burton, T. 2008. *Naming rights: Legacy gifts and corporate money.* Hoboken, NJ: Wiley.

Butcher, D. 2010. Tissot Swiss watches activates NASCAR sponsorship with QR codes. Mobile Marketer. October 8. Available: www.mobilemarketer.com/cms/news/advertising/7668.html.

Cornwell, T. Bettina 1995. Sponsorship-linked marketing development. *Sport Marketing Quarterly* 4 (4): 13-24.

Cowan, A. 1988. *Advertising; ad clutter: Even in restrooms now. New York Times.* [Online]. February 18. Available: www.nytimes.com/1988/02/18/business/advertising-ad-clutter-even-in-restrooms-now.html.

deLisle, L.J. 2009. Marketing. In *Creating special events,* 131-147. Champaign, IL: Sagamore.

Donner, M. E. 2012, February 14. Kings and Dodgers team for cross-promotion. Retrieved from www.examiner.com/article/kings-and-dodgers-team-for-cross-promotion? Retrieved from http://grantspace.org/Tools/Knowledge-Base/Funding-Resources/Corporations/Cause-related-marketing

Harrison, K. n.d. How you can calculate the sponsorship fee for an event. CuttingEdgePR.com. Available: www.cuttingedgepr.com/articles/sponsorship_calculate_fee.asp.

Harrison, K. n.d. Think of what you can do for a potential sponsor rather than what they can give you. CuttingEdgePR.com. Available: www.cuttingedgepr.com/articles/what-you-can-do-for-potential-sponsor.asp.

International Events Group. 2012. IEG's guide to why companies sponsor. Chicago, IL: IEG. Available: http://stjude.org/SJFile/alsac_ieg_guide_why_companies_sponsor.pdf.

Johnson, C. 2009. Cutting through the clutter. CBSNews.com. February 11. Available: www.cbsnews.com/stories/2006/09/17/sunday/main2015684.shtml.

Johnson, S. 1759, January 20. No. 40 The art of advertising exemplified. *The Idler.* Retrieved from www.readbookonline.net/readOnLine/29924/

Lavidge, R.A., and G.A. Steiner. 1961. A model for predictive measurements of advertising effectiveness. *Journal of Marketing* 25 (6): 59-62.

Lawrence, H., and M. Wells. 2009. Event sponsorship. In *Event management blueprint*, 119-126. Dubuque, IA: Kendall/Hunt.

Limpert, R. 2012. BB&T to extend sports sponsorships with Atlanta tennis championships. RickLimpert.info. April 23. Available: http://ricklimpert.squarespace.com/journal/2012/4/23/bbt-to-extend-sports-sponsorships-with-atlanta-tennis-champi.html.

Lough, N. L., Irwin, R. L. & Short, G. 2000. Corporate sponsorship motives among North American companies: A contemporary analysis. *International Journal of Sport Management* 1 (4): 283-295.

McCarthy, E.J. 1960. *Basic marketing. A managerial approach.* Homewood, IL: Irwin.

Mickle, T. 2012. Sponsors activate for Winter Youth Olympic Games. *Street and Smith's SportsBusiness Journal*, January 2, 7.

Mullin, B.J., S. Hardy, and W.A. Sutton. 2007. Promotional licensing and sponsorship. In *Sport marketing* (3rd ed.), 313-340. Champaign, IL: Human Kinetics.

Performance Research. n.d. Loyal NASCAR fans please stand up. Available: www.performanceresearch.com/nascar-racestat.htm.

PGA Tour. 2012. Official schedule. Available: www.pgatour.com/r/schedule.

Plunket Research, Ltd. 2012. Sports industry overview. Houston, TX.

Schmader, S.W., and R. Jackson. 1997. *Special events: Inside and out.* 2nd ed. Urbana, IL: Sagamore.

Shank, M.D. 2009. Sponsorship programs. In *Sports marketing* (4th ed.), 324-364. Upper Saddle River, NJ: Pearson Education.

Singh, V. 2009. Sponsorship proposals: 10 ideas that will get you cash in this recession. [Web log comment]. January 30. Available: www.allaboutpresentations.com/2009/01/sponsorship-proposals-10-ideas-that.html.

Skildum-Reid, K. 2010. Top ten tips for sponsorship seekers. Sydney, Australia: Available: www.powersponsorshipdownloads.com/powersponsorship/TopTenTipsForSponsorshipSeekers.pdf.

Skildum-Reid, K. 2011, April 5. K.I.S.S – keep it simple, sponsors. [web log comment]. Retrieved from http://blog.powersponsorship.com/index.php/2011/04/

Skildum-Reid, K., and A.-M. Grey. 2008. *Sponsorship seeker's toolkit.* 3rd ed. Sydney, AU: McGraw-Hill.

Solomon, J. 2002. *An insider's guide to managing sporting events.* Champaign, IL: Human Kinetics.

Spoelstra, J. 1997. *Ice to the Eskimos.* New York: Harper Business.

SponsorMap. 2008. Understanding sponsorship. Available: www.sponsormap.com/defining-sponsorship.

Stotlar, D. 2005. *Developing successful sport sponsorship plans.* 2nd ed. Morgantown, WV: Fitness Information Technology.

Ukman, L. 2012. *IEG's guide to sponsorship.* Chicago: IEG.

Ukman, L. 2012. Sport Sponsorship. In L.P. Masteralexis, C.A. Barr, and M.A. Hums, *Principles and practice of sport management (4th ed.)*, 362-389. Sudbury, MA: Jones & Bartlett Learning.

USTA.com. 2012. BB&T agrees to naming rights deal for Atlanta tennis championships. April 23. Retrieved from www.bbtatlantaopen.com/news/bbt_agrees_to_naming_rights_deal_for_atlanta_tennis_championships/

VanDen Heuvel, D. 2009. Marketing classics: The hierarchy of effects model. [Weblog comment]. June 16. Available: www.marketingsavant.com/2009/06/marketing-classics-the-hierarchy-of-effects/trackback.

CHAPTER 7

Event Marketing

Chapter Objectives

After completing the chapter, the reader should be able to do the following.

- Understand why event marketing provides different challenges and opportunities than traditional marketing.
- Understand the role of the marketing plan and the marketing planning process.
- Utilize multiple methods of identifying target markets for events.
- Understand multiple tools available for promoting events.
- Identify the key issues of developing an event brand.

Basil DeVito has more than 30 years of experience in the sport and television industries. Mr. DeVito has work experience with the National Basketball Association (Indiana Pacers), WWE, Breeders' Cup, and XFL. His experience runs the gamut from ticket sales and marketing to television production and management. For more than 25 years, he has been a vital part of the World Wrestling Entertainment (WWE) team. His WWE tenure began in 1985, when he created WWE's first marketing group. He subsequently managed several WWE departments, served as its chief operating officer, and served as the president of the XFL. Mr. DeVito received both his bachelor's degree in journalism (BSJ) and master's degree in sport administration (MEd) from Ohio University.

Q: How would you describe WrestleMania?

A: WrestleMania is a common shared experience for all our fans. For anyone who is interested in our event, our brand of entertainment, or the WWE brand, whether they are current, have lapsed, or have only a light interest, this is the one time where everyone would have the same opportunity to enjoy. It is our culminating event of the year. WrestleMania also adds the aspect of celebrities and entertainment. Having the involvement of non-WWE stars from sport, music, and entertainment allows a port of entry for a lapsed or nonfan to say, "I have some interest," and sample or tune in. If you are going to watch only one of our events, you will watch WrestleMania. You may love it or you may not, but you'll be entertained. And, if you are exposed to it and have some follow-up interest, you may follow it somewhere down the road.

Q: What is the most important consideration in marketing an event such as WrestleMania?

A: The most important thing is to understand the positioning of that event and how it fits both in the local marketplace and in that industry. This year (2012) is the 28th WrestleMania. The aspects of WrestleMania III at the Pontiac Sil- verdome in 1987 (the event drew an attendance of 93,173, which at the time was the largest recorded attendance for an indoor sporting event in the United States) are different from this year's event at Sun Life Stadium in Miami Gardens, Florida. Flexibility and innovation are important, so what we did for WrestleMania III bears no resemblance to what we will do for 28, 29, or 30.

Q: What is a challenge you face in growing your business?

A: We have four hours of weekly prime-time television programming on basic cable. Those hours, while highly entertaining, are the best infomercial ever created. Every one of those 15 million fans watching get all the information they need. They know how to buy tickets, and they know how to buy pay-per-views. Although that's a good number and plenty to sell to, we're not going to grow if we are reaching only 15 million fans per week. We have a goal to be bigger and broader.

Q: Beyond traditional methods, how do you promote the event?

A: Remember, we're a property that cannot be found in the newspaper. We are not on the sports page, and we're generally not in the entertainment section, so you won't know what happened last night at the big event unless you were there or you watch next Monday on TV. If you have no interest in the product, a big ad in the newspaper saying "Watch WrestleMania for $59.95 next Sunday" is not going to get you to watch. Our challenge is to utilize whatever the emerging opportunity is to connect. One of the things we did in 2012 was to have our own YouTube channel. What we were able to do was create an exclusive preshow live from the stadium and put it on the front of YouTube on their splash page. WrestleMania had the WWE Superstars tweeting from backstage live. It had a totally interactive Facebook and Twitter component, which we never had before.

We streamed different content on WWE.com from around the arena. We did our first fan festival at WrestleMania IV in Atlantic City, and this year (2012) we had 40,000 fans come through the convention center for WrestleMania Axxess. It's really the one time all year you can get close to the guys. In the end it is the connectivity and the ability to reach our core, involved, dedicated fans directly, specifically, and in a manner that they like.

Q: What are some tips you would offer when marketing an event?

A: The first tip is to ensure that everyone on your team and all the different departments have a clear and concise understanding of your event and your goals. It does not matter if you are a small event such as a street fair or if you are WrestleMania. All your departments must be coordinated with the vision. The second tip is to have an initial timeline plan to act as touch points on the way to the event. Even if you can't keep up with the timeline, those points in time (e.g., on-sale dates for tickets) allow different areas to understand what needs to happen and when those things need to happen. The third tip is that the event should have only one voice to the media and the public. It might not have to be one person, but everyone has to be singing in the same voice. It is important that the outbound messages throughout the entire preevent and postevent be singular.

Sporting events are unique products; therefore, marketers must consider differences between marketing sporting events and marketing other goods and services. Mullen, Hardy, and Sutton (2007) and Wakefield (2007) each provided a series of differences between sport marketing and marketing other goods and services. Many of those differences can be applied to the marketing of sporting events.

First, sporting events share many of the same characteristics of services in that they are perishable and simultaneously produced and consumed. Sporting events are perishable, meaning that once they are over, they are over (Van der Wagen and Carlos 2007). If tickets or sponsorships go unsold, they cannot be shelved and sold later. This aspect of sporting events puts a premium on timing and scheduling because marketers must make the most of opportunities before they are lost. Similarly, the product (the event) is simultaneously produced and consumed, meaning consumers are involved in producing the event. Sports spectators help create the environment, and other participants help create the competition. Thus, event marketers must have skill in managing consumers and the staff who interact with their consumers.

Second, consumers of sporting events tend to be highly identified with the product. Spectators may travel great lengths and spend more than they should to attend events featuring their favorite athletes or favorite teams. For example, a college student may stay up all night for tickets, skip class, and spend a week's salary to see his team play in the NCAA basketball tournament. You do not see that type of behavior with the purchase of toothpaste or socks. Similarly, event participants may also be highly identified with the sport in which they participate. Given that sport is part of their identity, they may follow it more closely, be more aware of upcoming events, and be more willing to invest their time and resources to participate in a specific event.

Third, the cost of attending an event is often much greater than just the ticket prices. Spectators attending sporting events may have to account for travel and lodging expenses in reaching the event, food and beverages at the event, and souvenirs and entertainment surrounding the event. Therefore, event marketers must consider the total cost of attendance when setting prices. For example, many of the hotels near the Talladega Superspeedway significantly increase their room rates and require minimum stays during race week, which dramatically increases the spectators' cost of attendance. These costs have an effect on what event organizers charge for ticket prices, souvenirs, and concessions (Graves 2008).

Fourth, sport is social in that most consumers prefer to attend or participate with other consumers. Sport consumers like the idea of being part of a large crowd, and event participants tend to prefer the events with more players or more teams. As Wakefield (2007) suggests, a line at the grocery store is a bad thing, but a line at a ballgame is a good thing.

DEVELOPING A MARKETING PLAN

The marketing plan is the written document detailing the marketing activities that need to happen for an event to reach its objectives. In other words, the marketing plan is your game plan (Stotlar 2005). Developing a marketing plan is a step-by-step process where organizations first consider their objectives, analyze relevant data, and then develop strategies accordingly. A typical marketing plan contains the following sections.

Data and Analysis

The data and analysis section encompasses the information necessary to make wise marketing decisions. This section should include detailed analyses of the following:

- Event description: What is the purpose of the event, and who are our stakeholders? What is it that makes the event or location unique, attractive, and exciting to potential participants or spectators?
- Customers and potential customers: Who are our customers, and what are their needs?
- Competition: Who are our competitors? What gives us a competitive advantage?
- Environment: External influences such as social trends, technological advances, legal restrictions, demographic trends, and economic issues should be analyzed so that you understand factors that may affect your marketing strategies (Shank 2008; Stotlar 2005).
- SWOT analysis: This is related to the previous analysis, with an additional emphasis on marketing strengths, weaknesses, opportunities, and threats.

Marketing Goals and Objectives

Using data from the analyses, event marketers should set performance goals consistent with the organization's overall goals (discussed in chapter 2). If the organization's goal is to generate revenue, then the marketing plan should be designed to maximize the amount of money that comes in through registrations, ticket sales, sponsorships, and so on. However, if the focus of the event is to promote a cause, the plan will be much different. Typical marketing goals may be related to revenue, attendance, participation numbers, media coverage, fund-raising targets, or room nights. Specific, measurable objectives define targets that need to be reached to achieve each marketing goal. For example, a local runners' organization may set the following goal and objectives for its annual event:

Marketing goal: Increase participation in the annual Spring Fun Run.

Objective 1: Retain 95 percent of last year's participants.

Objective 2: Recruit 50 new runners.

Objective 3: Recruit 10 more organizational groups.

Objective 4: Increase number of youth participants by 15 percent.

Target Markets

Market selection involves identifying potential targets and selecting target markets. Target markets are selected based on careful analysis of consumer data, and selections should be consistent with marketing objectives. A discussion of targets and segments is found in the next section of the chapter.

Marketing Tactics

In this section of the marketing plan, event marketers identify the different marketing tactics according to the marketing mix necessary for each target. Tactics are based on the four Ps: product, place, price, promotion. The marketer's aim is to create a product at an acceptable price, in appropriate places, that can be promoted to target consumers (Masterman 2009).

Implementation

This section of the plan includes a thorough detailing of what needs to take place to successfully implement the marketing plan. Having good ideas is not enough to be successful. Instead, marketers have to execute those ideas. Planners should identify and address issues related to budget, organizational support, leadership, resource acquisition, resource allocation, coordination, and timing (Mullin, Hardy, and Sutton 2007).

TARGET MARKETING

No event can provide all benefits to all people. Even the Super Bowl, with an average audience of almost 100 million viewers in the United States, reaches less than half of the population. Think about an extreme sport event. Would it make sense to try to market the event to the entire community? Given that most people in the community would not be interested in the event, a broad marketing campaign would be wasteful because many resources would be expended on people with no intention of ever attending the event.

Instead of marketing to everyone (mass marketing), events should be tailored to meet the needs of specific segments of the population (target marketing). Segments are groups of consumers or potential consumers with similar attributes, attitudes, or behaviors. By segmenting the population into groups with similar attributes, event marketers are able to develop efficient marketing plans to reach those groups. Segments are often identified using the following criteria:

- Demographic segmentation—identifying groups based on population characteristics such as age, gender, ethnicity, geographic location, income, and education
- Psychographic segmentation—identifying groups based on psychological characteristics such as lifestyle, personality, opinions, and values

- Product usage—identifying groups based on how often or how much consumers use the product
- Product benefits—identifying groups based on the benefits consumers seek from an event

After identifying segments, event marketers select target markets. Target markets are the segments to which the event will be marketed. They are selected based on the segment's interest in the event, likelihood of buying, size, and accessibility. Once targets have been selected, event marketers can develop specialized marketing activities and messages designed to appeal to and meet the specific needs of the target.

One common mistake is to target overly broad segments or target segments based solely on size. Think back to the extreme sport event. Organizers may have identified a large segment of senior citizens in the community. Although this segment may be large, it would not be appropriate to target this group because they would not be interested in the event, and no amount of marketing genius would be sufficient to get them to attend. This example illustrates that just because a segment is large, it may not necessarily be the best to target. In fact, smaller, well-defined segments are often the most attractive targets. Niche markets are typically small, focused segments whose needs may not be currently served by larger events. A good example of this strategy comes from the cable television industry. Although ESPN and Fox Sports Net reach wide audiences with a variety of events, smaller networks such as The Golf Channel, The Tennis Channel, The Outdoor Channel, and SpeedTV have emerged and experienced success in marketing to smaller, focused audiences. Similarly, the NBA has had some success targeting niche markets. In late 2009, the NBA rolled out advertisements and a new website targeting the Hispanic market. Even though the Hispanic market makes up only 15 percent of NBA viewers, the league has identified it as an important and growing market (Hall 2009).

THE MARKETING MIX

Sporting events are no different from other businesses in that effective use of the marketing mix is important for reaching marketing objectives. The marketing mix is a set of marketing tools that work together to achieve an event's objectives. Traditional definitions of the marketing mix consist of elements related to the sport product, price, promotion, and place. Strategies based on the marketing mix are typically developed with the specific needs of each target market in mind.

Product

The sport product is the unit of exchange designed to satisfy needs and provide benefits to the event participant or spectator (Shank 2009). Successful event marketers know how to identify what people want and provide them with a little more (Goldblatt 2008). To do this, event marketers must understand what makes sporting events different from other products.

First, every event is a unique experience for the spectator or participant, adding an element of unpredictability for the event marketer. As such, event marketers cannot promise a close game, a competitive tournament, or good weather. However, Mullin, Hardy, and Sutton (2007) argue that it is the uncertainty that makes sporting events attractive. Further, sporting events are characteristically intangible (basketball game, golf tournament, or bicycle race) rather than tangible (basketball, golf club, or bicycle). The implication here is that participants and spectators typically consume sporting events for the experience instead of some tangible factor. Therefore, event marketers have to focus on the experiential nature of the event in order to attract and retain customers. For example, the 2008 Beijing Organizing Committee incorporated state-of-the-art lighting, multimedia video, and giant LED screens into the Olympic opening ceremony to produce a memorable, over-the-top event (Weiss 2008).

Second, product benefits can be delivered through a variety of means because the product package for an event may be complex. Sporting events may consist of core offerings (e.g., basketball game, volleyball tournament) as well as extensions (e.g., halftime show, awards ceremony, music, tailgating). The challenge for an event marketer is to develop an acceptable mix of activities to meet the needs of participants and spectators. Consider the Circle City Classic, a college football game featuring two historically black institutions. Although the game itself may be the central product, fans often attend the games for the entire experience, which includes the Classic Sports X-Perience, the halftime show, and a battle of the bands. Similarly, people who attend AVP volleyball tournaments do not attend just for the volleyball but also for the music, beach atmosphere, and AVP dancers.

Price

Price is what you ask from your customers in order to watch or participate in your event. Pricing decisions are important to event managers because price balances attractiveness and value with organizational revenue. Setting the price is especially difficult for sporting events in that marketers are associating a price with an experience rather than a tangible good. You have to consider what the experience is worth to the customer, which can be difficult considering the subjective nature of intangible benefits.

To make effective pricing decisions, event marketers need to consider several factors such as the cost of producing the event, consumer demand (what people are willing to pay), and competitors' prices (how your event compares with others). Event marketers also have to consider organizational objectives when setting price. Events may set their prices to maximize profits, generate exposure, meet competitive threats, or provide participation (Shank 2009). For example, each of the following events will use different pricing strategies to meet different objectives.

- Championship boxing event: Set a high price to maximize revenue.
- Charity fun run: Set the price at a level that would encourage people to attend and give to the cause.
- Volleyball tournament: Set a price that would be comparable to other tournaments.
- Intramural softball tournament: Set a low price to encourage as many people as possible to participate.

Sporting events have many pricing options to meet these objectives, including the following:

- Charge each person for admission or participation.
- Charge teams or groups rather than individuals.
- Base the price on a package of benefits. For example, spectators could either pay per game or pay for an all-tournament or all-access pass.
- Bundle the admission price with other attractions or activities.
- Provide free admission. Free admission can be profitable if you can generate revenue through sponsorships or media. In addition, customers attending for free may generate revenue through concessions, parking, merchandise sales, or, depending on the type of event, donations.

Place

Place (or distribution) refers to important issues related to time (when is the event) and location (where is the event). Distribution strategies are typically focused on making the event timely and convenient for the customer. In regard to location, event marketers need to consider access to the location, perceived safety of the location, and proximity to transportation when designing marketing efforts. Event managers also have to manage different intermediaries (also called distribution channels) that make the event available to consumers. Examples of these intermediaries include the venue where the event is held, the media that broadcast the event, ticket agents, and retail partners. A great example of how place can influence the perception of an event is the inaugural Carrier Classic, which featured a basketball game between North Carolina and Michigan State on the deck of the USS *Carl Vinson*, a Navy aircraft carrier. The choice of such a unique location allowed active-duty military personnel to be honored in conjunction with Veterans Day (Witz 2011).

Technology has dramatically changed how sporting events are delivered. NBC, the official Olympic broadcast partner in the United States, provided more than 3,600 hours of coverage through a variety of media platforms such as the Internet, podcasts, RSS feeds, and e-mail alerts. Whereas prior Olympics were accessed mostly through television, the Beijing Games were transmitted to viewers when they wanted it in the platform they wanted (Horovitz, Petrecca, and Howard 2008).

Promotion

Promotion embodies the methods marketers use to communicate with customers. The purpose of promotion is to stimulate interest in, awareness of, and ultimately purchase of your product (Mullin, Hardy, and Sutton 2007). Large and small events alike require strong promotional campaigns to ensure a successful event (Goldblatt 2008). Promotion is a broad category because it covers elements such as advertising, public relations, sales, and sales promotion. These methods are discussed further in the next section.

EVENT PROMOTION

Few events sell themselves. To be successful, an event promotion plan should effectively communicate with various targets through multiple methods. Promotion planning is often one of the more important elements of the event marketing mix. Event marketers must effectively utilize promotional tools to create demand, resulting in attendance, participation, sales, or other revenue.

Event marketers need to set objectives for their promotional programs. Promotional objectives are statements about what marketers want to accomplish through the promotional program. For a new event, promotional objectives may be to inform people about the event and make them aware of what the event offers. For events people are already aware of, promotional objectives may focus more on persuading people to attend or participate. Popular events may focus on reminding people about the event and reinforcing consumers' commitment to the event. Ultimately, the objectives should result in some action.

Choosing the right message will go a long way in meeting promotional objectives. Effective messages will appeal to the target market and give the target market reason to listen. Therefore, marketers must carefully identify what they want to promote and to whom. This is often accomplished by focusing on the needs of the consumers. For example, an event targeting families will be most effective if it focuses on issues relevant to families, such as opportunities for family fun at a low price. The message also depends on the type of event. Think about what makes the event exciting or attractive. Is it the history of the event, the location, or the participants? What makes this event relevant to the target market? Demonstrating the key benefit of the event is another characteristic of an effective message. For example, ESPN used the message "More ping, less bling" to promote the 2003 College Baseball World Series; the message reinforced the idea that college baseball fans like the fact that college players play for the love of the game rather than for the money. Although short, this message effectively communicated what consumers liked about this event.

Once the message has been developed, the event marketer has to choose communication tools that will achieve the promotional objectives. Some of the most-used communication tools include advertising, public relations, sales promotion, and personal selling. Typically, an event marketer will use multiple tools to communicate the event. However, care should be taken to ensure the same message is getting across regardless of the tool being used. An integrated marketing communication (IMC) approach means the event will utilize several promotional elements to deliver a consistent message about the event.

Advertising

Advertising is a paid, nonpersonal, clearly sponsored message (Mullin, Hardy, and Sutton 2008). Advertising is often the most visible tool available to event marketers, and it can be effective in creating awareness and building an image (Shank 2009). Choosing the right media is critical to the success of advertising. When choosing media, it is important to consider whether it is appropriate for your message, whether it reaches your target market, and how much it will cost to reach your target market. Although we typically think of

advertising as an advertisement in the newspaper, a television commercial, or a billboard, a variety of other media such as newsletters, transportation ads, and yard signs can effectively reach target markets. In addition, new technologies have changed advertising. For example, events trying to reach younger markets are finding that advertising on websites and through social media may be more effective than traditional newspaper advertising. The following is a list of some of the media commonly used to promote sporting events:

Electronic media: television, radio, websites, mobile devices

Print media: newspapers, magazines, newsletters, trade publications

Outdoor media: billboards, buses, benches, posters, fliers

Publicity

Publicity is media exposure that is not paid. A positive story in the newspaper or in a magazine can be very effective in influencing public opinion. Publicity has an advantage over advertising in that it may stimulate more attention, consumers often see it as more credible, and it is much less expensive. However, the media have more control over the message.

Media coverage can often be the difference between a successful event and an event that comes and goes without anyone knowing it even happened. According to Acosta Hernandez (2002), major events such as the Olympics and the FIFA World Cup would never have been possible without media exposure. This exposure motivates public imagination and brings life to athletes and rivalries.

To generate positive coverage, event promoters must know how to identify newsworthy stories and pitch them to reporters and editors. Most story ideas never make it to press or air. Stories that are timely, different, or important have a better chance of being published. Consider an event on the Legend's Tour (the Official Tour of the LPGA). Story pitches about the date of the event or the rules of the event will probably never get any attention. However, story pitches about rivalries between golfers, records about to be broken, or human interest stories about extraordinary players are more likely to get picked up by the media.

Sometimes planned activities can create publicity for an event, generating awareness or interest. For example, in 2005 WWE used an 11-market mall tour to promote WrestleMania, its premier annual event. The tour included several interactive displays along with opportunities to meet and greet current and former WWE Superstars. As expected, the promotional tour created numerous opportunities for media coverage in each city. Similarly, celebrities can be used to generate additional publicity. In 2012, the struggling Humana Challenge Golf tournament leveraged its association with former president Bill Clinton and the Clinton Foundation to generate a surge of positive attention, which helped change the profile of the event (Montgomery 2012).

Sales Promotion

Sales promotion consists of many different techniques used to engage the consumer, such as discounts, special offers, coupons, samples, premiums, contests and sweepstakes, demonstrations, and exhibitions. In event management, sales promotion is often used to create interest or generate purchases through reduced-price or value-added incentives.

When your consumers are price sensitive and will respond to price changes, you may consider a price incentive such as a ticket discount, coupon, or free trial. For example, Utah State University did a price promotion selling football tickets for the same price as a gallon of gasoline. They were able to sell more than 2,000 tickets in one day. Although price promotions can be quite successful, you have to be careful that you do not cheapen your product.

If price is not an issue with customers, or you are concerned about cheapening your product, adding value may be the best option. A variety of tools can be used to add value such as premium giveaways (hats, T-shirts, collectable items), special attractions (postgame concerts, autograph sessions), and theme nights. A great example comes from the San Francisco Giants. To capitalize on the large Filipino population in the area,

the team staged Filipino Heritage Night. Before the game, popular Filipino boxer Manny Pacquiao threw out the first pitch, ticket buyers received a Pacquiao bobblehead doll giveaway, and the team provided cultural entertainment. As a result of the added value, the team drew a crowd of 39,314 fans that night, which included a large walk-up of more than 11,000 (Nightengale 2009).

Numerous types of sales promotions can be used to promote an event. The key is to identify which types of promotions will resonate with your target market and deliver results. The following is a list of some common techniques used to promote sporting events.

Price Promotions

- Discounts
- Coupons
- Buy-one-get-one promotions
- Family packages
- Group discounts
- Bundling parking or other amenities with tickets

Value-Added Promotions

- Premium giveaways
- Trivia contests
- Sweepstakes entries
- Meet and greet events
- Theme promotions
- Camps and clinics
- Pre- and postevent entertainment
- Autograph sessions
- Cross-promotion with other events
- Product sampling
- Point-of-purchase displays
- Open houses
- Exhibitions
- Celebrity appearances
- Loyalty programs
- Honors and celebrations
- Interactive experiences
- Fan appreciation promotions

Direct Sales

Direct sales involve direct contact between the event and the consumer. Direct sales techniques most often include personal selling, direct mail or e-mail, and telemarketing and are most often used for larger purchases such as season tickets, premium seating, and sponsorship. Often, the key to direct sales is the list of prospects. These activities rarely work unless you are contacting the right people. Smaller and less frequent sporting events do not have the luxury of full-time sales staffs, so they utilize volunteer sales staffs, sponsors, and the Internet to facilitate sales.

Word of Mouth

Activities designed to generate word-of-mouth communications can be effective for communicating with hard-to-reach or hard-to-influence consumers (Greenwell and Andrew 2007). Event organizers use a variety of tactics to proactively encourage word of mouth. Word of mouth can be generated by working with other organizations to get their members talking about your event, providing recruiting incentives to current customers who spread the word and enlist new customers, and giving coupons or premium items to customers to pass along to new customers. Technology has produced additional methods to stimulate word of mouth such as viral marketing, organizational weblogs, and social networks.

Social Media

In recent years, many sporting events have begun to embrace nontraditional media, such as social media, to connect with customers and promote events. This type of media can provide instant communication before, during, and after events. Social media allow organizations to bypass traditional media and communicate directly with consumers. Further, the communication is more user driven and community oriented. This type of communication is especially effective for events that do not tend to get as much print coverage or broadcast coverage as mainstream sports. For example, organizations such as Women's Professional Soccer (WPS) and Ultimate Fighting Championship (UFC) have been active in leveraging nontraditional media to compensate for the lack of mainstream media attention given their sports.

The following are a few examples of how social media can be used to promote events:

- HBO Sports put fighter interviews, press conferences, and other promotional activities on social media sites such as Twitter and Facebook to keep boxing fans constantly abreast of the events and stories leading up to the Manny Pacquiao and Antonio Margarito fight at Cowboys Stadium in order to reach younger viewers and spur pay-per-view sales (Umstead 2010).

- The University of Michigan created an offer requiring fans to "like" a page to unlock a ticket presale code, resulting in more than $74,000 in ticket sales in one day (Butler 2011).

- The Louisville Lightning, a professional arena soccer club, used Facebook extensively to promote its inaugural season. Realizing they did not have the budget to extensively promote the team through traditional methods, team managers filled their Facebook page with player introductions, embedded video clips, photos, and a promotion for children. Most important, they used the page to urge soccer fans to buy tickets. The result was an opening-night sell-out.

- Several college football programs including Texas Christian University (TCU) and Boston College have used Groupon to promote the sales of discounted football tickets. The site has helped football programs induce new customers to attend games at lower prices (Muret 2011).

- NASCAR uses social media to keep fans engaged between races. Fans who are engaged are more likely to watch race broadcasts (Busch 2011). Similarly, the NHRA has begun providing more compelling content through social media, with the goal of creating engaged fans who will buy tickets and watch televised events (Mickle 2011).

- The Marine Corps Marathon uses Facebook to connect directly with participants, which allows the event to bypass traditional media.

In addition, the Facebook postings allow participants to publicize the causes for which they are running (Nearman 2009).

ATTRACTING SPECTATORS

To attract spectators, event marketers must first ask what consumers want from the event. Do they want to see the top athletes? Be a part of history? Enjoy time with family and friends? The only way to accomplish this is to research your customers to identify what they want and what they value. Consumer groups may be quite diverse, so it is important to identify what each target market wants so you can attract them to the event (Solomon 2002).

Sporting events have many features, benefits, and attributes; however, only a few are important to consumers. For example, a World Cup soccer match could be described as being two hours long and featuring two teams and a ball. This description is accurate, but it misses the aspects of the event that are attractive to customers. If you were to describe the event as two teams comprising the best athletes in their sport, playing the most important games of their lives in front of a world stage, you would be providing a description better reflecting why spectators are attracted to the event.

Several researchers have identified important attributes of sporting events. Ferreira and Armstrong (2004) identified attributes that attract college students to college sporting events: popularity of the sport, attractiveness of teams and players, offerings and promotions, pregame and in-game entertainment, convenience and accessibility, facility quality, and cost. Mullin, Hardy, and Sutton (2007) identified level of excitement, price, proximity to action, level of performance, authenticity, affiliation, and socialization as key attributes that differentiate one event from another. The event marketer's task is to identify what aspects of an event are relevant to consumers, highlight the appealing aspects, and illustrate how this product is different from other entertainment options.

In addition to identifying event characteristics that are important to spectators, event marketers need to identify what motivates consumers to attend their events. Fan motivation is often defined as the internal drive that leads to behavior. Wann and colleagues (2008) found that motivation differs according to the sport. Specifically, motivation will be different for individual versus team sports, aggressive versus nonaggressive sports, and stylistic versus nonstylistic sports. Therefore, it is important for marketers to identify what it is about their respective sports that motivates consumers to watch and attend. Although the list of motives for event attendance is extensive, a few are common to most sporting events. Funk and colleagues (2009) defined five core motivations for sport event attendance:

1. Socialization—attend to socialize and interact with others at events.
2. Performance—attend to appreciate the grace and elegance of events.
3. Excitement—attend to enjoy the excitement sports provide.
4. Esteem—attend to feel a sense of accomplishment when a team or athlete wins.
5. Diversion—attend to get away from the tension of life's everyday routines.

ATTRACTING PARTICIPANTS

Although participants are much different from spectators, the same two questions need to be addressed: (1) What do participants want from the event, and (2) what makes the event attractive to participants?

The type of event will often dictate what participants want. For example, runners in a charity road race are likely participating to support a cause or to just have fun, while competitors in a triathlon are more likely to be participating to challenge themselves and to gain a sense of achievement. In addition, different types of participants will want different things. A professional athlete will want different things than a youth team coach.

Marketers of poker events have done a good job identifying what participants want from their experiences and have used that knowledge to attract players. Poker offers two main inducements: the opportunity to win big money and the opportunity for everyday people to compete with professionals. By focusing on these aspects of the event, major events such as the World Series of Poker (WSOP) Tour and the World Poker Tour (WPT) have seen dramatic growth in the number of players in recent years (Bradford 2009).

To make events attractive to participants, Wanda Rutledge of the National Council of Youth Sports encourages event planners to focus on the entire experience rather than just the event (Martin 2009). Athletes most likely have participated in other events and will have expectations of what their experience should be like. Make sure you understand why people are participating and what they want out of their entire experience. From that knowledge, try to turn your event into an unforgettable experience. Further, Solomon (2002) argues that events should have a player-friendly mentality and that events should be designed with the athlete in mind. In addition to the competition itself, scheduling, transportation, and accommodations can make a big difference to participants. Extra touches such as welcome parties, activities, and goody bags may make for memorable experiences.

Peavy (2008) provides a list of hints for being a gracious host:

- Thank participants for registering, and include special offers as a thank-you for registering for the event.
- Keep participants informed as the event approaches.
- Arrange for billboards or posters around the community to welcome participants and make them feel special.
- Have friendly and efficient staff greet guests.
- Train your staff to respond to visitors' needs.
- Have a big send-off when the event ends to show your appreciation and to encourage participants to return.

BRANDING THE EVENT

A brand is the combination of names, symbols, slogans, or logos that identifies a product and distinguishes it from other products (Aaker 1991).

Brands also communicate an identity or image of a product. When someone sees the brand name *McDonald's* or sees symbols such as the restaurant's golden arches, they automatically associate them with the fast-food giant. Brands also communicate quality because consumers may consider brand name products (e.g., Starbucks, Coca-Cola, Google, IBM) to be superior in quality to less recognizable brands. Similarly, an event's brand generates the associations consumers connect to the event. Events' brand names (e.g., Olympic Games, Super Bowl, the Masters, Ironman Triathlon) and marks (e.g., Olympic rings, Super Bowl logo, the green jacket, Ironman M-Dot symbol) help consumers identify the event and differentiate the event from competitors.

When branding an event, an organizer's goal should be to build up the event so that the mention of the name generates recognition, attention, and awareness (Hoyle 2002). Event organizers should try to communicate certain images or values in order to create the impression that the event is unique or important. NASCAR has been especially effective in creating and managing its brand. The NASCAR brand has been built to represent more of a lifestyle than a sport. As such, NASCAR works to communicate that it provides thrilling entertainment and that its drivers are role models and regular, down-to-earth people. This approach has allowed the sport to connect with the target markets and build a loyal audience (Bernhardt 2006).

The brand is often communicated through the event's name. A strong name is especially important because it is often the center of marketing and promotional campaigns. For example, in 2002 the Senior PGA Tour, a series of golf events for professional golfers 50 years of age and older, changed its name to the Champions Tour. Whereas the former name was effective in describing the event, the new name communicates an image of quality and experience.

In addition, event branding involves creating an experience that gives an event name recognition and longevity (Chavis 2008). The brand equity of an event will be boosted by notable or memorable experiences. A great example of a strong event brand is the Flying Pig Marathon in Cincinnati,

First of all, the name *Flying Pig* and the winged pig logo distinguish the event from all the other marathons across the country (Olberding and Jisha 2005). Second, the event is different from other marathons in that organizers tried to appeal to a new breed of runners by offering experiences and interactions unlike what traditional marathons were offering.

ELECTRONIC EVENT MARKETING

More and more, technology has become an important tool in marketing events. Websites and e-mail have become essential sources of communication, and in recent years, social media have become an important tool in connecting with spectators and participants.

Event marketing often starts with a good website, as consumers now depend on the Internet for information about events and activities surrounding them. Further, organizations depend on the Internet to build their brands and generate sales. Considering the importance of your website, it is essential to make sure the site is effectively marketing your event. In the early days of the Internet, many event organizers designed and maintained their websites themselves. However, changes in technology now demand professional skills to develop sites that look and function at a level site visitors expect. In fact, a poorly designed website may suggest a poorly organized event in the minds of many consumers. Outsourcing your web management may be expensive; however, when the price is weighed against the value of the expertise, it may be worth the cost. Regardless of whether you design a website yourself or outsource your web needs, it is important to keep the end consumer in mind. According to Graham, Neirotti, and Goldblatt (2002), there are several keys to successful event websites:

• A marketable URL: Your URL, or web address, must be something people will remember. Sometimes it is something as simple as usopen.com for the USGA's U.S. Open Golf Championship.

• Usability: Usability refers to how easily your visitors can use your site. Visitors should be able to find what they need or do what they want quickly without becoming frustrated (Pedersen, Miloch, and Laucella 2007). Take time to find out what your visitors want from your site. You cannot assume you know what your site's visitors are looking for.

• Extensive and updated content: Your site should provide content that is interesting enough to keep people coming back. In addition to basic information about schedules, statistics, and records, event sites can provide unique content by publishing exclusive news, features, and videos that cannot be found elsewhere (Irwin, Sutton, and McCarthy 2008).

In addition to providing information, your website can be used to target specific customers for specific products. The Los Angeles Lakers enlisted an online marketing agency to help sell 2,500 premier seats at the Staples Center. Using computer technology, they were able to identify market niches by analyzing what people were looking for on the Internet and targeting those people for high-end tickets (Muret 2009).

E-mail provides event marketers a way to target and reach customers beyond their immediate area. Many events now use e-mail to keep in touch with customers, update customers on various activities, and sell tickets for events. A great example of using e-mail to reach new fans comes from the Milwaukee Brewers baseball team. The Brewers sent an e-mail to their season ticket holders offering an opportunity to purchase tickets for an upcoming game. The recipient could also forward the e-mail to a friend, and if the friend bought tickets, the recipient was rewarded with free club seats to an upcoming game (Walker 2008).

CREATING COMMUNITY SUPPORT

Another good way to promote your event is through partnerships with community organizations. A wide variety of community partners can be utilized to create community support, promote your event, and involve the community. Community leaders and local politicians can provide high-profile support, and your work together is likely to generate media attention. Local agencies such as sports commissions, convention and visitors bureaus, and chambers of commerce are in the business of promoting economic activity; therefore, they are likely to have the networks, manpower, and know-how to promote events. In addition, local businesses that cater to tourism such as restaurants and tourist attractions make good partners because they also stand to benefit from your success.

To better engage the community, organizations will often create advisory boards made up of local leaders to help them promote the event. Advisory boards bring contacts and knowledge of the community to the table and play a role in advising event organizers on these matters. Advisory boards can also establish legitimacy for events lacking awareness or recognition in the community. By utilizing trusted and respected community leaders, advisory boards can emphasize the significance of the event (Supovitz 2005). Similarly, events may recruit host committees or local organizing committees. These groups differ from advisory boards in that they assist in specific functions beyond advising (Supovitz 2005). The role of a local organizing committee is to provide on-location support for the event. For some events, such as the Olympic Games, much of the day-to-day decision making is governed by the local organizing committee (Andranovich, Burbank, and Heying 2001).

A great example of an event that generates considerable community support is the PGA's St. Jude Classic. This PGA Tour event benefitting St. Jude Children's Research Hospital has been in Memphis, Tennessee, for more than 50 years and has an undeniable bond with the city. FedEx, a local company, has been either the title or presenting sponsor for more than 20 years, and according to tournament organizers, about 1,850 volunteers contribute more than 25,000 hours of service to the event each year. Y.O.U.T.H Program, Inc., an organization made up of local business and political leaders, serves as the host organization.

SUMMARY

Effective event marketing does not happen by accident. Merely "getting the word out" is not enough to meet most marketing objectives. Instead, it takes extensive planning and forethought. Marketers need to identify what their customers want and systematically develop marketing plans to meet those customer wants. Effective marketing plans require careful analysis of internal and external influences, meaningful goals that support organizational objectives, selection of appropriate target markets, strategies that incorporate the four Ps, and a plan for implementation. Event marketers have numerous tools at their disposal. A strong event brand and various promotional tools allow marketers to communicate that their events will meet consumers' needs.

LEARNING ACTIVITIES

Assume you are in charge of marketing a senior women's professional golf tournament in your town. The organization's goal is to maximize ticket sales to ensure the event is a financial success.

1. What kind of data will you need to make your marketing decisions?

2. Who will you target to sell tickets to this event?

3. What will be unique or attractive about the product that will attract spectators?

4. What would be your pricing strategies?

5. What would be your distribution issues?

6. Outline your promotional strategies to attract spectators.

    A. What is your message?

    B. How will you communicate the message?

    C. What types of sales promotions and sales strategies would be effective for an event like this one?

    D. How can you generate word of mouth?

    E. How can you use social media to promote your event?

Now, assume you are in charge of marketing an amateur junior women's team golf tournament in your town. The organization's goal is to maximize the number of junior golf teams to register for the event.

1. What kind of data will you need to make your marketing decisions?

2. Who will you target to register teams for this event?

3. What will be unique or attractive about the product that will attract participants?

4. What would be your pricing strategies?

5. What would be your distribution issues?

6. Outline your promotional strategies to attract participants.

   A. What is your message?

   B. How will you communicate the message?

   C. What types of sales promotions and sales strategies would be effective for an event like this one?

   D. How can you generate word of mouth?

   E. How can you use social media to promote your event?

REFERENCES

Aaker, D. 1991. *Managing brand equity.* New York. Free Press.

Acosta Hernandez, R. 2002. *Managing sport organizations.* Champaign, IL: Human Kinetics.

Andranovich, G., M.J. Burbank, and C.H. Heying. 2001. Olympic cities: Lessons learned from mega-event politics. *Journal of Urban Affairs* 23 (2): 113-131.

Bernhardt, K. 2006. NASCAR's marketing prowess a biz model. *Atlanta Business Chronicle.* [Online]. May 26. Available: http://atlanta.bizjournals.com/atlanta/stories/2006/05/29/smallb2.html.

Bold, B. 2009. Lance Armstrong uses Twitter to invite fans on cycle tour. *Brand Republic*, August 21, 1.

Bradford, M. 2009. High stakes poker: Winning hands, gaining fans. *SportsEvents* (January): 27.

Busch, G. 2011. How NASCAR can maintain its early-season momentum. *Street and Smith's SportsBusiness Journal*, March 14, 22.

Butler, D. 2011. How to revolutionize team communications with ticket buyers. *Street and Smith's SportsBusiness Journal*, October 24, 14.

Chavis, S. 2008. Branding sports events: Creating a sports event identity that lasts. *SportsEvents* 5 (2): 22-23.

Ferreira, M., and K.L. Armstrong. 2004. An exploratory examination of attributes influencing students' decisions to attend college sport events. *Sport Marketing Quarterly* 13:194-208.

Funk, D.C., K. Filo, A.A. Beaton, and M. Pritchard. 2009. Measuring the motives of sport event attendance: Bridging the academic-practitioner divide to understanding behavior. *Sport Marketing Quarterly* 18:126-138.

Goldblatt, J. 2008. *Special events: The roots and wings of celebration.* Hoboken, NJ: Wiley.

Graham, S., L. Delpy Neirotti, and J.J. Goldblatt. 2001. *The ultimate guide to sports marketing.* New York: McGraw-Hill.

Graves, G. 2008. Rising fuel, hotel costs the pits for NASCAR fans. *USA Today*, April 24, 1C.

Greenwell, T.C., and D.P.S. Andrew. 2007. Communicating with different customer segments: A case from minor-league baseball. In *Sport marketing across the spectrum: Selected research from emerging, developing, and established scholars*, ed. J. James, 157-164. Morgantown, WV: Fitness Information Technology.

Hall, V. 2009. New NBA campaign is first major Hispanic effort. *Street and Smith's SportsBusiness Journal*, October 19, 4.

Horovitz, B., L. Petrecca, and T. Howard. 2008. Faster, higher, stronger—and digital; Ad spending buzzes to social networks, cellphones. *USA Today*, August 8, 1B.

Hoyle, L.H. 2002. *Event marketing: How to successfully promote events, festivals, conventions, and expositions.* New York: Wiley.

Irwin, R.L., W.A. Sutton, and L.M. McCarthy. 2008. *Sport promotion and sales management.* Champaign, IL: Human Kinetics.

Martin, M. 2009. 2008 S.P.O.R.T.S. report: Education, conversation, networking & more. *SportsEvents* (January): 11-14.

Masterman, G. 2009. *Strategic sports event management: Olympic edition.* Oxford, UK: Elsevier.

Mickle, T. 2011. NHRA rolls out greatest moments contest to boost Facebook fan base. *Street and Smith's SportsBusiness Journal*, March 12, 6.

Montgomery, G. 2012. Former president Clinton saves Desert Classic Humana Challenge. Blackvoicenews.com. January 26. Available: www.blackvoicenews.com/inside-pages/sports/47374-former-president-clinton-saves-desert-classic-humana-challenge.html.

Mullin, B.J., S. Hardy, and W.A. Sutton. 2007. *Sport marketing.* 3rd ed. Champaign, IL: Human Kinetics.

Muret, D. 2009. Targeted web ads help AEG move Staples Center club seats. *Street and Smith's SportsBusiness Journal*, October 19, 13.

Muret, D. 2011. Social media sites redefine cheap seats. *Street and Smith's SportsBusiness Journal*, May 23, 20.

Nearman, S. 2009. Race using social media to click with the public. *The Washington Times*, October 23, C4.

Nightengale, B. 2009. Promotions punched up for fans seeking knockout. *USA Today*, May 12, 5C.

Olberding, D.J., and J. Jisha. 2005. The Flying Pig: Building brand equity in a major urban marathon. *Sport Marketing Quarterly* 14:191-196.

Peavy, P. 2008. Helpful hints for being a gracious host. *SportsEvents* (November): 14.

Pedersen, P.M., K.S. Miloch, and P.C. Laucella. 2007. *Strategic sport communication.* Champaign, IL: Human Kinetics.

Shank, M.D. 2008. *Sports marketing: A strategic perspective.* 4th ed. Upper Saddle River, NJ: Pearson.

Solomon, J. 2002. *An insider's guide to managing sporting events.* Champaign, IL: Human Kinetics.

Stotlar, D. 2005. *Developing successful sport sponsorship plans.* 2nd ed. Morgantown, WV: Fitness Information Technology.

Supovitz, F. 2005. *The sports event marketing and management playbook.* Hoboken, NJ: Wiley.

Umstead, T. 2010. HBO jabs digital media behind Pacquiao-Margarito ppv bout. Multichannel News. November 6. Available: www.multichannel.com/article/459509-HBO_Jabs_Digital_Media_Behind_Pacquiao_Margarito_PPV_Bout.php.

Van Der Wagen, L., and B.R. Carlos. 2005. *Event management for tourism, cultural, business and sporting events.* Upper Saddle River, NJ: Pearson.

Wakefield, K. 2007. *Team sports marketing.* Oxford: Elsevier.

Walker, D. 2008. The Brewers try viral marketing. *Journal Sentinel.* [Online]. May 8. Available: www.jsonline.com/blogs/sports/31887829.html.

Wann, D.L., F.G. Grieve, R.K. Zapalac, and D.G. Pease. 2008. Motivational profiles of sports fans of different sports. *Sport Marketing Quarterly* 17:6-19.

Weiss, J. 2008. Beijing puts on a grand show. *The Boston Globe*, August 9, E4.

Witz, B. 2011. Carrier Classic more than just a game. Fox Sports Carolinas. November 12. Available: www.foxsportscarolinas.com/11/12/11/Carrier-Classic-more-than-just-a-game/landing.html?blockID=602366&feedID=3736.

CHAPTER 8

Media Promotion and Relations

Chapter Objectives

After completing the chapter, the reader should be able to do the following:

- Understand the role of the media, media promotion, and media relations.
- Recognize the critical Rs of media relations: relating, retaining, and repairing.
- Understand the symbiotic relationship between the media, sport, and events.
- Value the role of the promotional mix with regard to the marketing mix.
- Appreciate the value of social media in event management.
- Understand how to evaluate the success of a promotion and media relations campaign.

Scottie Rodgers is the associate executive director for communications at the Ivy League Office. Rodgers leads the media relations, website and multimedia, and other communications efforts for the Ivy League's 33 men's and women's sports and assists with other external areas including marketing, sponsorships, television, and branding as a member of the executive director's senior management team. Before joining the Ivy League, Rodgers spent two years as senior director of university relations at CBS Interactive (formerly CBS College Sports Network and CSTV) in New York City, where he served as the primary marketing, sales, and account manager for a number of online clients including the Heisman, the Big East Conference, Louisville, Marquette, St. John's, Pittsburgh, Villanova, and two Ivy League members (Brown and Yale). Before joining CBS Interactive, he spent five years at the NCAA national office in Indianapolis with the Division I Women's Basketball Championship. He began his career with the Southeastern Conference as media relations assistant after graduating from the University of Alabama, where he worked as a student SID (sports information director).

Among his many accomplishments, he has also served in the following capacities during his career: 2002 FIBA men's world basketball championship and 2004 FINA World Swimming Championships (25 m); as publicity assistant coordinating celebrity interviews at the Kentucky Derby from 2002 to 2007; on the media operations staff for the AT&T Cotton Bowl Classic since 2000 and with media operations for the New York Yankees for the 2008 Major League Baseball All-Star Game; 2007, 2008, 2009, and 2011 American League Division Series; 2009 and 2010 American League Championship Series; and 2009 World Series.

Q: What was it about media promotion and relations that enticed you to this field?

A: My interest started with sport journalism, but once I was introduced to the media relations side, I thought it was more of a fit with what I wanted from a career in sports. Over my time in the profession, what entices me to still enjoy it is the diversity of the job description and job skills needed on a daily basis. It's not just all about writing. I have been able to gain understanding and experience in so many other areas including event logistics, game operations, management, and marketing and promotions.

Q: What special skills are necessary to compete for jobs in this field?

A: I think you almost have to be a jack of many trades and the master of none in the media relations profession to be successful. You also have to be a flexible and evolving person because so much of the profession has changed in recent years with the advent of social media and multimedia.

Q: What has been the most exciting moment of your career so far?

A: That's a hard one to say because I have been lucky in my experiences to work several major sporting events, from the men's and women's Final Four to the World Series to the Kentucky Derby. If I had to say one, I would go back to the one that first got me hooked. My first year as a student assistant in the Alabama athletics media relations office was the 1992 football national championship season for the Crimson Tide. I was fortunate enough to get a media credential to the Sugar Bowl game against Miami and spent the last eight minutes of the game on the Alabama sideline. When the game was over and Gene Stallings was being carried on the shoulders of the players, I glanced up at the Jumbotron and saw myself on the screen. That's the moment I knew I wanted to figure out a way to have a career in college athletics.

Q: Sport is competition, winning and losing. How difficult is it to remain positive when the team you work for isn't winning?

A: As a media relations professional, you have to remain positive and be consistent in your approach to serving as the spokesperson for a team, athletic department, or conference office. In that role, there are more things to promote about your program, coaches, and student-athletes beyond the wins and losses, so it's important to always maintain a good balance of trying to promote all aspects of the team, department, or office you are managing the media relations efforts for.

Q: Working with the media has its challenges. What would you say is the most difficult challenge you have encountered thus far in your career?

A: The biggest challenge is probably happening now with the changing landscape of media, especially in sports, as the traditional media outlets and people are being replaced by online publications and independent bloggers who may or may not practice the traditional tenets of journalism.

Q: You have worked the Cotton Bowl for many years now. How important is volunteering and gaining practical experience to work in this field?

A: I think it is vitally important to volunteer for other sporting events beyond your team, school, or conference because it gives you opportunities to grow as a professional and expand your network of colleagues. Working the Cotton Bowl Classic has been one of the highlights of my professional experience. The 2012 game was my 13th straight to work, and I still look forward to it every year.

Q: What advice would you offer to up-and-coming sport management students who select this career path?

A: Get involved and volunteer! Whether that is assisting at games or spending time with office tasks, just get involved. The best way to get into sports is gaining experience by working events and figuring out what areas you like more than others.

Q: If you could go back to college and select another career path, would you? Why? Why not?

A: I would not change a thing. I found the career that makes me the most happy and satisfied professionally and personally, so I would do it all over again if given the chance.

For an event to experience success, there are some necessary steps and processes that must occur beforehand. Communicating with your target audience will give them the necessary information to make an informed decision to purchase tickets, attend, and participate or, at a minimum, to increase chatter about the impending event. This process of communication takes on many forms and falls in line with the marketing concepts discussed in the previous chapter. Whether functioning independently or in unison, the traditional elements of the promotional mix (also known as integrated marketing communication) have been categorized as advertising, direct marketing, personal selling, public relations, sales promotions, and sponsorship (Shank 2009; Mullin, Hardy, and Sutton 2007; Irwin, Sutton, and McCarthy 2002). We contend that social media are now a necessary promotional consideration, and they will also be addressed here.

This chapter focuses on media promotion and relations, two highly visible avenues utilized by companies to accomplish their marketing and promotional goals. Sport organizations and events employ media promotion and relations as successful means of communicating with their target markets. Media promotion refers to integrating the various communication strategies to convey the organization's message, while media relations is defined as the give-and-take relationship that must be groomed and nurtured by the sport organization in an effort to maintain a favorable position with the media outlet, which in turn promotes and broadcasts the sporting event. This relationship is discussed later in the section Symbiotic Relationship: Working Together to Achieve Greatness.

THE CRITICAL RS

Three processes that are critical to the success of an organization's media relations efforts are the relationship with the media, the retaining of that relationship, and the repairing of any issues that arise that could negatively affect the relationship. Their status as the critical Rs of media relations shows the importance of the role of the media in the sport industry.

Relating

Media relations, according to Stoldt, Dittmore, and Branvold (2012), are the most popular form of public relations in the sport industry. The goal of media relations is to develop positive relationships with members of the media and the sport organization (Mullin, Hardy, and Sutton 2007). Tuckwell (2011) described this as the process of garnering public support and acceptance. Media relations are founded on the principle of generating positive publicity while lessening the impact of negative publicity for a sport entity (Stoldt, Dittmore, and Branvold 2012). Publicity is a free form of communication for an organization, and since a legitimate media outlet is reporting the information, consumers believe what they hear (Tuckwell 2011).

Event managers rely on publicity to spread the word about their events. Depending on the setting, this could be as simple as a sports information director producing a press release, a facility manager listing upcoming events on a billboard or marquee, or an event manager setting up an interview to discuss her event and how it will affect the local community. In an effort to relate to the media, practitioners must be willing to work at building a relationship with the local media that is above reproach. This requires providing the media with access to information. Practitioners have multiple tools that allow for this flow of information, such as press releases, feature articles, press conferences, and Internet sites.

Retaining

Retaining favor with the media requires special care. The extending of courtesy is not only required but also expected. Remember, a media outlet is your friend until you do something to tarnish that friendship. The same rules that apply to a friendship such as mutual respect, honesty, fair treatment, and openness are essential for maintaining a positive relationship with the media. You must supply accurate and timely information both in good times and during controversy. We are very much aware of the flow of positive information when things are going great. Nowhere is the process more evident than in the role of the college sports information director (SID). In a constant fight to garner media attention, SIDs work feverishly to create press releases, media guides, and feature articles that provide the media with much needed content for little effort on their part. The constant flow of information from the SID to the media outlets establishes a positive rapport and in most cases captures the attention of the media, and thus the story is reported.

Repairing

Media relations can be tricky. A minor miscue or bad timing can thwart all of the time and energy you have put into building your relationship. Building a positive relationship requires an investment of time and energy; repairing a severed relationship will require much more. In times of crisis, the media will turn on you if you don't respond accordingly. Often this is a result of a breakdown in the communication process. Take care to properly manage your relationships and to be proactive in times of crisis. Crisis communication sets the tone for your relationships.

SYMBIOTIC RELATIONSHIP: WORKING TOGETHER TO ACHIEVE GREATNESS

The adjective *symbiotic*, derived from the root word *symbiosis*, is defined as a cooperative relationship between two entities. For event managers, the symbiotic relationship shared between the media and an institution is critical to the success of the event. The relationship is best personified as one that garners the most benefit for both the media and an organization, despite the fact that both could function independently. In other words, media outlets and the sport industry form a very lucrative partnership. This partnership is fed through the advent of sporting events that need media relations tactics and promotional efforts to fulfill their potential.

The Kansas State High School Activities Association *Media Relations Guide* says that "positive exposure is often the result of good preparation and providing media representatives with information and/or ideas they need and then allowing them to do their job" (p. 2). This epitomizes how the relationship with the media should proceed. It is imperative that you get to know the media assigned to cover your event so you can begin to forge the relationship. Remember, the media need content to fill the pages of their newspapers and the segments of their broadcasts. They rely on you just as much as you rely on them. You must be diligent in distributing your information in a timely manner, respecting the media's deadlines (Kansas State High School Activities Association 2012).

Bussell (2011) says the following regarding media relations:

> *As one element of the public relations equation, media relations, when combined with the other element, community relations, provides organizations with powerful tools for creating positive exposure. Organizations must be proactive in establishing media relations by providing information for them to scrutinize and utilize. The media possess a powerful influence over public opinion so great care must be taken in providing timely and accurate information. Open, honest communication will help to build this relationship.*

DIFFERENTIATING THE PROMOTIONAL MIX FROM THE MARKETING MIX

In chapter 7, you were introduced to the concepts of marketing and promotion as they relate to the sport industry. Marketing, as it applies to sport, has been defined as "the specific application of marketing principles and process to sports products" (Shank 2009, p. 3) and as "consisting of all the activities designed to meet the needs and wants of sport consumers through exchange processes" (Mullin, Hardy, and Sutton 2007, p. 11). The previous chapter also describes the process of capturing the four Ps (product, place, price, promotion), with the intent of creating products at acceptable prices, and in appropriate places, that can be promoted to target consumers (Masterman 2009).

Pitts and Stotlar (2002) expanded on the traditional Ps of marketing, stating that sport marketers must address elements outside of the four Ps if they are to create and implement a successful marketing plan. Pitts and Stotlar devised a two-tier, 10-step approach to the sport marketing process that identifies strategies and tactics. Their 10 Ps include purpose, product, projecting the market, position, players, package, price, promotion, place, and promise (Pitts and Stotlar 2002). Of the 10 Ps, positioning, promoting, placing, and promising are key in media promotion and relations. These four concepts most directly relate to the dissemination of information.

Positioning is defined by Shank (2009) as "fixing your sports entity in the minds" of those people you are targeting with your product or service (p. 198). A sporting event must compete with other events and attractions for consumers' discretionary funds. Positioning your event in a way that creates a memory and thus action on their part to participate in or attend your event over other options is the desired outcome. This process requires some creative strategies and careful planning.

As discussed in chapter 7, promoting is how marketers communicate with customers. Kaser and Oelkers (2008) define the promotional mix as the blending of the promotional elements of "advertising, sales promotion, publicity, and personal selling" (p. 246). Kotler (1975) labeled it a form of communication dedicated to persuading. For our purposes, we define promotion and the promotional mix as the communication process that utilizes varied communication tools such as advertising, publicity, public relations, community relations, media relations, selling, and sponsorship to convey a message and entice action. As you work through this chapter, you will begin to see the important role the media play in fulfilling the expectations of a sport organization's promotional goals. The media are critical for success because event marketers cannot rely on an "if you build it, they will come" approach to marketing.

In traditional terms, placing refers to the distribution strategies (Shank 2009). But we contend that placing also relates to the various media used in promoting an event. Identifying the optimal channels for promoting an event is critical. Technology continues to shape how we engage with others and obtain information. The various social media such as Facebook, Twitter, YouTube, and smartphone applications have reshaped how we disseminate information. These, as well as traditional media communication channels, are discussed later in this chapter.

The final P to consider is the promise. Typically, the promise refers to evaluating. How well did you do what you said you were going to do? How well did you follow your plan for doing it? In terms of the media, built-in mechanisms such as ratings and shares help determine both return on investment (ROI) and return on objectives (ROO). ROO measures the achievement of goals and objectives and are a viable alternative to ROI (Silvers 2007). Yes, money—specifically a profit—is an indication of financial success, but sometimes we seek more than just monetary gains; we seek attainment of marketing plan goals and objectives. ROO will provide this information.

Sport entities rely on these processes to convey their offerings to fans to entice and inform. Successful promotional efforts will take the fan through the hierarchy of effects model discussed in chapter 6. This process moves the intended consumers through the phases of awareness, interest, desire, and action in an effort to move them from being in the target group to being a purchasing consumer. In terms of the event, the goal is that the event experience be enjoyable and that fans become repeat customers. Media relations and promotional efforts are significant tools in making this the desired outcome for event managers.

PROMOTIONAL TOOLS

Promotion is all about persuasion. Your intent is to drive customers to want to attend your event. Well, now that you understand the role the media can play in this process, you can turn your attention to developing and designing those tools that will help promote your event. What does it need in order to be successful, aside from the typical patrons and performers? Do you need to generate interest, or is interest already peaked? What is your target audience, and how will you best reach them?

These questions and others are discussed, modified, and implemented through your promotional plan. A promotional plan embodies the promotional goals, strategies and tactics, budget, and evaluation processes defined in the planning stage. This is when your advertising, direct marketing, personal selling, public relations, sales promotions, and sponsorship ideas are fashioned (Shank 2009; Mullin, Hardy, and Sutton 2007; Irwin, Sutton, and McCarthy 2002). Chapter 6 introduces you to sponsorship, while chapter 7 discusses marketing and its related components, including promotion. Chapter 7 also describes two types of sales promotions, those associated with price and those that are value added. Let's take a look at some specific examples of each.

Price promotions include such things as discounts, coupons (money off or buy one, get one), family or group discounts, and bundling of amenities (tickets plus parking pass). Value-added enticements such as premium giveaways, sweepstakes, meet-and-greet events, theme nights, pre- and postevent entertainment, autograph sessions, interactive experiences, and fan appreciation promotions are fan lures. No other sector of the sport industry relies on these promotions like minor league baseball does.

Fans at minor league baseball games have come to expect the added value of a special event or giveaway when attending a minor league game. Minor league ball clubs are cognizant of this expectation. Most of them on a regular basis provide fans with more than just a baseball game. They offer them entertainment activities, free souvenirs, or ticket and concession discounts. (Hixon 2005)

NASCAR, the one sport in which you can "see" sponsor activation before, during, and after the event and even hear it in the winner's circle, is a huge marketing success. What a tremendous visual a car is as it tools around the track or visits the local grocery store for a meet and greet. Because of NASCAR's integrated approach to marketing, its promotional efforts have paid off, literally. NASCAR fans are more likely to be loyal purchasers of products "their" driver represents. Ukman (2012) reports that more than 70 percent of NASCAR fans would purchase a sponsor's product over the product of a competitor who was not affiliated with NASCAR. That is powerful!

SOCIAL MEDIA: A "NEW" TOOL FOR SUCCESS

Jackson (2012) boldly claimed that "social media and sports are natural teammates" (para. 1). Who can argue that? You would be hard-pressed to find a sport entity that has not jumped on the social media bandwagon. Jackson contends that baseball was slow to migrate to the new medium, but once MLB tested the waters, it too was hooked. According to Jackson, "the New York Yankees, with an estimated marketing worth of $340 million, are becoming as aggressive online as they are on the field. With more than 500,000 Twitter followers, nearly 5 million Facebook fans. . ." (para. 7).

Qualman (2011) asserts that "social media transforms the way you live and do business" (p. 278). He also professes that using social media is not "wasting time"; instead, it motivates productivity. Social media allows us to live and work transparently in a world that can be summed up in 140 characters (Twitter), Facebook posts, or YouTube videos. We no longer seek information, information finds us. The social media have infected our lives, and we are gracious hosts. Sanderson (2011) asserts that social media are "embedded in the fabric of everyday life" (p. 3).

Sports teams and athletes understand the importance of social media. According to Sanderson (2011), the connective ability of social media promotes a more intimate rapport for fans, athletes, and sport entities. NBA superstar Lebron James' very public announcement of his move to Miami was immediately followed by his establishing a Twitter account. ESPN.com news services reported on July 6, 2010, that within an hour of establishing an account, James had 18,000 followers and more than 90,000 by 4:30 p.m. that day.

How do you harness the power of social media for your event? You take your message to the people. Frost (2012) identified the following 10 reasons why you should engage in social media.

1. Cost-effectiveness: There is little to no cost to use the established social media platforms. A great example is the Texas Christian University (TCU) volleyball program. Drosos (2011) highlighted the impact of Facebook on the TCU program and summer camps. TCU utilized Facebook as a research tool, searching for and identifying more than "50,000 people within 50 miles of the Fort Worth campus on Facebook that stated in their profile they liked volleyball" (para. 7). From this information they began a campaign to reach out to those people, and in the first year they generated more than 7,000 fans on Facebook, increased attendance by 85 percent, and grew summer camp registrations by 30 percent.

2. Reach: In the previous TCU example, the impact of reach is easily seen. Reach, as defined by Shank (2009), is "the number of people exposed to an advertisement in a given medium" (p. 308). Utilizing social media to connect with current and potential customers is just one of its benefits. It makes even greater sense when you consider the following statistics. Bullas (n.d.) offers that Facebook reaches more than 850 million people per month online and 425 million mobile users; Twitter has 465 million established accounts, with another 1 million added daily; and YouTube has more than 2 billion views a day. Now, do you get it? Social media's reach is far greater than public releases, but the social media augment rather than replace the traditional media.

3. Connectivity: Or better yet, getting personal with customers. What better way to stay in touch during the off-season or downtime? The WWE has positively exploited this engagement tool. In an effort to maintain emotional hype between events, the WWE and its members began

tweeting so that the plots and the conflicts among the Superstars would not fizzle (Cummins 2012).

4. Timeliness: The social media deliver instantaneous information. Just as sport is a unique product (produced and consumed at the same time), social media can be produced and disseminated just as quickly (Frost 2012; Mullin, Hardy, and Sutton 2007). In 2008, the University of Utah, in a last-ditch effort to sell its remaining 500 football tickets, posted to Facebook, and within two hours the tickets were sold (Steinbach 2010).

5. Flexibility: The ability to share more than you would with traditional avenues such as advertising creates a more flexible promotions approach. Giving updates, altering information, and offering supplemental information are possible within seconds if utilizing social media. Many schools have turned to social media as a way to extend their sales promotions. For example, Louisiana State University has capitalized on their mascot, Mike the Tiger, by creating Facebook and Twitter accounts that allow students to interact with the feline (Tomko 2011).

6. Promotional opportunities: Mass distribution of your promotional efforts is now more accessible with social media. Two such promotions come to mind. First, the National Football League's Carolina Panthers held a citywide scavenger hunt fashioned after *The Amazing Race* to engage fans. According to Hepburn (2010), participants met at Bank of America Stadium, followed clues to prescribed points, and checked in with location-based applications such as Foursquare. Participants had fun and earned points for each check-in, businesses that participated experienced an influx of people, and in the end prizes were awarded. The second example comes to us from Bowling Green State University's Stroh Center grand opening. In an effort to generate hype for the new facility, BGSU students created a music video chronicling the funding of the building. Kielmeyer (as cited in Goss 2011) reported that the school was looking to do something different that would create a lasting impression for BGSU students, fans, and supporters. I think they hit this one out of the park! You can watch the video at www.youtube.com/watch?v=YxNJJgs08Xg.

7. Easier referrals: The social media let you engage in a more global outreach through word of mouth, or as Qualman (2011) puts it, "world of mouth."

8. Increased web traffic: The various forms of social media allow you to cross-promote all the outlets you use, thus driving web traffic, smartphone application downloads, and virtual retail opportunities.

9. Branding opportunities: Honigman (2012) stated it best when he said that "most of the time, only fans interested in your athlete or brand will see your content on Facebook or Instagram since it's their choice to follow you or not, giving you the opportunity to connect with your real brand advocates" (para. 11). In February 2012, the Philadelphia Wings, a National Lacrosse League (NLL) franchise, decided to spice things up a bit by using the players' Twitter monikers on their jerseys instead of their last names (Olenski 2012).

10. Hiring: Actively using social media engages potential employees who are also utilizing the media. This allows you to identify highly qualified employees and also to screen their social media etiquette.

It's evident that the social media are an integral part of the integrated promotions mix. Using social media is not "outside the box" thinking, nor is it a fad as Qualman (2011) stated; social media offers a powerful tool that must be embraced and utilized to its fullest potential.

EVALUATING SUCCESS

As with all forms of communication, feedback from customers is always appreciated. Feedback in its many forms allows us to know if our message was received and understood. Actions such as purchasing tickets, apparel, or other sport-related products are the most tangible forms of feedback (Shank 2009). Intangible forms of feedback such as attitudinal changes and nonverbal cues speak just as loudly as a lack of purchasing.

As you began your journey into the field of media relations and promotions, you established specific goals in your planning phase. Now those goals need to be measured against your actual performance.

Keep in mind that along the way you have picked up new fans and (hopefully) maintained your previous ones. The goal now is to retain all those customers. According to Mullin et al. (2009), you must view customers "as assets" (p. 174). Listen to what they are saying, change if necessary, and keep the lines of communication open. If this sounds cyclical, it is. Planning, executing, and evaluating are constants in business and sport. To maintain the attention of fans, you must constantly engage them at every opportunity. Communication and transparency are critical.

Super Bowl XLVI in Indianapolis is a great example of how the flow of information and the transparency of the host committee helped create a spectacular mega-event, without incident. Utilizing all forms of the promotional mix, the host committee was committed to keeping residents, volunteers, tourists, and the media abreast of the happenings in Indianapolis and the surrounding communities (Schoettle 2012). Billboards, signage, mall kiosks, smartphone applications, and Twitter were all utilized to help with everything from the events of the day to which restaurant had the shortest wait line. For Indianapolis, the real promotional plan will not be realized until well after the actual game, which was won by the New York Giants. Indianapolis is hoping that its Hoosier hospitality wowed the visitors to the city to the point that they will someday return.

SUMMARY

We create events because we want to share with the public what we have to offer. These events may be as simple as a fund-raiser for a charity or a carnival at a local elementary school, or they could be mega-events such as the Super Bowl. Regardless of the size of your event, developing a presence through positive interaction with the local media and through your own promotional efforts is a must for event planners. Media relations are fundamental to an organization's ability to maintain public support, support that builds a reputation (Bussell 2011). We have all heard the old adage that reputation is everything. Reputation—what others think about you—is critical to an event's survival.

Remember, never underestimate the power of the press; keep them happy and seek their partnership. Using social media is now a necessity, not just a fad. Engaging your fans early and often and where they are (by virtue of smartphones) is now the expectation.

LEARNING ACTIVITIES

Select an event to review. Gather as much information about that event as you can. Create a promotions chart to identify the vehicles or channels used to promote the event. See the example that follows.

Medium	Description
Television	
Radio	
Newspapers	
Magazines	
Billboards	
Posters and fliers	
Direct mail	
Social media	

Once you have decided on the event and created your chart, answer the following questions.

1. How did you hear about the event? Once you selected the event, what was your first impression of the promotional efforts of the organizers? (Did the advertising catch your attention, or was it more low key?)

2. On a Likert scale (1 to 10, 10 being the best), rate how well you think the promoters did in enticing customers to attend. What did they do well? What could they have done better?

3. What forms of media were utilized to deliver the message?

4. If this had been your event, what would you have done differently and why? What lessons from this event can you take and use in a future event you may host?

5. How did the event staff determine if their efforts were successful? If they did not assess their performance, how would you evaluate the success of a media promotion and relations campaign?

REFERENCES

Bullas, J. n.d. 48 significant social media facts, figures and statistics plus 7 infographics. Available: www.jeffbullas.com/2012/04/23/48-significant-social-media-facts-figures-and-statistics-plus-7-infographics.

Bussell, L.A. 2011. Media relations. In *The encyclopedia of sports management and marketing*, 890-891. Thousand Oaks, CA: Sage.

Cummins, L. 2012. The social media smackdown. Band Digital. April 10. Available: http://banddigital.com/node/222.

Drosos, M. 2011. Using Facebook to engage with your fans, alumni . . . and your recruits! Tudor Collegiate Strategies. February. Available: http://dantudor.com/2011/02.

Frost, S. 2012, January. Top 10 reasons a business should use social networking in its promotional plan. Houston Chronicle. Retrieved from http://smallbusiness.chron.com/top-10-reasons-business-should-use-social-networking-its-promotional-plan-20337.html

Goss, N. 2011, October 22. Bowling Green video: Watch Falcon's Stroh center rap video. *Bleacher Report*.

Hepburn, S. 2010. The Panthers Purrsuit is on—A social media challenge! Media Merging. September 2. Available: www.mediaemerging.com/2010/09/02/the-panthers-purrsuit-is-on-a-social-media-challenge.

Hixon, T. 2005. Price and non-price promotions in minor league baseball and the watering down effect. *The Sport Journal* 8 (4). [Online]. Available: www.thesportjournal.org/article/price-and-non-price-promotions-minor-league-baseball-and-watering-down-effect.

Honigman, B. 2012. How sports brands are using stars and social media. Businessinsider.com. April 23. Available: http://articles.businessinsider.com/2012-04-23/news/31385406_1_twitter-and-facebook-brand-audience.

Irwin, R.L., W.A. Sutton, and L.M. McCarthy. 2002. *Sport promotion and sales management*. Champaign, IL: Human Kinetics.

Jackson, J. 2012. Social media and sports: Natural teammates. Time.com. January 26. Available: http://techland.time.com/2012/01/26/social-media-and-sports-natural-teammates.

Kansas State High School Activities Association. 2012. *Media relations guide: Tips on working with the media and increasing awareness of your school activities program*. Topeka, KS. Available: www.kshsaa.org/Media/Media%20Guide.pdf.

Kaser, K. and Oelkers, D.B. 2008. Sport and entertainment marketing (3rd ed.) Independence, KY: Cenage Learning.

Kotler, P. 1975.Marketing for nonprofit organizations, Englewood Cliffs, NJ: Prentice-Hall, Inc.

Masterman, G. 2009. *Strategic sports event management: Olympic edition*. Oxford, UK: Elsevier.

Mullin, B.J., S. Hardy, and W.A. Sutton. 2007. *Sport marketing*. 3rd ed. Champaign, IL: Human Kinetics.

Olenski, S. 2012. The lines between social media and sports continue to blur. Forbes.com. February 13. Available: http://owl.english.purdue.edu/owl/resource/560/10.

Pitts, B. G., and Stotlar, D. K. 2002. Fundamentals of sport marketing (2nd ed.). Morgantown, WV: Fitness Information Technology.

Qualman, E. 2011. *Socialnomics*. Hoboken, NJ: John Wiley & Sons, Inc.

Sanderson, J. 2011. *It's a whole new ballgame: How social media is changing sports*. New York: Hampton Press, Inc.

Schoettle, A. 2012. City leaders determined to use global Super Bowl spotlight to build cachet. *Indianapolis Business Journal*. [Online]. January 30. Available: http://indianaeconomicdigest.com/Main.asp?SectionID=31&SubSectionID=121&ArticleID=63766.

Shank, M.D. 2009. *Sports marketing: A strategic perspective*. 4th ed. Upper Saddle River, NJ: Pearson.

Silvers, J.R. 2007, October 27. Return on objectives (ROO).

Retrieved from www.juliasilvers.com/embok/return_on_objectives.htm.

Steinbach, P. 2010. Colleges use social media to sell sports tickets. Madison, WI: *Athletic Business*. August. Available: http://athleticbusiness.com/articles/article.aspx?articleid=3599&zoneid=40.

Stoldt, G.C., S.W. Dittmore, and S.E. Branvold. 2012. *Sport public relations: Managing stakeholder communication*. 2nd ed. Champaign, IL: Human Kinetics.

Tomko, M. 2011, October 19. College athletic departments use social media to increase fan engagement. Retrieved from http://news.medill.northwestern.edu/chicago/news.aspx?id=190560

Tuckwell, K.J. 2011. *Integrated marketing communication: Strategic planning perspectives*. Toronto: Pearson.

Ukman, L. 2012. *IEG's guide to sponsorship*. Chicago: IEG.

CHAPTER 9

Contract Considerations

Chapter Objectives

After completing the chapter, the reader should be able to do the following:

- Comprehend the legal environment as it relates to event management operations.
- Understand the contract law fundamentals and the importance of contracts in event management.
- Develop negotiation strategies for various event contracts. Identify typical contractual arrangements for events.
- Comprehend the federal laws that must be a consideration for event managers.

Lee Lonzo is an education consultant specializing in school transition issues, antihazing and antibullying, sporting behavior, risk management, and student-athlete leadership training. Lee has experience in both teaching and administration in interscholastic sport and has frequently been called on as an expert consultant for both the Indiana High School Athletic Association (IHSAA) and the National Collegiate Athletic Association (NCAA). He is also co-owner of Lonzo Enterprises, LLC, doing business as the Kick-Off Program, which is a freshman transition and mentoring program at Carmel High School, Carmel, Indiana. He has also served as a consultant and presenter on a variety of legal, athletic, and education topics. Before opening his consulting business, Lee was the athletic director at Carmel High School and also taught history.

Q: What would you say are the top legal considerations for someone who is planning an event?

A: The most important consideration must be the safety of all involved in the event—participants, coaches, officials, spectators, and so on. This must be thought through from beginning to end, taking into consideration such issues as transportation, ingress and egress, parking, weather, the facility, equipment, emergency plans, first aid and medical response, and supervision.

Q: Contract negotiations are critical to events. What advice would you offer an event planner with regard to this process?

A: A high school athletic director may oversee as many as 800 athletic events per year. There is typically a contract for the contest and, where appropriate, also for officials. The most important consideration for these is to have a good tracking system. Since many of these contracts are signed years in advance, it is far more important to verify the details of all contracts before the event. High school athletic directors have been fired for sending teams to a contest that the other school does not have on its schedule (whether there is a contract or not) and for having thousands of spectators show up for a contest but no officials show up.

Q: During your career in the sport industry, what has been the most interesting legal concern you have addressed?

A: It's hard to pick out one or even a few, but here are some examples:

- I once received notice on a Thursday that several key members of the football team had been arrested months before on charges of illegal consumption in a northern Indiana county. The players were notified that they would be suspended as per the athletic code of conduct. A judge issued an order late Friday afternoon that they were to be allowed to play on Friday night. Many involved thought we should ignore the order of the court. Allowing an athlete to participate in a state championship competition under a court order would risk later having the state championship vacated under the IHSAA restitution rule.
- Coaches being accused of abuse because of language or treatment of athletes during practices.
- Anything involving a Title IX accusation.
- Hazing incidents that occur off school grounds and are not associated with any official school or team activity.
- Criminal investigations of coaches accused of having sexual relations with a student-athlete.
- Parents encouraging and signing off on participation of an injured athlete and then suing the school, coach, and trainer for negligence.

Q: There have been many instances where weather has been blamed for injury or death. What recommendations would you offer to an event planner to be proactive in this area?

A: Safety first. I have seen reasonable adults argue over whether or not to start or continue an event in dangerous conditions based on what they perceived to be a competitive edge. I ask coaches to always err on the side of safety. I often said they should imagine their own family members being involved when deciding issues about practices or events under circumstances of lightning, travel in icy or snowy conditions, and extreme heat.

Q: We have all heard the adage "the devil is in the details." Discuss this in terms of legal liability for event managers.

A: It is difficult to articulate, but the event planner has to be able to envision the event from start to finish. Who will arrive first, how will they get to the venue, where will they park, where will they enter, who will greet them, what happens before the event starts, what problems might come up during the competition, what happens after the event?

Q: Any words of advice for someone looking to plan or host and event?

A: Get as much input as possible on the things that have gone wrong in the past and what could go wrong. Try to have a plan to minimize risk for each scenario. Don't make the same mistake twice. Hire a go-to person to handle issues as they arise so you can take care of the big picture. Take notes on everything you should have done differently.

Of great concern to event managers and planners is keeping all who are participating in, watching, or working an event within a safe and secure environment. Great pains are taken to ensure that all potential legal considerations have been addressed appropriately before the event. Legal concerns require that intricate details be identified and protection for the event, facility, and workers be provided. From the hiring of staff, to the serving of food, to the actual contract negotiations, each process must be exhaustive and designed for the event or facility involved. Throughout this chapter and chapter 10, Risk Management and Negligence, we explore the contractual elements that are critical considerations before, during, and after an event, identifying who is responsible for what in an effort to offer protection from legal recourse.

According to Goldblatt (2008), there are four main reasons to conduct your event in accordance with the established laws and regulations: (1) to protect your legal interest, (2) to operate ethically, (3) to provide a safe and secure environment, and (4) to protect your financial investment. A contract is a tool that protects your interests and helps foster partnerships between the various entities critical for producing events.

CONTRACT LAW 101

Agreements between events and facilities, events and vendors, and events and ancillary contrac-tors must be negotiated and formalized. The standard relationship is formalized through the creation of a contract. Van Der Wagen and Carlos (2005) contend that the "contracts between the parties involved in an event is crucial" (p. 56). Matthews (2008) claims that contracts consist of two parts: (1) the specifics of the terms and conditions that establish the relationship and (2) the clauses that provide more specific details. In simplistic terms, a contract is a promise. This promise requires that an offer be presented and accepted, that there be some form of consideration, that the parties have the capacity to enter into a relationship, and that it be legal (Cotten and Wolohan 2010; Sharp, Moorman, and Claussen 2010; Spengler et al. 2009).

- Offer—The initial promise that is made by one party to another party to either do something or not do something. This offer usually has a price tag attached. For example, event tickets are contractual; you give up something in order to get something (e.g., you exchange $40 for a ticket to attend a University of Alabama nonconference football game).

- Acceptance—When the person being offered something of value accepts the conditions. Only that person to which the offer was extended may accept the offer. Should the offer not be accepted, then the offer is voided (Ammon, Southall, and Nagel 2010).

- Consideration—Without consideration the contract would not be binding (Ammon, Southall, and Nagel 2010). Both parties must give to get. Consideration involves one person offering something of value in exchange for something of value from the other person. In most instances, the exchange is a product or service traded for money.

- Capacity—Each party to a contract must have the capacity to enter into the contract. Capacity is determined by such factors as being of legal age (minors cannot sign) and being mentally capable of understanding the conditions of the promise.

- Legality—The promise must be based on a legal transaction. Sharp, Moorman, and Claussen (2010) emphasize that both state and federal laws must not be broken in the formation of a contract.

When the promises made in the formation of a contract are not kept, then a breach of contract occurs. Remedies for a breach can either be monetary or the party in breach could be ordered to perform the expectations of the contract (Ammon, Southall, and Nagel 2010; Sharp, Moorman, and Claussen 2010). There are two types of contractual agreements, bilateral and unilateral. A bilateral contract involves two parties engaging in a promise; both parties have expectations. A unilateral contract represents the offering and accepting of a promise. A unilateral contract is one directional, with an offer being made without an acceptance; the party does not have to agree to the terms. As a precautionary measure, Spengler et al. (2009) propose the following tips for managing contracts:

- Get it in writing.
- Read the contract thoroughly.
- Keep copies of all contract documents.
- Use good faith when negotiating contracts.
- Note deadlines for performance.
- Ensure the performance of third parties.
- Share contract information with those who need to know, and educate staff on the consequences of contract breach.
- Resolve ambiguities as quickly and fairly as possible.

TYPES OF CONTRACTS

According to Spengler et al. (2009), a standard contract, "to be enforceable, must contain an offer, acceptance and considerations." There are also typical provisions that are customary in most contracts such as clearly identified parties involved, the terms of the agreement, the promises made, the responsibilities of all parties involved, and a clause for terminating the agreement. With regard to events, there are many potential partnerships that will need to be negotiated via contractual agreements. Allen and colleagues (2011) and Bladen and colleagues (2012) identified the following typical contracts associated with an event:

- Venue
- Game or entertainment
- Sponsorship
- Media
- Security
- Vendors and suppliers
- Food and beverage
- Waivers and releases

Because most facilities do not put on their own events, they look to lease or rent their facilities to event managers and planners in order to utilize their space as often as possible. Million-dollar multipurpose facilities do not want to stand idle. When planning an event, selecting the venue can be a cumbersome task. The type of venue will depend on the type of event you are producing: sports, entertainment, or charity. A venue contract is the most complex contract to negotiate (Bladen et al. 2012). Essential elements of this type of contract include the parties involved, the event (name and type), the date(s) and time(s) of the event, rental fees, cancellation stipulations, and costs (Cotten and Wolohan 2010). What makes it complex are the various clauses and addendums that are specific to your needs for your event. For example, Allen et al. (2011) list indemnification, security deposits, signage, and change orders (additions or alterations to the original contract) as possible clauses. Bladen et al. (2012) add to that list of clauses payment terms, security, food and beverage, and any additional venue staff that might be required and at what cost. Lawrence and Wells (2009) offer ancillary clauses that include any activities associated with the event but not part of the main attraction. Examples of ancillary events are banquets, awards presentations, and autograph signings scheduled around the event.

The main attraction of your event can be a game, a concert, or a performance. Regardless of the entertainment form, you will need to formalize a contract for participation. Entertainment contracts contain the common elements just discussed, but they also carry two unique items, an exclusivity clause and a rider. The exclusivity clause protects the event manager from the talent's scheduling an event close by that could affect the event's success (Allen et al. 2011). Exclusivity would potentially offer a geographic boundary from which to work. A rider is an amendment that spells out the requirements of the talent (Allen et al. 2011). The rider can involve any items the talent "must have," such as specific food or beverage items, transportation requirements, and dressing room necessities.

Game contracts are established so there will be no discrepancy in the terms of the agreement between teams participating in a single game or series of games. Certain necessities to be included are the date, time, location, rules and regulations that will be followed, compensation for playing, any travel reimbursement, and any other items negotiated by the two parties. Many state high school associations have created fillable forms for their respective schools to utilize. An example of a football game contract from the Georgia High School Association can be reviewed at www.ghsa.net/sites/default/files/documents/forms/OfficialContract-Football.pdf.

Chapter 6 outlines the various sponsorship opportunities for event managers. Sponsorship agreements and contracts are specific to the events and parties involved, so a standard fillable form for the agreement is not advised. Each sponsorship agreement or contract is established to "protect the best interests of all parties involved" (Ammon, Southall, and Nagel 2010, p. 116). Expectations, rights, benefits, fees, terms, governing laws, marks and logo usage, and duties should be expressed in the contract. Any items unique to the relationship should be spelled out, especially the critical component of establishing liability. In reviewing a sponsorship agreement from Florida International University (2009) (see figure 9.1), you begin to realize the complexity of a sponsorship agreement or contract and the need to involve legal counsel to ensure the protection of each party.

As you have learned, there are other types of sponsorships besides financial investments. Agreements can include trades between the parties or in-kind donations. This does not preclude the need for a contract. As Lawrence and Wells (2009) indicated, this is a "mutually beneficial partnership" (p. 50) and should be carefully crafted.

Should you have the fortune of negotiating a media contract, you will find yourself involved in an intricate and complex negotiation that could result in a large financial gain for your event. Because your event likely will not garner national or international media attention, you should consider the relationships with local media outlets and how you can encourage them to partner with you to air your event. Solomon (2002) claims that "the growth in television means that what once was not even thinkable is today at least a possibility" for broadcasting (p. 133). Networks, regional and local stations, pay-per-view, and streaming over the Internet could all be viable options as many media outlets look for content to broadcast. Your "event is a tool" for a media outlet "as much as television is a tool for you" (p. 137). Initial negotiations should include the air date, the time slot for airing, the length of the event, and whether you will have it aired live or have it recorded for future broadcasting (Solomon 2002). Once those particulars are finalized, then you can start discussing finances. You can pursue various financial options in an effort to televise your event. You can negotiate rights fees; you can barter your way on; or you can pay for the production, which is risky and pricey (Solomon 2002).

According to Allen et al. (2011), you should address some important clauses in your media and broadcasting contracts such as reach (region or territory), access, credits, and merchandising. Solomon (2002) also stresses that you secure the

FIU ATHLETICS SPONSORSHIP AGREEMENT

The Florida International University Board of Trustees ("FIU") on behalf of its FIU Athletics Department thanks _____ ("Sponsor"), with a principal place of business at _____, for its commitment as a _____ level Sponsor of the FIU Athletics program, with a cash contribution of _____ and an in-kind contribution as outlined below.

1. **Sponsorship Rights and Benefits.** As an official sponsor, _____ will receive a generous package of signage, print, electronic and other benefits which are outlined in Exhibit A attached hereto.

2. **Sponsorship Term.** This Agreement shall commence as of _____ and continue through _____. This agreement may be renewed for two successive one-year periods, by mutual agreement of the parties, in writing, at any time prior to the end of the initial term or any renewal period.

3. **Sponsorship Fee.** In consideration for entering into this Agreement, Sponsor agrees to pay FIU the sum of $_____ for the initial term, and the amount of $_____ for each renewal period. All payments due from Sponsor shall be in the form of checks made payable to "Florida International University" and shall be due on or before _____. In addition, as further consideration for the sponsorship benefits conferred herein, Sponsor agrees to provide the following in kind contribution: _____.

4. **General Conditions:**

   A. **Licensing Rights**

      i. Grant of Rights. Sponsor will have the limited, non-exclusive, right to use FIU marks and logos ("Marks"), on a royalty-free basis, in promotions, advertising and website identification for the limited purpose of leveraging its sponsorship position. Sponsor must obtain the prior written approval of FIU's Athletics Department and Marketing Department as to all proposed promotional, advertising, identification or other logo applications prepared by Sponsor pursuant to this paragraph prior to their publication, circulation, or display. Sponsor shall place the indicia "SM" or "TM" next to each use of any Mark. FIU will have the limited, non-exclusive right to use Sponsor's trademarks and logos on a royalty-free basis, in promotions, advertising and website identification as specified herein.

      ii. License Term. On the date of termination of this Agreement, all rights and privileges granted to Sponsor and FIU by this limited license shall immediately terminate.

      iii. Goodwill. Sponsor and FIU recognize the great value of the goodwill associated with each party's intellectual property. Each party recognizes that the other party has an interest in maintaining and protecting the image and reputation of its respective intellectual property, and that the other party's intellectual property must be used in a manner consistent with the standards established by that party.

      iv. No Assignment. This limited license and all rights and duties hereunder are personal to Sponsor and shall not, without the written consent of the University, be assigned, mortgaged, sublicensed or otherwise encumbered or transferred by Sponsor or by operation of law.

OGC – Form Athletics Sponsorship Agreement – 5-08

■ **Figure 9.1** Sample sponsorship agreement.

Reprinted, by permission, from Florida International University.

v. No Joint Venture. This Agreement does not authorize Sponsor to do business under the name of "Florida International University" or "FIU Athletics" or any name similar thereto, or to enter into any contracts or agreements of any type in the name of, or on behalf of any of these parties. The Sponsor is not empowered to state or simply imply, either directly or indirectly, that Sponsor or its activities, other than pursuant to the limited license permitted herein, are supported, endorsed or sponsored by the University and upon the direction of the University shall issue express disclaimers to the effect. Nothing herein shall be construed to place the parties in the relationship of partners or joint venturers, nor shall any similar relationship be deemed to exist between them.

B. **Recognition Rights**. All copy and graphics proposed for display by Sponsor for the recognition referred to in Exhibit A, attached, are subject to approval by the University. The University shall have the right to decline to display any copy or graphics which is in violation of any statute, regulation or ordinance, or which the University reasonably considers to be misleading or offensive or in violation of any University contract obligation. The University shall not display any logo, sign, banner, or other visual display nor shall it print, publish, or distribute any written or visual material from Sponsor which contains a comparative or qualitative description of Sponsor's product, price information or any other indications of savings or value about Sponsor's product, any message that otherwise endorses Sponsor's product or induces one to purchase or use Sponsor's product, or any message that causes Sponsor's payments to not be treated as "qualified sponsorship payments" as that term is defined in Section 513(i) of the Internal Revenue Code and related regulations.

C. **Indemnification.** Sponsor shall indemnify and hold harmless the University, its Board of Trustees, the FIU Athletics Finance Corporation, the Florida Board of Governors, the State of Florida, and their respective directors, officers, agents and employees, from and against any and all damages, losses and all claims, counterclaims, suits, demands, actions, causes of action, setoffs, liens, attachments, debts, judgments, liabilities or expenses including, without limitation, attorney's fees and legal costs by reason of any claim, suit or judgment arising or alleged to arise from, or relating to: (1) this Agreement; (2) the negligent acts or willful misconduct of Sponsor, its employees, agents or contractors; or (3) any liability for fraud, misrepresentation, copyright or trademark infringement in connection with Sponsor's name and/or logo displayed pursuant hereto.

D. **Governing Law.** This Agreement shall be construed and governed in accordance with the laws of the State of Florida and any dispute arising hereunder shall be resolved in a court of competent jurisdiction in the State of Florida.

E. **Notices.** Any notices to be made hereunder shall be made in writing and shall be sent by hand delivery, facsimile with confirmation receipt, overnight courier or certified United States mail, return receipt requested, with postage prepaid. Each party may, by notice to the other party as provided herein, change the address to which notices or payments thereafter shall be sent:

a. Notices to Sponsor shall be sent to:

_____

_____

_____

_____

_____

_____ (fax)

(continued)

(continued)

    b. Notices to University shall be sent to:
Mr. Jose Velasco
Executive Director, FIU Athletic Association
Florida International University
11200 S.W. 8th Street, _____
Miami, FL 33199
(305) 348-_____ (fax)

F. **Waiver.** The failure of either party hereto to insist in any instance upon the strict performance of any provision of this Agreement or to exercise any election contained herein shall not be construed as a waiver or relinquishment for the future of such provision or election. No waiver or modification by any party shall have been deemed to have been made unless expressed in writing by such party.

G. **Force Majeure.** If either party is unable to perform any obligation hereunder by reason of any event beyond such party's reasonable control, including but not limited to fire, flood, epidemic, earthquake, explosion, act of God or public enemy, riot or civil disturbance, strike, lockout or labor dispute, war (declared or undeclared), terrorist threat or activity, or any federal state or local government law, order, or regulation, order of any court or jurisdiction, or other cause not reasonably within either party's control (each a "Force Majeure" event or occurrence), such party shall be excused from performance and may terminate this Agreement upon written notice to the other party.

H. **Entire Agreement.** This Agreement supersedes all prior negotiations, understandings and agreements between the parties hereto and constitutes the final and complete understanding of the parties regarding the subject matter hereof, and both parties acknowledge and agree that neither party has relied on any representations or promises in connection with this Agreement not contained herein. This Agreement may not be amended or modified except by a subsequent written instrument evidencing the express consent of each of the parties, duly executed by the parties.

I. **NCAA Rules Violation.** The University has the right to terminate this Agreement immediately if, in the University's reasonable discretion, Sponsor has violated NCAA rules or otherwise taken any action that jeopardizes the eligibility of the University's programs or its student-athletes.

J. **Termination.** FIU may terminate this Agreement without cause upon fourteen (14) days written notice to Sponsor.

K. **Logo and Sponsorship Acknowledgement Guidelines.** The parties agree to utilize the following guidelines with respect to the use of each party's logos and the sponsorship recognition conferred herein:

    i. Logo/trademark

        1) Definition: an official, registered symbol that represents and/or identifies the sponsor.

        2) Criteria: submitted as Black & White and color versions (converted for 4/C Process printing). EPS (vector) format (Illustrator or Freehand) **preferred** (1-2" diameter). Hi-res (300 dpi or higher) TIFF or JPEG format (3-4"diameter) also accepted. Printed versions must be supplied as samples for color proof. It is Sponsor's responsibility to provide FIU with printed color proofs.

OGC – Form Athletics Sponsorship Agreement – 5-08

3) FIU will evaluate the submission of Sponsor's logo for use by the FIU Athletics Department and will notify Sponsor of any problems. Logo/trademark usage may include materials produced for FIU Athletics for advertising, promotion and programming purposes. Logo/trademark size will vary.

ii. Line Listing

1) Definition: an official, registered corporate identification to be used for copy purposes (press releases, etc.).

iii. Program Advertisement/Acknowledgement

1) An advertisement promoting Sponsor's product or service will not be accepted if it includes:

a) Qualitative or comparative language of sponsor's products;

b) Price information or other indications of savings or value associated with the product or service;

c) A call to action;

d) An endorsement; or

e) Inducements to buy, sell, rent or lease the sponsor's product or service.

2) An acknowledgement supporting FIU Athletics will be accepted if it includes or conforms as follows:

a) Sponsor logos and slogans that do not contain comparative or qualitative descriptions of the sponsor's products, services, facilities or company;

b) Sponsor locations, telephone numbers, and Internet addresses;

c) Value-neutral descriptions, including displays or a visual depiction of a sponsor's product line or services; or

d) Sponsor brand or trade names and product or service listings.

3) Suggested acknowledgments of sponsorship include:

a) "(Sponsor) is a sponsor of the _____"

b) "A proud sponsor of the _____"

c) "(Sponsor) is proud to be a sponsor of the _____"

d) "(Sponsor) is a proud supporter of the _____" and

e) "(Sponsor) is proud to support the _____"

AGREED: AGREED:

_____   _____
Name   Name

Title   Title
                                                 The Florida International University
                                                 Board of Trustees

Date: _____   Date: _____

OGC – Form Athletics Sponsorship Agreement – 5-08

proper clearance for music or video you want to include in your event. A great example of a broadcasting contract for high school football playoffs can be found at www.mpssaa.org/assets/media /MPSSAA%20Broadcasting%20Contract.pdf. Many times an event will contract with a third party for goods or services. You will want to spell out the arrangements with this third party in a contract. According to Kuse (2012),

> the key elements that your agreement should contain are the cost or price, services or products provided, what happens if something goes differently than planned, and dates for delivery. An agreement is hammered out so that, ideally, the consequences to be suffered for any possible scenario will be spelled out specifically. (para. 4)

Security is one of the many services you could contract for your event. Risk management and negligence (see chapter 10) are essential considerations when planning an event. Since 9/11, the event industry has had to rethink and rewrite many of its policies and procedures with regard to the safety of all vested parties at an event. Security is the area that has garnered the most attention because venues will not compromise on the safety of patrons, participants, and their own staff. With heightened security comes not only the expense of offering a safe environment but also the need to negotiate contracts for coverage. You must weigh the cost of not properly securing your event against the cost of contracting with a service provider. In your venue negotiations, you can address whether the facility will provide security or whom facility managers would recommend that you contract.

By reviewing the Unarmed Event Security Services contract for the University of Wisconsin-Madison, you can begin to understand the scope of security and the details that must be contained in such a contract. Areas such as ticket takers, ushers, general security personnel, parking lot personnel, and various supervisors are addressed.

This negotiated contract provides the cost of each unit of security requested as well as the facility information and the scope of events to be covered. This comprehensive Division I athletic department contract with a security firm can be found online at www.bussvc.wisc.edu/purch/contract /wp5059.html.

Anyone who has attended an event knows that concessions are a must. Many people form an opinion of an event around the food and beverages it offers. It is important that you give this contractual agreement full consideration because it will forever be a part of your event's reputation. Some venues have standing contracts with food service companies, and you will have to negotiate with them for your concession needs. Steinbach (2008) says that concession agreements can be "sliced and diced" in many ways. It is strongly recommended that you utilize a service provider that is either the current concessionaire with the venue or from a venue-approved list. Because certain requirements and restrictions apply, you need to ensure that the utmost care is taken in the preparation of the food. Some of those requirements are food-handling regulations, licenses and permits, health department inspections, and employee hiring requirements. When negotiating with the venue, you can include concessions in that contract, making sure the financial arrangements are detailed, specifically with regard to payments or the percentage of monies you will receive from concession sales (if this is part of your venue contract).

Figure 9.2 is a simple concession stand contract template used by the ConocoPhillips Sports Complex in Ferndale, Washington. This contract represents the expectations that you will provide your own staff and concession food and beverages. This is a great example of a food and beverage contract for a small-scale event. For a more sophisticated concession contract, visit the North Carolina State University concessionaire contract at www.fis.ncsu.edu/materialsmgmt/purchasing /Concessions.pdf.

If you host a participatory event such as a sports competition, an athletic event with entries, or a

CONOCOPHILLIPS SPORTS COMPLEX
CONCESSION STAND CONTRACT

Tournament/Event name: _____

Dates: _____

Director/Contact: _____ Phone: _____

Address: _____ City/Zip: _____

Please read and understand the rules and responsibilities associated with the rental of the ConocoPhillips Sports Complex concession stand.

The City of Ferndale will supply the following:

- Concession building, electricity, water, garbage cans, and cleaning supplies

Duties of the concession operator:

- Concession building key must be checked out the Friday before the tournament at Ferndale City Hall and returned Monday morning after the tournament.
- Deposit and rental fees must be paid before the tournament.
- Supply all utensils, coolers, food products, and supplies as needed.
- Maintain a neat and clean concession area.
- Empty concession stand garbage in the outside dumpster.
- Post and maintain established prices throughout the tournament.
- At least one adult must be present at all times the concession stand is open.
- No alcohol is allowed at the park or to be sold at the concession stand.
- Complete the cleaning checklist for the concession building before leaving.

Rental agreement (concessionaire agrees to pay the following rates):

- Damage/cleaning deposit of $200.00, which will be refunded after an inspection of the concession building. (Submit the refund request form with the deposit. Processing of the refund could take up to two weeks.)
- A $100.00 per day building rental fee for use of the concession stand.
- No refunds will be given unless the tournament is rained out before the completion of more than half of the games scheduled for the tournament.

Please make checks payable to: City of Ferndale.

    Concession fees (to be paid before the tournament):

    Damage/cleaning deposit fee: $200.00

    (Will be refunded upon approved inspection after the tournament) $ _____

    Building rental fee: $100.00 per day

    $100.00 × _____ days = $ _____

    Total: $ _____

    Record of payment:

    Total: $ _____ Receipt #: _____ Date: _____

■ **Figure 9.2** Example of a concession stand contract.

Reprinted, by permission, from Gary Jensen, Mayor of the City of Ferndale.

recreational activity, or if members of the crowd are invited to participate in a game promotion, it is important that you utilize waivers and releases. A waiver, which a participant signs before an event, releases the organization from liability should the participant become injured during the event (Spengler et al. 2010). Kozlowski (1996) described a waiver as "a valid and enforceable agreement" whereby a "participant waives or releases any future negligence claim he or she may have against the provider of a sport or recreational services in exchange for an opportunity to participate" (para. 1). Waivers do not cover the misconduct of a person or representative of the organization with whom the patron signed the waiver. According to Glover (2009), "the term waiver is sometimes used to refer [to] a document that is signed before any damages actually occur. A release is sometimes used to refer [to] a document that is executed after an injury has occurred" (para. 1). Waivers will incorporate an assumption of risk by the participant, whereas a release will, in detail, explain the risks associated with participation in an activity.

Minors are precluded from signing a waiver because it is a contract, and as discussed earlier in this chapter, minors do not have the capacity to sign. Parents of minor athletes are familiar with signing waivers in order for their children to participate in an activity. Even though parents may sign a waiver, Glover (2009) cautions that the "law is unclear as to whether parents who sign waivers on behalf of their children will release a potential defendant from liability to the minor. The trend is to enforce such waiver arrangements signed by parents on behalf of a child." (para 1). Because state laws apply to waivers, it is important for you to use due diligence in researching them. Figure 9.3 is a waiver used for a recreation program at Purdue University.

TIPS FOR NEGOTIATING CONTRACTS

Each contract you negotiate requires finesse. Venues will differ, games or entertainment will vary, sponsorships may be specific, but the need to formalize a relationship with a contract will remain constant as a means of protecting the parties' interests. Being prepared for a negotiation is your best asset. Identify your needs, express your wants, and firmly discuss the nonnegotiable items. Mandel (2012) offers the following tips for a successful negotiation:

- Don't be afraid to ask.
- Never negotiate against yourself.
- Get it in writing.
- Prepare.
- Listen to the other side.
- There is no substitute for discussion.
- Avoid form contracts.
- Make sure the decision makers are in the room.

"The ability to negotiate vendor contracts effectively—getting the right products and services at the right price and with the right terms—is a crucial skill" (Ambrose 2010, p. 1). Remember to remain flexible. Don't get stuck on costs, but rather value and prioritize what you want and need; ask questions instead of making demands (Gerber 2011; Stim n.d.) The more negotiations you are involved in, the better you will become.

AN ATTORNEY'S PERSPECTIVE: NEIL BRASLOW, JD, ON CONTRACTS

For a valid sport contract to be formed, there must be an offer, acceptance, consideration, mutual assent, capacity, and legality. A contract in the sport world is no different from a contract in the rest of the legal world. Most sport contracts, and in particular professional services or standard players' contracts, are in boilerplate form. This means the same standard terms and wordings can be used over and over without any modifications. Arenas and teams alike usually have standard contracts that are slightly altered each time.

WAIVER, RELEASE AND HOLD HARMLESS AGREEMENT

In consideration of permission granted by Purdue University allowing me to participate in the [INSERT ACTIVITY NAME] (the "Activity"), which will occur on [INSERT ACTIVITY DATES], which is sponsored by [INSERT SPONSOR NAME], I (together with my parent or guardian, if I am under the age of eighteen (18) or under a legal disability) represent, covenant and agree, on behalf of myself and my heirs, assigns, and any other person claiming by, under or through me, as follows:

1. I acknowledge that participating in the Activity involves certain risks (some of which I may not fully appreciate) and that injuries, death, property damage or other harm could occur to me or others. I accept and voluntarily incur all risks of any injuries, damages, or harm which arise during or result from my participation in the Activity, including any associated travel, regardless of whether or not caused in whole or in part by the negligence or other fault of Purdue University, The Trustees of Purdue University, and/or its or their departments, trustees, affiliates, employees, officers, agents or insurers ("Released Parties").

2. I waive all claims against any of the Released Parties for any injuries, damages, losses or claims, whether known and unknown, which arise during or result from my participation in the Activity, regardless of whether or not caused in whole or part by the negligence or other fault of any of the Released Parties. I release and forever discharge the Released Parties from all such claims.

3. I agree to indemnify and hold the Released Parties harmless from all losses, liabilities, damages, costs or expenses (including but not limited to reasonable attorneys' fees and other litigation costs and expenses) incurred by any of the Released Parties as a result of any claims or suits that I (or anyone claiming by, under or through me) may bring against any of the Released Parties to recover any losses, liabilities, costs, damages, or expenses which arise during or result from my participation in the Activity, regardless of whether or not caused in whole or part by the negligence or other fault of any of the Released Parties.

4. I have carefully read and reviewed this Waiver, Release And Hold Harmless Agreement. I understand it fully and I execute it voluntarily.

EXECUTED this _____ day of _____, 20_____.

_____   _____
Participant Signature   Participant Printed Name

_____   _____
Parent/Guardian Signature   Parent/Guardian Name
(required if participant is under the age of 18 or disabled)

■ **Figure 9.3** Sample agreement from Purdue University.

Reprinted, by permission, from Purdue University. Available: www.purdue.edu/recsports/programs/club_sports/forms/Waiver_Release.pdf

Athletes will often create addendums to their contracts, which are additions usually found at the end. This is particularly true for elite athletes. For example, a stipulation in a standard team contract may give an average baseball player two tickets to every home game his team plays. A superstar player may add additional terms to the contract to read that he is to receive a luxury box for every home game his team plays. An average player is usually offered the standard team contract and told to take it or leave it. For elite players, in addition to the differences in the amount of salary, deviations from the standard team contract are usually bonuses and the option to renegotiate. Because of the addendums and modifications made to the contract, it is sometimes beneficial for the player to have an agent who is an attorney during the negotiation process. However, not all professional leagues require that agents be lawyers, and many players choose to use agents who are not lawyers.

In addition to agents, leagues and teams have their own set of attorneys working on contracts. Although many leagues and teams have been outsourcing their legal work for years, with the current economic climate many are either bringing in attorneys to work in-house or adding additional lawyers to already existing teams. Although agents do work on contracts for their clients, the role of an in-house attorney generally requires more contractual work. In-house attorneys must deal with all player contracts in addition to apparel, contest, licensing, media, merchandise, sales, sponsorship, vendor, and venue contracts, to name a few.

In-house attorneys deal with many of the legal issues relating to event or game logistics. For example, the Green Bay Packers are playing at Soldier Field in Chicago. On the day of the game, Aaron Rodgers is nowhere to be found and fails to show up. Can the Chicago Bears and Soldier Field sue Aaron Rodgers? The answer is no. Aaron Rodgers did not sign an appearance contract with the Bears that would have compensated him for showing up to an event. Aaron Rodgers has a professional services contract with the Green Bay Packers. They are the only party that Aaron owes an obligation to. Although the Chicago Bears may not be able to sue Aaron, the Packers could take action according to the terms of his contract since they are the organization that entered into the agreement.

What if Rodgers had said he assigned his contract to Brett Favre to play in Chicago that day? This would not have worked because personal service contracts cannot be assigned to anyone else. An assignment is a transfer of rights that a party has under contract to another person. A personal service contract cannot be assigned because the talents of an athlete, in this case Aaron Rodgers, are unique. The Packers would not have allowed such an assignment to take place.

What if the next day the Packers decided to trade Aaron Rodgers to the Dolphins? Could Rodgers argue that since he was not allowed to assign his rights to Favre, why should the Packers be allowed to assign his rights to the Dolphins? Any contract, including personal service contracts, may be assigned as long as there is permission from both parties. In almost all player contracts, the right to assign is part of the contract. Some players, however, have what is known as a no-trade clause, which keeps the team from assigning their rights to a team they do not want to play for. Teams have become increasingly less willing to award no-trade clauses because this prevents them from trading a player without their approval.

Regardless of the position the attorney has with an employer, all lawyers must pay great attention to detail when drafting a contract. Contracts should not be ambiguous; they should be easily interpreted by a third party. If there is a dispute over a contract, courts will seek to enforce the intent of the parties to the contract. The intent to be enforced is what a reasonable person would have believed that the parties intended. In sport, contracts often involve millions and millions of dollars. Attorneys need to proceed with caution and ensure they are drafting unambiguous contracts where the intent can clearly be inferred. For many contracts, the process of drafting and editing could take weeks before the final edition is signed by the parties to be charged.

FEDERAL LEGISLATION

Events must conform to the rules and restrictions of the facility in which they will operate as well as the local ordinances and laws. In addition, event managers must consider various federal laws when planning an event.

Americans With Disabilities Act (ADA)

The Americans with Disabilities Act of 1990 was instrumental in mainstreaming people with disabilities into all aspects of society. Facilities (places of public accommodation) are required to provide barrier-free accommodations, which could require modifications to the existing layout (Ammon, Southall, and Nagel 2010). According to the International Association of Exhibitions and Events, event planners should be aware of ADA requirements. Everything from event forms to hotel accommodations to assisted listening devices need to be addressed by the event planners. Visit www.ada.gov for comprehensive information that may pertain to your event.

Occupational Safety and Health Administration (OSHA)

Specific directives and policies regarding workplace safety and health are administered through the federally created Occupational Safety and Health Administration. OSHA was created by Congress when they passed the Occupational Health and Safety Act of 1970. The primary focus of OSHA is to reduce the number of job-related illnesses, injuries, and deaths. Since many of your events may require the constructing of scaffolding or rigging, it is important that you understand and abide by the guidelines issued by OSHA as well as the state OSHA guidelines where the event is held.

The tragedy of the Indiana State Fair in August 2011 provides us with validation of the critical nature of OSHA guidelines and why they must be followed explicitly. While fans were gathering and waiting for the band Sugarland to take the Hoosier Lottery Grandstand stage, a line of strong thunderstorms with wind gusts up to 70 miles per hour (110 km/h) made its way to the fairgrounds. As announcements were made regarding a possible evacuation, a strong gust of wind blew through the venue, collapsing the stage and the rigging. The collapse led to seven deaths and more than four dozen injuries (Winick, Claiborne, Gray and Schabner 2011). An ensuing investigation by the Indiana OSHA resulted in fines to three contractors hired to construct the stage. It was determined that key risk-assessment planning and inspections were not performed and that the safety of workers was compromised (one of the persons killed was an employee of the contracted companies cited for violations).

This tragic incident illustrates why, as an event manager, you must perform due diligence in hiring qualified and competent staff and subcontractors. Just as risk management relates to a safe and secure environment, the OSHA guidelines are designed to protect employees.

SUMMARY

Protecting your investment is your first consideration when planning an event. You must prepare for potential legal issues that could prove detrimental if not addressed. First and foremost, you are to provide a safe and secure environment for the event. From the conception of the event through to its end, measures should be taken to ensure an incident-free experience for all involved. Through the formation of your agreements and contracts and the hiring of competent and trained staff, you will put together a team of event workers who will execute your plans as you have devised. Careful consideration of the local, state, and federal laws that are applicable to your event will help provide the safeguards necessary to host a successful event or to protect you should there be an incident.

Remember that all things are negotiable in a contract. You must do your homework and generate your wants and needs list before negotiations so that you enter those meetings well informed and ready to formalize your agreement. Always keep in mind the old adage of "when in doubt, write it out." Contracts must be written and details outlined so there are no discrepancies that could result in legal action.

LEARNING ACTIVITIES

Having decided to run a concession stand for a Little League organization, you are now charged with acquiring the requisite permits, licenses, and insurance. Not having done this before, you turn to legal counsel for guidance. Create a to-do list so you have all the items covered. Once you do that, answer the following questions.

1. What do you see as the necessary legal concerns of running a concession stand?

2. What permits, licenses, or insurance have you determined you will need to acquire?

3. How does employment law and food handling apply to a temporary business such as a concession stand? (This may require a little more research on your part.)

4. What types of contracts would you be entering into with a concession stand operation?

5. Are there any OSHA or ADA concerns? If so, how will you address them?

6. What will be a critical element to the success of your concession stand with regard to food handling and customer service?

REFERENCES

Allen, J., W. O'Toole, R. Harris, and I. McDonnell. 2011. *Festival and special event management.* 5th ed. Queensland, AU: Wiley.

Ambrose, C. 2010. Negotiating vendor contracts. Available: www.gartner.com/it/initiatives/pdf/KeyInitiativeOverview_NegotiatingVendorContracts.pdf.

Ammon, R., R. Southall, and M. Nagel. 2010. *Sport facility management: Organization events and mitigating risks.* 2nd ed. Morgantown, WV: Fitness Information Technology.

Bladen, C., J. Kennell, E. Abson, and N. Wilde. 2012. *Events management: An introduction.* New York: Routledge.

Cotten, D., and J. Wolohan. 2009. *Law for recreation and sport managers.* 5th ed. Dubuque, IA: Kendall/Hunt.

Florida International University. 2009. FIU Athletics sponsorship agreement. Available: http://generalcounsel.fiu.edu/downloads/2008-2009/Athletics%20Sponsorship%20Agreement%20Template%205-08.pdf.

Gerber, S. 2011. How to negotiate vendor contracts. [Weblog comment]. April 1. Available: www.huffingtonpost.com/scott-gerber/young-entrepreneur-counci_1_b_843800.html.

Glover, W.H. 2009. Waivers and releases regarding sports activities with forms. [Weblog comment]. Available: http://williamhgloverjd.wordpress.com/2009/03/11/waivers-and-releases-regarding-sports-activities-with-forms.

Goldblatt, J. 2008. *Special events: The roots and wings of celebration.* 5th ed. Hoboken, NJ: Wiley.

Kozlowski, J.C. 1996. Can you say "exculpatory agreement"? *NRPA Law Review.* March 1996. Available: http://class-web.gmu.edu/jkozlows/p%26r396.htm.

Kuse, K.R. 2012. Vendor contracts: What are they and do you need them? Available: http://integratedgeneralcounsel.com/vendor-contracts-what-are-they-and-do-you-need-them.

Lawrence, H., and M. Wells. 2009. Event sponsorship. In *Event management blueprint,* 119-126. Dubuque, IA: Kendall/Hunt.

Mandel, J.R. 2012. Top 10 negotiation tips. September 4. MeetingsNet. Available: http://meetingsnet.com/negotiatingcontracts/top-10-negotiation-tips.

Matthews, D. 2008. *Special event production: The process.* Oxford, UK: Butterworth-Heinemann.

Sharp, L., A. Moorman, and C. Claussen. 2010. *Sport law: A managerial approach.* 2nd ed. Scottsdale, AZ: Holcomb Hathaway.

Solomon, J. 2002. *An insider's guide to managing sporting events.* Champaign, IL: Human Kinetics.

Spengler, J.O., P.M. Anderson, D.P. Connaughton, and T.A. Baker III. 2009. *Introduction to sport law.* Champaign, IL: Human Kinetics.

Steinbach, P. 2008. Concessions: Concessions contracts capitalizing on consumers' brand loyalty. *Athletic Business* 32 (8). [Online]. Available: www.athleticbusiness.com/articles/article.aspx?articleid=1838&zoneid=37.

Stim, R. 2012. Contract negotiation: 11 strategies. Available: www.nolo.com/legal-encyclopedia/contract-negotiation-11-strategies-33340.html.

Van Der Wagen, L., and B. Carlos 2005. *Event management for tourism, cultural, business and sporting events*. Upper Saddle River, NJ: Pearson Prentice Hall.

Winick, T. J., Claiborne, R., Gray, K., and Schabner, D. 2011, August 14. Indiana state fair death toll of 5 could go higher after 'fluke' storm fells stage. Retrieved from http://abcnews.go.com/US/indiana-state-fair-death-toll-higher-fluke-storm/story?id=14302288

CHAPTER 10

Risk Management and Negligence

Chapter Objectives

After completing the chapter, the reader should be able to do the following:

- Describe risk management.
- Identify the risk management process and generate a risk management plan.
- Recognize risks that could hinder an event.
- Understand crowd control.
- Devise an emergency plan.
- Understand that a competent, trained staff is critical for securing a safe environment.

Kenneth S. Trump, MPA, is the president of National School Safety and Security Services, a Cleveland-based national consulting firm specializing in school security and emergency preparedness training and consulting. He has written three books and more than 80 articles on school security and crisis issues. Ken has 25 years of experience in the school safety profession and has worked with school and public safety officials from all 50 states. Ken began his school safety career as an officer, investigator, and Youth Gang Unit supervisor for the Cleveland Public Schools' safety division, after which he served as a suburban security director and assistant gang task force director. He is one of the most widely quoted school safety experts, appearing on all network and cable TV news channels and regularly in national print media. Ken has served four times as a U.S. Congressional hearing witness on school security and crisis issues, testified on the federal role in bullying in 2011 before the U.S. Commission on Civil Rights, and was an invited attendee at the 2006 White House Conference on School Safety. For more information, see www.school security.org/school-safety-experts/trump.html.

Q: What critical skills allow an event manager to provide a safe and secure environment for patrons, staff, and participants?

A: Security must be viewed as a specialized professional field. Too often event managers believe that anyone can do security, and so emergency preparedness plans end up being put together by well-intended persons with minimal to no training or expertise to do so. Event managers also too often must choose between the costs for adequate security and saving their proceeds taken in at the gate. Event managers either must have specialized training and experience in professional security and emergency preparedness best practices or must hire someone who has such expertise.

Q: The events of 9/11 forever changed the landscape of security and planning. Obvious changes have occurred such as pat-downs and bag checks, but what changes may not be so obvious to the general public?

A: The terror attacks of 9/11 created a new normal by bumping up public expectations of security and the responsibility of entities to take reasonable security measures. Whether we are talking about security at our nation's airports or safety at a high school basketball game, the public expects the event managers to evaluate threats and security needs and to take reasonable risk reduction and preparedness steps.

Q: Realizing that sport is just one of the extracurricular activities that happen in an educational setting, do you see any differences in planning and preparing for this type of event over others?

A: The level of security for different types of extracurricular activities will vary event by event. Many factors go into decisions about the type and amount of security at an event, including the number of expected spectators, the size of the venue, past history of the type of event, rivalries, current security issues in the school or community, and related considerations. It is not logical to provide the same level of security for a 100-attendee volleyball game inside a high school gym as you would for a 5,000-attendee football game housed at a school stadium with large parking lots, concession stands, and a history of intense rivalries.

Q: What challenges do event planners face with regard to risk management and security?

A: The greatest challenge to risk management and security is that we have roller-coaster public awareness, public policy, and public funding on public safety issues. We legislate and fund by anecdote, and people have short memories when the threats to our safety are no longer staring us right in the face. So we have an incident, get alarmed, and throw money at it. Two or three years (and sometimes two or three months) down the road, we have forgotten about it and begin complaining about the inconveniences created by the heightened security. As a society, we want it both ways: We want heightened security, but we don't want the inconvenience. But you cannot have it both ways. Whether you are talking about an airport or your local high school football game, if you want heightened security, by definition there will be heightened inconvenience.

Q: What opportunities have presented since 9/11 that have helped shape the United States' response to safety and security?

A: In general, there have been significant investments in security training, staffing, and technology since 9/11. The problem is that the commitment to security by organizational and government leaders is, at best, inconsistent. So the good news is that we are better off than we were before 9/11. The bad news is that we are not as far ahead as we could be because of wavering organizational and governmental commitment to consistent security policy and funding.

Q: What advice do you offer to current or future event planners and managers with regard to risk management and safety?

A: Future event planners and managers need to view risk management and security as professional disciplines requiring professional skills. They need to set policies and budgets accordingly and hire people with the education, training, experience, and expertise to professionally implement and institutionalize security and preparedness best practices into their organizational culture.

Risk management concerns are inextricably woven into managerial responsibilities, whether you are a coach, teacher, recreation program administrator, or manager in a high school, college, Olympic, or professional sport organization. For many who attend events, the inner workings of producing an event are seldom known. The countless hours and efforts that go into running an event are not realized by the general public. What the public sees and expects is a safe and secure environment in which to enjoy the event.

A deep appreciation for identifying and addressing the potential risks associated with an event is vital. Spengler, Connaughton, and Pittman (2006) defined risk management as "reducing or eliminating the risk of injury and death and potential subsequent liability that comes about through involvement with sport and recreation programs and services" (p. 2). DeLisle (2009) claimed it is the "exercise of common sense and prudent responsibility [in] minimizing threats" (p. 149). Sharp, Moorman, and Claussen (2010) describe risk management as being preventive in nature, playing the "what if" game to determine potential threats and address them in the planning phase. Risk management at its simplest is a "process for managing the risks that you can identify—and insuring those you can't manage" (Ashley and Pearson 1993, p. 1).

Regardless of the risk management definition you subscribe to, aggressively identifying potential hazards is a must. Many times we become too comfortable with the way things are because we have not been confronted with an incident to challenge our response. According to Trump (2009), "the most challenging obstacle . . . is complacency. Time and distance from a major high-profile tragedy breeds complacency and fuels denial" (para. 7). This complacency and denial could position an event manager on the wrong side of a lawsuit. Take a cue from the Boy Scouts of America: Be prepared.

RISK MANAGEMENT PROCESS

Risk management is not a one-and-done exercise but rather a process utilizing everyone involved in the planning and execution of an event in order to create the safest possible environment for patrons. A risk management plan entails all the necessary elements of a crisis management plan, an emergency action plan, and a communication plan, all developed and coordinated by the people responsible for each area. Planning for risk is more like the adage that anything can happen and probably will.

Tarlow (2002) outlines the risk management process in the following way: identifying risks, projecting potential issues related to the risk, identifying remedies, doing what is necessary to prevent injuries, anticipating the reaction to the crisis, and creating a plan for both the crisis and how it will be communicated to the public. Sharp, Moorman, and Claussen (2010) offered the following elements of risk management:

• Identification: Conducting a legal audit identifies the deficiencies that need to be addressed or corrected during the planning process of a risk management plan (discussed later in this chapter).

• Assessing and classifying: Documentation of previous incidents is of great use when assessing

SEVERITY OF RISK

Category	PROBABILITY THAT SOMETHING WILL GO WRONG				
	Frequent Likely to occur immediately or in a short period of time, expected to occur frequently	**Likely** Quite likely to occur in time	**Occasional** May occur in time	**Seldom** Not likely to occur but possible	**Unlikely** Unlikely to occur
CATASTROPHIC May result in death	E	E	H	H	M
CRITICAL May cause severe injury, major property damage, significant financial loss, and/or result in negative publicity for the organization and/or institution	E	H	H	M	L
MARGINAL May cause minor injury, illness, property damage, financial loss and/or result in negative publicity for the organization and/or institution	E	M	M	L	L
NEGLIGIBLE Hazard presents a minimal threat to safety, health and well-being of participants; trivial	M	L	L	L	L

RISK DEFINITIONS

Many events, without proper planning, can have unreasonable levels of risk. However, by applying risk management strategies you can reduce the risk to an acceptable level.

E	**Extremely High Risk**	Activities in this category contain unacceptable levels of risk, including catastrophic and critical injuries that are highly likely to occur. Organizations should consider whether they should eliminate or modify activities that still have an "E" rating after applying all reasonable risk management strategies.
H	**High Risk**	Activities in this category contain potentially serious risks that are likely to occur. Application of proactive risk management strategies to reduce the risk is advised. Organizations should consider ways to modify or eliminate unacceptable risks.
M	**Moderate Risk**	Activities in this category contain some level of risk that is unlikely to occur. Organizations should consider what can be done to manage the risk to prevent any negative outcomes.
L	**Low Risk**	Activities in this category contain minimal risk and are unlikely to occur. Organizations can proceed with these activities as planned.

■ **Figure 10.1** University of Wisconsin at River Falls risk-assessment matrix.

Reprinted, by permission, from University of Wisconsin - River Falls.

issues and attempting to classify them. The risk matrix in figure 10.1 defines the levels of risks and provides a basis for determining the severity of the potential issues uncovered during the identification phase. Once identified, they will need to be classified.

• Treating and managing: Risk treatment refers to the process of identifying the options for addressing potential risks. Four specific options available for treating risks are retaining, reducing, avoiding, and transferring. Retaining the risk refers to accepting the risk and working around it. Reducing the risk is accomplished by putting measures in place such as supervision and staff training. Avoiding risks is possible when a decision is made to not proceed with an event because of the potential risk. The final treatment involves transferring liability to a third party (Cotten and Wolohan 2009).

The management of risks requires the generation of standard operating procedures (SOPs), which provide consistency and uniformity for job performance. Parkhouse (2005) defined SOPs as a "strategic plan that will provide the most efficient and effective way to decrease the occurrence of risks" (p. 160). These SOPs become guiding principles for events that outline the processes to be followed for each potential risk.

RISK MANAGEMENT PLANNING

Proactively identifying and classifying potential risks will assist in the development of risk management plans. The DIM process is a way to remain proactive rather than reactive during a crisis situation. The DIM process involves developing, implementing, and managing the plan.

Developing the Plan

The first step in developing a risk management plan is identifying the potential risks that could be associated with an event (Ammon, Southall, and Nagel 2010; Cotten and Wolohan 2009). Various methods can be utilized to collect this informa-

tion, from fans reporting potential hazards to a full-fledged walk-through of the host venue. Most venues will already have standard operating procedures in place for addressing potential situations, but anything that has not been previously experienced may require special attention. Involve as many people as necessary to ensure the safety of all involved. This process is also referred to as a risk assessment.

Once the venue, whether indoor or outdoor, has been carefully considered, the identified risks must be classified (Ammon, Southall, and Nagel 2010). Classification of potential risks into a hierarchical order allows for understanding of their frequency and seriousness (Spengler, Connaughton, and Pittman 2006). As mentioned earlier in the section on assessing and classifying risks, a risk matrix is a common tool used by event and facility personnel for this purpose. Barringer (2006) summed up a risk matrix as a graphical tool that highlights the chance of a risk with the consequence of the risk. Next, event managers need to decide how to manage or treat the identified risks. Various authors have identified the four possible treatments as retaining, reducing, avoiding, or transferring to a third party (Ammon, Southall, and Nagel 2010; Spengler, Connaughton, and Pittman 2006; Cotten and Wolohan 2009).

Implementing the Plan

Implementation of a risk management plan requires that all involved understand the expectations the plan has established and their role in making sure these expectations are met. If properly trained, event staff should be confident and able to do what is expected of them. Buy-in is critical. This can be achieved by involving the staff in the development of the plan or, if utilizing volunteers, asking for suggestions during training (Ammon, Southall, and Nagel 2010). A key ingredient in the facilitation of a risk management plan is the effectiveness of communication. Handbooks, e-mails, posters, fliers, and other forms of conveying information are essential for maintaining open lines of communication and consistency in expectations.

Managing the Plan

All the hard work put into devising the plan is now ready to pay off. You've hired the staff, trained them, and prepared them for potential risks. It is crucial that you have confidence in the person or persons hired to oversee the risk management process. The risk management plan is an evolving document. Over the course of an event, things will happen that may not have been addressed in the plan. The risk manager will document these incidents and develop strategies for addressing them in the future. Each event should end with a formal evaluation. The final step in most processes—evaluation—allows for pinpointing where something went wrong and, more important, where things went right. Do not assume that an incident-free event means the plan is foolproof. Event managers must be constantly considering what can be done to best serve patrons, keeping them safe and secure while at an event. Remember, a satisfied customer is a repeat customer!

THREATS TO EVENTS

When attending an event, a patron does not plan to become part of the action, but sometimes a foul ball or broken bat ends up in the stands; or a hockey puck misses the Plexiglas and sails 12 rows up; or a patron spills a drink and it goes unreported, or the custodial staff does not respond immediately. All these non-event-related incidents have the potential to cost the event and facility managers in legal fees. Spengler, Connaughton, and Pittman (2006) outlined those areas that require special consideration in risk management planning: medical attention, heat-related illnesses, lightning safety, bloodborne pathogens, equipment and supervision, and insurance.

Medical Attention

The medical attention an event manager needs to provide is dictated by the type of event and the governing body. In sport, we know that injuries are inherent and that we can prepare for what might happen. At the very least, staff should be certified in CPR, first aid, and AED use. Event personnel should carry cell phones in case they need to call 911. In a medical emergency, response time can be the difference between life and death. Establish a clear communication plan for every situation, including who will be the designated caller (Spengler, Connaughton, and Pittman 2006).

Heat-Related Illnesses

According to the National Oceanic and Atmospheric Administration (2012) the most common weather-related killer in the United States is heat. The NOAA works diligently with local National Weather Service (NWS) offices to report weather conditions. As the weather becomes warmer, the NWS will begin to issue excessive heat outlooks, watches, warnings, and advisories. Identify someone from the event management staff who will be responsible for checking the extended forecast so that alternative plans can be considered if necessary.

Reports of well-conditioned athletes collapsing from heat-related causes are far too common. An estimated 2,100 people sought treatment for exhaustion and dehydration at the 2012 Boston Marathon. During the summer of 2011, six high school football players died from heat-related injuries in Texas, and in November 2011, a University of Miami football player was found unconscious on the field at an early-morning practice (Siegel 2011; Kercheval 2011).

Lightning Safety

In March 2012, four members of the Seymour (Indiana) High School softball team were injured, one critically, from a lightning strike on what was described as a hot, sunny day (WRTV 2012). The NOAA calls this phenomenon a bolt from the blue. A serious concern for event managers, lightning can travel as far as 25 miles (40 km) from its origin before it strikes. Consulting the various organizations that address lightning safety such as the National Athletic Trainers' Association, National Lightning Safety Institute, National Collegiate Athletic Association, and state high school sports associations is highly recommended (Spengler, Connaughton, and Pittman 2006).

Bloodborne Pathogens

In many sports, injuries are a given. Some injuries involve the muscles and joints, while others involve the loss of blood. Strict precautions regarding handling blood are specified by the Occupational Safety and Health Administration (OSHA). OSHA guidelines exist to prevent the spread of diseases through contact with blood. Using latex gloves and thoroughly washing hands are two preventive measures. Sports such as boxing and the martial arts are scrutinized when it comes to bloodborne illnesses.

Equipment and Supervision

Equipment is essential in sport for protection of the participants. Safety inspections must be performed to ensure that equipment is maintained and in proper working order. It is critical to make sure that equipment and supervision are adequate for the age of the patrons (Cotten and Wolohan 2009). Both equipment and supervision, from a legal perspective, fall within the realm of liability law. Sharp, Moorman, and Claussen (2010) reported concerns of liability with regard to supervision. The quality of the supervision (a competent, trained staff) and the quantity of supervisors (ratio of supervisors to participants or attendees) must be adequate for the activity or event.

Hiring competent staff and conducting a thorough screening process, including background checks, are necessary. Although events rely heavily on volunteers, every person who applies does not need to be hired. Training, according to Van Der Wagen and Carlos (2005), should address three areas: event objectives, the facility, and each staff member's job duties. Becoming familiar with expectations allows the staff to fully grasp the intent of the event. Touring the facility gives them a sense of familiarity with exits, evacuation routes, concessions, and any other aspects necessary for them to properly do their jobs. Be sure to provide employees and volunteers with the expectations of their specific jobs and how they fit into the overall experience that patrons will have while at the event.

As a shining example of how properly trained staff make for a spectacular event, we need only look at the 2012 Super Bowl in Indianapolis. The Super Bowl Host Committee provided numerous training sessions over the course of a year for its 8,000-plus volunteers. Volunteers were subjected to background checks by Homeland Security and were trained on how to respond to certain issues, should they arise. Communication was critical to the success of the Super Bowl volunteer program, and text messages, e-mails, and websites were vital tools for disseminating the necessary information about schedule or venue changes.

Insurance

Insurance needs are determined by the type and location of your event, but at a minimum event organizers need to secure liability insurance to protect their financial investment and protect against potential legal action related to civil or criminal law (deLisle 2009; Supovitz 2005). Liability insurance is necessary because facility owners will require you to purchase it to protect their interests in your event and because of the duty owed to participants, spectators, and workers (Supovitz 2005). This duty refers to the requirement of the party hosting the event to provide a safe environment for all involved. Due diligence in the planning process should account for potential issues that could result in injury or worse to participants, spectators, or workers. According to Van Der Wagen and Carlos (2005), liability claims "can be reduced by careful risk analysis and prevention strategies" (p. 52). It is especially important that event planners allocate the funds necessary to procure the appropriate amount of liability coverage. Each event is different and will require insurance coverage based on the size, complexity, and location of the impending event (Supovitz 2005).

CROWD CONTROL

Among the many skills required of facility managers is an understanding and appreciation of crowd dynamics and the relationship of crowding to facility design and management. Fruin

(1984) reported that good crowd planning and management improves the public's enjoyment of events and encourages attendance. It also reduces crowd-related accidents, their associated liability claims, and the possibilities of more serious and costly incidents. This is a management skill that is critical for both the patron and the manager. Understanding the differences between crowd management and crowd control is imperative for event planners. Berlonghi (1994) defined crowd management as those measures taken to facilitate the movement and enjoyment of people. He contended that properly managing a crowd reassures people that they will get what they paid for and will return home safe and sound.

CROWD MANAGEMENT PLANS

Crafting a crowd management plan (CMP) that includes the strategies necessary for creating a successful and safe event is one part of the overall risk management plan. A CMP helps provide a safe and enjoyable environment for patrons. An effective plan addresses the following:

- Number of people at the venue
- Behavior of spectators
- Layout of the facility
- Movement and activities of guests
- Emergency response
- Specific concerns of guests visiting the facility

Following are some key terms related to crowd management.

- Crowd expectations: Patrons have the expectation that the environment they are entering has been prepared for the event and is safe and secure. They assume that every precaution has been taken to prevent accidental, intentional, or negligent acts that could cause harm.
- Crowd dynamics and demographics: Each crowd has its own unique qualities. Fell (2003) stated that crowd dynamics refers to "the management and the flow of pedestrians in crowded venues and situations" (p. 1). The demographics of the crowd also play a role in the dynamics.

- Movement theory: How people move within and without a facility relates to pedestrian traffic flow. As an equation, movement theory takes into account the speed at which a crowd is moving multiplied by the density and the width of the crowd, which will tell us the flow. Hoogendoorn and Bovy (2003) asserted that certain factors contribute to walking speeds, such as "personal characteristics of pedestrians (age, gender, size, health, etc.), characteristics of the trip (walking purpose, route familiarity, trip length), properties of the infrastructure (type, grade, attractiveness of environment, shelter), and finally, environmental characteristics (ambient and weather conditions)" (p. 154).
- Evacuation procedures: Mass exodus of crowds requires that adequate exits be unlocked and ready for use. Tragedies such as the Rhode Island nightclub disaster of 2003 are preventable if evacuation routes are not blocked or locked, preventing people from exiting the building. Pyrotechnics were set off during a rock concert, catching the nightclub on fire and creating chaos within the crowd. Several exits to the facility were chain-locked from the inside, preventing escape from the burning building and resulting in the deaths of nearly 100 people (CNN 2003).
- Alcohol policy: Selling alcohol requires careful consideration. If the decision to sell alcohol is made, an alcohol policy must be in place to manage the sale of alcohol and address the handling of intoxicated and obnoxious fans. Removing the patron as quickly as possible, without incident and without becoming the main attraction, is the goal.
- Training: Ammon, Southall, and Nagel (2010) contend that properly training staff is the first component of an effective CMP. Ticket takers, ushers, and bag-check personnel are the first line of defense in controlling risks and crowds, and these employees should be trained accordingly. Training should also include the scope of their duties and cover the second component of an effective CMP, activation and implementation of an emergency plan. Procedures for dealing with unruly or intoxicated fans should be well thought out and explained. In devising your emergency plan, consider creating a working document that

all employees will have access to. The table of contents of Purdue University's emergency plan is a good example of what to include (figure 10.2).

• Crowd control: Crowd control more directly relates to the actions implemented once a crowd begins to act in a way that was not planned. Examples include engaging in unsafe activities, becoming rowdy, pushing or shoving, and fighting. The 2004 "Malice in the Palace" fiasco helps up better understand how a situation can turn ugly in a matter of seconds. The Pacers–Pistons brawl originally started on the court but ended up in the stands, with players and fans battling it out Wild West style (Lage 2004; Associated Press 2004).

• Signage: A key ingredient of crowd control is adequate signage inside and outside a facility. Signage is one aspect of the communication plan that gives patrons necessary information to maneuver to and from and within an event. Two typical types of signage are as follows:

• Directional signs: These signs provide patrons with directions to important locations such as interstates, main roadways, and parking areas. Inside a facility, directional signs help patrons navigate the facility.

• Informational signs: These signs inform patrons of things such as prohibited items, facility rules, and locations of importance within the facility.

TABLE OF CONTENTS

Section 1: Introduction

Section 2: User Items

Emergency Contact Information

Nonemergency Contact Numbers

Automatic External Defibrillator (AED)

Response to Alarms

Detailed Emergency Evacuation Procedures

Detailed Emergency Shelter in Place Procedures

All-Clear Procedures

Class Suspension or Campus Closure

Section 3: Building Information

Building Deputy/Alternate Building Deputy Information

Building Description

Building Departments

Building Safety Committee

Building Critical Operations

Building Alarm(s)

Section 4: Responsibilities and Requirements

Department Head or Designated Representative

BEP Developer (building deputy or an individual designated by the department head)

Building Occupants

Training

BEP Requirements

Section 5: Evacuation Guidelines for People Requesting Additional Assistance

Appendices

Appendix A: Acronyms and Term Definitions

Appendix B: Resource List

Appendix C: Voluntary Registry for Persons Requesting Additional Assistance

Appendix D: Supplemental Evacuation Guidelines for People With Disabilities

Appendix E: Revision Log

■ **Figure 10.2** Purdue University's emergency plan, table of contents.

Reprinted, by permission, from Purdue University.

NEGLIGENCE

For the most part, events are produced with minimal cause for concern. Most of the issues that arise are behind the scenes and are unknown to participants and spectators. But in the event something happens that places participants and spectators in harm's way, you must have a plan in place to remedy the situation. This can be addressed during the initial planning phase, where it is critical for you to take the initiative and consider the potential hazards that might interfere with hosting a safe and secure event. Specifically, the tort of negligence must be visited. You can decrease your liability with proper planning.

Cotten and Wolohan (2009) define negligence as an unintentional wrongdoing that results in injury to a person, property, or reputation. They go on to state that this is the area of law in which the sport industry sees most of its lawsuits. Simply put, negligence is failing to provide a safe environment, resulting in someone or something being injured or harmed.

Establishing negligence is not as simple as it may seem. There is no guarantee that a person injured at an event will be able to recover a monetary reward. In our sue-happy society, too many people believe that something as simple as slipping and falling is cause for compensation. But in order to make such a claim and potentially receive restitution, negligence must be proven. To prove negligence, four elements must be present: "duty, breach, cause, and damage" (Owen 2007, p. 1673).

• Duty: The term *duty* refers to a recognized social norm regarding how you should conduct yourself with others (Cotten and Wolohan 2009). The relationships covered by a duty are those that are viewed as inherent to the situation, such as a facility owner and invitees, coach and athlete, or teacher and student. Bell (1995) highlighted the following groups as those that must be afforded special relational considerations: (a) students, (b) employees, (c) volunteers, (d) tenants, (e) authorized visitors, and (f) trespassers. Specifically with regard to your event, you must consider the following duties: "the duty to protect against foreseeable dangers, the duty to provide adequate security and the duty to warn about known dangers" (Bell 2005, pp. 2-3).

• Breach: As mentioned already, you are expected to provide a safe and secure environment for all involved in the production of your event. If you fail to provide such an environment, you are considered in breach of your duty. A breach can involve misconduct that occurred or a person's action or oversight (Owen 2007). Breach of duty is centered around two risks: (1) those that are inherent to the activity (audience participation in a halftime game) and (2) those that are negligent behaviors (climbing on a railing at a facility and falling).

• Cause: To determine if a defendant's actions or lack of actions were responsible for the plaintiff's injuries, the plaintiff must prove cause and effect. In other words, if someone claims he was injured while attending your event, he must prove that you (event manager or facility manager) created the situation that caused the injury (negligent behavior), either by not taking the necessary precautions or by failing to warn. It is best that event managers work closely with the facility to ensure that all potential situations are addressed before the event or that a plan is in place to address them as they arise.

• Damage: For recovery, there must be damages. The damage is typically either physical or emotional injury. Compensable damage can be a financial loss, an emotional distress, or an impairment.

Because sporting events involve competition, with some being very physical in nature, and spectators who have a tendency to become rowdy, it is no wonder that event managers need to diligently prepare for charges of negligence. Rowdy fans can become verbally violent, which may lead to a physical altercation. On the other end of this spectrum, jubilant fans can also become rowdy as they express unbridled emotion for their teams. Either can develop into a crowd management issue that could turn deadly. From soccer matches in Europe to concert-goers in the United States, it is hard to manage a mobile crowd, and thus injury or death could occur. Far too often we hear of tragic situations in which people are trampled by out-of-control crowds.

As an event manager, you need to consider all potential areas of liability that are within your purview, including spectators, participants, and event workers. Ultimate liability lies with you. Liability laws vary from state to state, so you need to be aware of your responsibilities if you are managing a mobile event (Cotten and Wolohan 2009). According to Cotten and Wolohan (2009), there are three potentially liable parties to consider: employees, the administrators or supervisors, and the corporate entity (owners). For these reasons, it is critical that you hire competent staff that are responsible and trustworthy and then train them for their specific tasks.

Spectators and participants must also share some of the burden for potential problems. Spectators assume the risk of attending an event knowing that some sports have potential dangers, such as a puck clearing the Plexiglas and entering the seats, a baseball or bat flying into the stands, or an errant golf ball finding its way into a gallery. Situations such as this can be addressed through various means such as a disclaimer on the back of a ticket or signage around the event that provides warnings for spectators.

Participants in your event should be required to sign a waiver or release form before competing. Considered contracts, waivers and releases inform participants of the potential dangers associated with participating. Upon signing these forms, the participant assumes the potential risk for participating, and they surrender the right to sue if injured during the activity (Cotten and Wolohan 2009). It is advisable to secure the services of a lawyer to help you create the necessary forms (waiver and releases) and provide counsel for local and state laws.

SUMMARY

Providing a safe and fun experience for patrons is not only expected but also legally required. Risk management strategies help address any potential issues before an event is held. Creating an overarching risk management plan, inclusive of crowd management strategies, emergency responses, and an effective communication plan, will offer protections against potential injuries and lawsuits.

Safety and security are sometimes used synonymously, but they are different. Peter Taylor, former lord chief justice of England and Wales, summed up that difference with the following quote: "You cannot create a safe environment without effective security. If a crowd gets out of control, safety will be compromised." Ultimately, facility management is responsible for maintaining order. Event and facility managers work attentively to create detailed crowd management plans that address crisis situations such as "fandemonium," the state of crowd chaos. Once a crowd reaches this level, law enforcement officers or security personnel will be called to action.

A popular quote is, "Failing to plan is planning to fail." Set an event up for success; be diligent in taking the necessary precautions to prepare for a successful event through proactive planning.

LEARNING ACTIVITIES

Select a facility of your choice, and attend an event hosted by that facility. During your visit, complete a checklist that will help you evaluate the facility's safety. Once you have assessed the safety of the facility, you are to construct an executive summary of your findings and submit it for grading. The purpose of this exercise is to challenge you to "see" things from a facility management perspective in order to focus on preventive rather than reactive management. Before your visit, do your homework. Consider the following regarding the facility you have chosen to visit:

- Age of the facility
- Location: rural, urban, inner city
- Renovated or new facility
- How the facility is or was financed
- The facility's competition

Use the following survey to record your observations during your site visit.

SAMPLE FACILITY INSPECTION CHECKLIST

This form is provided as a sample facility inspection checklist and is designed to help you develop a checklist specific for your facilities. This is an incomplete checklist.

Name of inspector: _____

Date of inspection: _____

Name and location of facility: _____

Facility Condition

Circle Y (yes) if the facility is in good condition and N (no) if it needs something done to make it acceptable. Fill in what needs to be done on the line to the right.

Gymnasium

Y N   Floor (no water spots, buckling, loose sections) _____

Y N   Walls (vandalism free) _____

Y N   Lights (all functioning) _____

Y N   Windows (secure) _____

Y N   Roof (no adverse impact of weather) _____

Y N   Stairs (well lighted) _____

Y N   Bleachers (support structure sound) _____

Y N   Exits (lights working) _____

Y N   Basketball rims (level, securely attached) _____

Y N   Basketball backboards (no cracks, clean) _____

Y N   Mats (cleaned, properly stored, no defects) _____

Y N   Uprights/projections _____

Y N   Wall plugs (covered) _____

Y N   Light switches (all functioning) _____

Y N   Heating/cooling system (temperature control) _____

Y N   Ducts, radiators, pipes _____

Y N   Thermostats _____

Y N   Fire alarms (regularly checked) _____

Y N   Directions posted for evacuating the gym in case of fire _____

Y N   Fire extinguishers (regularly checked) _____

Other (list) _____

Locker Rooms

Y N   Floors _____

Y N   Walls _____

Y N   Lights _____

Y N   Windows _____

Y N   Roof _____

■ **Figure 10.3**   This form provides a starting point for evaluating facility safety.

Reprinted, by permission, from ASEP, 1996, *Event management for sport directors* (Champaign, IL: Human Kinetics), 80-83.

Y N   Showers _____

Y N   Drains _____

Y N   Benches _____

Y N   Lockers _____

Y N   Exits _____

Y N   Water fountains _____

Y N   Toilets _____

Y N   Trainer's room _____

Other (list) _____

Field(s)/outside playing area

Surface

Y N   Not too wet or too dry _____

Y N   Grass length _____

Y N   Free of debris _____

Y N   Free of holes and bumps _____

Y N   Free of protruding pipes, wires, lines _____

Y N   Line markers _____

Stands

Y N   Pitching mound _____

Y N   Dugouts _____

Y N   Warning tracks and fences _____

Y N   Sidelines _____

Y N   Sprinklers _____

Y N   Garbage _____

Y N   Security fences _____

Y N   Water fountains _____

Y N   Storage sheds _____

Concession area

Y N   Electrical _____

Y N   Heating/cooling systems _____

Other (list) _____

Pool

Y N   Equipment in good repair _____

Y N   Sanitary _____

Y N   Slipperiness on decks and diving board controlled _____

Y N   Chemicals safely stored _____

Y N   Regulations and safety rules posted _____

(continued)

(continued)

Lighting—adequate visibility

Y N   No glare _____

Y N   Penetrates to bottom of pool _____

Y N   Exit light in good repair _____

Y N   Halls and locker rooms meet code requirements _____

Y N   Light switches properly grounded _____

Y N   Has emergency generator to back up regular power source _____

Exits—accessible, secure

Y N   Adequate size, number _____

Y N   Self-closing doors _____

Y N   Self-locking doors _____

Y N   Striker plates secure _____

Y N   No obstacles or debris _____

Y N   Office and storage rooms locked _____

Ring buoys

Y N   20-inch diameter _____

Y N   50-foot rope length _____

Reaching poles

Y N   One each side _____

Y N   12-foot length _____

Y N   Metal stress _____

Y N   Good repair _____

Guard chair(s)

Y N   Unobstructed view _____

Y N   Tall enough to see bottom of pool _____

Safety line at break point in the pool grade (deep end)

Y N   Bright color floats _____

Y N   3/4-inch rope _____

First-aid kit

Y N   Inventoried and replenished regularly _____

Stretcher, two blankets, and spine board

Y N   Inventoried and in good repair _____

Emergency telephone lights and public address system

Y N   Accessible _____

Y N   Directions for use visibly posted _____

Y N   Powered by emergency generators as well as regular power system _____

Y N   Emergency numbers on telephone cradle or receiver _____

Emergency procedures

Y N   Sign posted in highly visible area _____

Track

Surface

Y N   Free of debris _____

Y N   Free of holes and bumps _____

Y N   Throwing circles _____

Y N   Fences _____

Y N   Water fountains _____

Other (list)

Recommendations/observations: _____

_____

_____

_____

_____

_____

REFERENCES

Ammon, R., R. Southall, and M. Nagel. 2010. *Sport facility management: Organization events and mitigating risks.* 2nd ed. Morgantown, WV: Fitness Information Technology.

Ashley, S., and R. Pearson. 1993. Fundamentals of risk management. Available: www.sashley.com/downloads/articles/fundamentalsofriskmanagement.pdf.

Barringer, P. 2006. Risk matrix: Know when to accept the risk. Know when to reject the risk. [PowerPoint slides]. Available: www.barringer1.com/nov04prb_files/Risk-Matrix.pdf.

Bell, S.T. 1995. Legal issues affecting event management at colleges and universities. Proceedings from the 16th Annual Law and Higher Education Conference, Deland, FL: Stetson University.

Berlonghi, A. 1994. *The special event risk management manual.* Rev. ed. Dana Point, CA: Berlonghi.

CNN.com. 2003. At least 96 killed in nightclub inferno. February 21. Available: http://articles.cnn.com/2003-02-21/us/deadly.nightclub.fire_1_attorney-general-patrick-lynch-nightclub-stampede-rhode-island-nightclub?_s=PM:US.

Cotten, D., and J. Wolohan. 2009. *Law for recreation and sport managers.* 5th ed. Dubuque, IA: Kendall/Hunt.

deLisle, L. 2009. *Creating special events.* Champaign, IL: Sagamore.

Fell, A. 2003. *A study of modeling crowd dynamics.* Unpublished senior project. Available: www.sxs.carelron.ca/~arpwhite/documents/honoursProjects.

Fruin, J.J. 1984. Crowd dynamics and auditorium management. *Auditorium News* (May).

Hoogendoorn, S., and P.H.L. Bovy. 2003. Simulation of pedestrian flows by optimal control and differential games. *Optimal Control Applications and Methods* 24 (3):153-172.

Kercheval, B. 2011. Updated: Miami LB taken to hospital for heat exhaustion. NBC Sports. November 15. Available: http://collegefootballtalk.nbcsports.com/2011/11/15/miami-player-taken-to-hospital-for-heat-exhaustion.

Lage, L. 2004, November 19. Pacers-Pistons game halted by brawl. *USA Today.* Retrieved from http://usatoday30.usatoday.com/sports/basketball/games/2004-11-19-pacers-pistons_x.htm

National Oceanic and Atmospheric Administration. 2012. Heat: A major killer. Available: www.nws.noaa.gov/os/heat/index.shtml.

Owen, D.G. 2007. The five elements of negligence. *Hofstra Law Review* 35 (4): 1671-1686.

Parkhouse, B. 2005. *The management of sport: Its foundation and application.* New York: McGraw-Hill.

Sharp, L., A. Moorman, and C. Claussen. 2010. *Sport law: A managerial approach.* 2nd ed. Scottsdale, AZ: Holcomb Hathaway.

Siegel, J. 2011. High school football player dies; sixth athlete death this summer. ABC News. September 3. Available: http://abcnews.go.com/Health/high-school-football-player-dies-sixth-athlete-death/story?id=14442856#.T57kWvUw8TA.

Spengler, J., D. Connaughton, and A. Pittman. 2006. *Risk management in sport and recreation*. Champaign, IL: Human Kinetics.

Supovitz, F. 2005. *The sports event management and marketing playbook*. Hoboken, NJ: Wiley.

Tarlow, P. 2002. *Event risk management and safety*. New York: Wiley.

Trump, K. 2009. Columbine's 10th anniversary finds lessons learned. District Administration. April 1.

Available: www.districtadministration.com/article/columbine%E2%80%99s-10th-anniversary-finds-lessons-learned.

Van Der Wagen, L., and B. Carlos. 2005. *Event management for tourism, cultural, business and sporting events*. Upper Saddle River, NJ: Pearson Prentice Hall.

WRTV. 2012, March 16. Softball player improving after lightning strike. Retrieved from www.theindychannel.com/news/softball-player-improving-after-lightning-strike.

CHAPTER 11

Event Services and Logistics

Chapter Objectives

After completing the chapter, the reader should be able to do the following:

- Describe the logistical planning process and the timeline for a sporting event.
- Explain various logistical operations areas in the event process.
- Compare and contrast how logistics differ based on the type of sporting event.
- Prepare students to think critically about the numerous logistical activities that occur in a sporting event.
- Apply theoretical concepts that are important to event services and logistics.

Dave McGillivray is the founder and president of Dave McGillivray Sports Enterprises (DMSE), Inc. and the race director of the Boston Athletic Association (BAA) Boston Marathon and BAA Half Marathon. For the Boston Marathon, he manages and oversees all operational and logistical aspects of the event. He also either directs or has directed major mass-participation events such as the U.S. Women's Olympic Marathon Trials, TD Beach to Beacon 10K, the Denver Marathon, and the Marathon of the Palm Beaches. He was inducted into Running USA's Hall of Champions in 2005 and named one of *Runner's World* magazine's Heroes of Running in 2007.

Q: How do you see your role as the race director?

A: My role is more akin to the conductor of an orchestra, where the musicians know their instruments better than I know their instruments. I am there mainly to tie it all together, to communicate with all of them so that it all plays out on race day harmoniously as one well-oiled machine. That doesn't mean I don't get into the nuts and the bolts and minutiae of specific areas, but generally speaking, I let the experts do what they know how to do best.

Q: What are important skills for people-managing events such as the Boston Marathon?

A: The most important skill is being able to delicately, professionally, and sensitively balance all the personalities of all the people that make up the event. You are talking about people who live around the route, corporate sponsors, media, politicians from the cities and towns, and public safety. You are talking about the organizing committee and the staff who have been around a long time, all the volunteers, and all the runners themselves. I think the biggest challenge is being able to understand everyone's needs and how they do business and being able to get the most out of everybody, making sure it's a cohesive group. What I try to do is make myself available to anyone and everyone to help them out. My motto is always about preventing fires versus putting out fires. You can look like a hero by putting out a fire, but what people don't understand is perhaps that the fire could have been prevented. And maybe you are not really the hero, but you should be the villain for not preparing well enough in advance to have prevented that fire from even occurring. That takes vision. That takes preplanning. That takes meticulous detail.

Q: What are some of the challenges related to managing an event such as this one?

A: Because it's an outdoor event over 26 miles, it's the unforeseen or the uncontrollable aspects of the event. In particular, it's the weather. If it's an 80- or 90-degree day (27 to 32 degrees Celsius), that exacerbates the challenge, and we'll have many potential medical issues on our hands. A couple years ago, we had a nor'easter come through that we knew of in advance. And so a critical decision to go or not to go had to be made. Those are tough decisions when you are dealing with 27,000 to 30,000 people from all over the world, and this may be their only chance to do this. So if you pull the plug, they're not going to be happy. But if you don't pull the plug, and they get hurt, many more people are not going to be happy. Certainly, there's a lot of responsibility to make the right decisions and do the right things under difficult circumstances.

Q: What are some tips you would give for effectively planning the logistical aspects of an event?

A: I always trick myself; I tell my staff and other people to just pretend an event is two weeks before it actually is. Shoot for that date. Don't shoot for the event date. There are so many things that pop up at the last minute. Maybe someone was supposed to do something and did not do it. Well, you had better be prepared to fill in for her and get that job done. You can't if you are so busy doing what you have to do. But if you can get all your business done and give yourself some flex time in order to cover other things that might crop up, then you've put yourself in a really good position. It's really all about preparation more than anything else. You can never overprepare. I always put everything in writing, and I always disseminate the information. For every event I do, I create what's called an operations manual. It is the textbook. Anything and everything logistically, technically, and operationally that has to do with our event is in that manual. I try to get all those documents from all the

different committee people and put them in one manual and then pass that out a couple of weeks before the event. I think knowledge is important, and even if you are responsible for only a specific area of the event, the more you know about everything going on around you, the better run the event is. If people come to you and ask questions and you don't know, you are not being overly helpful to the event. But if you have the answers because you read the manual, that benefits everybody.

Event planners are responsible for coordinating the logistics of a sporting event, which entails making sure the right people, equipment, and services are available in the right place and at the right time. Some important logistical components of any sporting event include financial resources, equipment, ticketing, human resources, site selection, information, and sponsorship. But there is a lot more involved in planning an event than just these logistical components. For example, Allen (2009) suggests the following factors are important when considering where to hold an event: location (local, out of state, out of country), date (taking into account national or religious holidays), season (spring, summer, fall, winter), time of day, indoor or outdoor (how bad weather will affect your event), single or multiple locations, and budget considerations.

EVENT TIMELINE

A timeline is an important tool for successfully implementing a sporting event. According to Goldblatt (2011), an event timeline is a sequential listing of all the tasks and duties associated with an event, and it is divided into various phases

consisting of event research, planning, coordination, and evaluation (figure 11.1). The timeline provides all stakeholders with a tool for managing the event. It is important that the primary event planner receive a timeline from each vendor and stakeholder and that these be incorporated into a master timeline. One of the reasons events fail is insufficient time to research, plan, and coordinate.

Research Phase

The research phase is important because it provides information about previous events and assists in outlining the needs and resources of the current event. During this phase of the event timeline, the event planner is primarily gathering data that will help him plan the event. For example, the event manager may collect data from the last two years the event was held. Research before the event may be quantitative or qualitative in nature. Event managers gathering quantitative data may use a questionnaire or survey to retrieve information from prospective attendees. The questionnaire or survey is analyzed using some form of statistical analysis. Often, quantitative research provides the event planner

▪ **Figure 11.1** Phases of an event timeline.

with demographic information (e.g., age, gender, household income) and participation rates, which is helpful in appealing to these groups when they arrive at the event venue. Qualitative research is useful in event planning as a way to get deeper information from respondents. It may take the form of focus groups, case studies, content analysis, or participant observation.

Event Planning Phase

The planning phase should take into account the previous research conducted in relation to the event. It should also specify the objectives of your event, and a good plan should help those involved reach these objectives. A strategic plan outlines the key stakeholders, the necessary steps for hosting a successful event, and the event's time frame. The planning process starts with a meeting involving all key stakeholders in the sporting event network. It is important to include those people who have responsibilities and the authority to make decisions.

Coordination Phase

In the coordination phase, the event planner synchronizes and integrates activities, responsibilities, and organizational structures to ensure that resources are used efficiently to achieve organizational objectives. Some activities that may transpire during the coordination phase are identifying prospective vendors, contracting vendors, and developing and implementing production schedules. Goldblatt (2011) suggests that event planners use critical analysis along with professional training during this phase to make correct decisions. He recommends the following six steps as simple but effective ways to make decisions:

1. Collect all the information because many problems have multiple sides to review.
2. Consider the pros and cons of decisions, especially in terms of who will be affected.
3. Consider the financial implications of your decisions.
4. Consider the moral and ethical implications of your decisions.

5. If possible, do no harm to others or yourself.
6. Make your decision and move forward.

Evaluation Phase

According to Myhill and Phillips (2006), evaluating an event helps the event planner determine whether the event objectives were met, and it also provides guidance for planning future events. Some of the tasks during the evaluation phase include preparing and distributing surveys or questionnaires; collecting, tabulating, and analyzing data; preparing reports of findings and recommendations; and submitting a final report (Goldblatt 2011). Myhill and Phillips provide the following purposes of evaluation:

- To determine success in accomplishing event objectives
- To identify the strengths and weaknesses in the event management process
- To compare the event costs to the benefits
- To decide who should participate in future events
- To identify which participants were the most successful
- To reinforce major points to event participants
- To gather data to assist in marketing future events
- To determine if the event was appropriate for and met the needs of participants

EVENT REGISTRATION

The need for event registration varies depending on the type of event being planned. For example, a marathon runner or participant in a youth volleyball tournament may register at the event site at a participant check-in. In contrast, a professional baseball game would not have a registration area for participants. Generally speaking, events catering to active participants are more likely to have some type of registration process in comparison to a regular-season contest attracting passive spectators. Registration is an important component of these types of events because it is the first interactive experience the participant has with the event. Many events offer the participant the opportunity to register in advance. Advance registration requires database software along with careful planning and skilled organization to prevent problems such as misplaced checks or incorrect paperwork, which ultimately results in angry customers (Carlisle 2006).

TICKET SALES

Ticketing is an important element of a sporting event, and the event manager must be concerned with both the raw material (i.e., the tangible tickets) and the distribution and human resource systems needed to sell them (Shonk 2011). As Fried (2010) suggests, ticket sales have changed over the years with new marketing techniques. Sports fans and spectators now have a variety of choices in terms of ticketing inventory, including everything from general admission, reserved seating, and box seating to more luxurious seating inventory such as club seats and luxury suites. In some cases, a customer must purchase a personal seat license (PSL) in order to buy a season ticket. PSLs refer to "a contractual right a person acquires for a fee that allows the person to purchase tickets for a specific seat; others cannot acquire tickets for that seat as long as the PSL contract is in effect" (Fried 2010, p. 336). The convenience for consumers in terms of purchasing tickets has also been greatly enhanced. The secondary ticket market and websites such as stubhub.com and livenation.com provide consumers with easy accessibility to tickets for numerous events. In addition, many teams now allow season ticket holders to sell unused tickets via their websites.

It is important that event managers research the various ticket options that will be used to sell the event. The physical ticket is an important part of the experience, and the ticket represents the patron's first tangible contact with the sporting event. A ticket on cheap paper stock, one that is poorly designed, or one that has spelling or grammatical errors portrays the event in a negative light. A number of automated ticketing systems are now available that make the distribution of tickets much easier for event managers. Ticketmaster, Live Nation, TicketCity, and tickets.com are examples of companies that compete in the ticketing and live entertainment industry. Because of bar-coding technology, tickets can now be printed on letter-size paper by the consumer and scanned at entry into the event.

FOOD AND BEVERAGE OPERATIONS

It is rare to find any large events that do not have some type of meal function. Even youth events often include a postgame snack or beverage provided by a parent or coach. Food and beverage operations at an event are vitally important and can be a significant source of revenue. An event planner has a number of considerations in terms of food and beverage services. Most events require a meal for active participants and concession operations for spectators. Hospitality suites are also common at many sporting events. Shock (2006) outlines the following types of food and beverage services:

- American service: Food is portioned and plated in the kitchen and then served by attendants. This is the most common, economical, functional, and efficient type of service.

- Buffet: Food is arranged on tables, and guests serve themselves and then move to a dining table to eat.

- Butler service: Usually offered at receptions, whereby servers offer a variety of both hot and cold hors d'oeuvres on platters or trays to guests.

- Cafeteria service: Similar to a buffet, except attendants serve food to guests, and the guests carry the food to their tables on trays.

- English service: A tray of food is brought to the table.

- French banquet service: Platters of food are prepared in the kitchen. The servers take the platters to the dining tables and place the food onto the guests' plates.

• French cart service: Service involves the use of silverware; heating and garnishing of food table-side by a captain; and the placement of food on a heated plate, which is then served to the guest by a server. Plated entrees and beverages are usually served from the right, and bread and butter and salad from the left.

• Preset service: Some food is already on the table when guests arrive. Foods may include bread and butter, water, salad, and cold appetizers.

• Russian banquet service: Food is fully prepared in the kitchen, and all courses are served either from silver platters or from an Escoffier dish. The server places a plate in front of each guest; after the plates are placed, the server returns with a tray of food and, moving counterclockwise around the table, allows guests to help themselves from a platter presented from their left.

Meals for Participants

Many sporting events have meal functions for the participants that take place at the host hotel, the sport venue, a local restaurant, or a banquet area. Meal functions may include breakfasts, luncheons, refreshment breaks, receptions, seated served dinners, seated buffet dinners, and even theme parties.

According to Shock (2006), breakfast may be served in various ways:

• Continental: A fast breakfast that may include coffee, tea, juice, bread, pastries, bagels, and muffins. This style of breakfast is good for participants because it is quick and encourages prompt attendance before daily events.

• Full breakfast buffet: Two or three types of meat, two or three styles of eggs, one potato dish, three to six types of bread or pastry, hot and cold cereals, fresh fruit, yogurt, juices, coffee, and tea. This style usually runs about an hour and is often more filling for event participants than the continental style breakfast.

• English breakfast: The same foods as the full breakfast buffet plus action stations with attendants serving foods such as waffles, omelets, or crepes made to order. Once again, this type of breakfast lasts about an hour, and participants must have enough time to truly enjoy.

• Full served breakfast: A full-service breakfast where participants order off the menu and servers deliver the meal. This style of breakfast may be best suited at the beginning or the conclusion of an event when participants are more relaxed and not running from one place to another. Some events may have a full served breakfast that also includes an awards presentation or a special speaker.

Depending on the type of event, refreshment breaks may vary. Refreshment breaks for participants in less strenuous events may include beverages such as coffee, tea, bottled waters, and soft drinks. For sports teams, refreshment breaks in between or after a game may include sport drinks and water and sometimes may also include some type of fruit such as oranges to provide energy to the players. Luncheons can be served in a variety of formats, including box lunches, seated lunch, luncheon buffets, and deli buffets. Many sporting events have some type of reception either before or at the conclusion of the event. Often receptions include entertainment along with hors d'oeuvres, and some events have an open bar. Although the reception can be catered to the needs of your event, guests are usually not encouraged to sit and eat during the reception.

Seated served dinners are normally planned for a time when there are no other imminent events (e.g., workout, press conference, team meeting) so that the guests can enjoy the experience. They normally last about two hours but can run as long as four hours if entertainment, dancing, awards, or other activities are included. A seated buffet dinner may be more appropriate if the participants have activities scheduled later in the evening such as a program, meeting, or press conference. If the event has a particular theme or if it is taking place in a certain geographic region, you may consider having a theme party. For example, when the National Football League Pro Bowl is held in Hawaii, often there is an official Pro Bowl Welcome Luau. Theme parties in New Orleans during the Super Bowl may resemble the laid-back and relaxed culture of the area.

Concession Operations

Concession operations over the years have changed dramatically. Sport venues in the 1970s and 1980s ran a concession operation that included fare such as hot dogs, hamburgers, french fries, popcorn, and other snacks and beverages, including alcohol. Today's sport venues offer more upscale amenities including sit-down restaurants, bars, and themed concession stands that offer meals such as Mexican, Chinese, Italian, or local favorites. For example, Oriole Park at Camden Yards in Baltimore offers Maryland crab cakes and a specialty concession named after Oriole great Boog Powell called Boog's BBQ. In 2011, the Orioles spent $11 million adding new concession foods with Maryland flavor such as crab enchiladas, beer-battered soft shell crabs, Little Italy meatball subs, Old Bay wings, and Berger cookies (Kartalija 2011).

The need and sophistication of concession operations will vary based on the type of event being planned. Youth sporting events may run a fairly simple concession setup operated by volunteers such as players' parents, whereas larger professional events will include all the amenities of the concessions at some of the newer professional sport venues. Local, state, and federal health and safety regulations should be consulted when food is served at any event, and vendors should have the proper licensing (Fried 2010). Event planners should take into account the following factors regarding concession operations during the initial site visit to the sport venue:

- How many spectators are expected to attend the event?
- How sophisticated a concession operation does your event require?
- How many points of purchase are there in the sport venue?
- Is the concession operation outsourced to a vendor (e.g., Aramark), or does the sport venue operate concessions in-house?

- What are the policies in terms of participants bringing food into the sport venue?
- As the event organizer, what is your role in concessions?
- Will you need to train concession workers?
- Will alcohol be served at the event? If so, do you have the necessary permits for the sale of alcohol? Is it appropriate to sell alcohol at the event based on the age of event attendees?
- Are concession operations a considerable source of revenue for your event, or is it simply an added service for participants and spectators?

It is important to understand the role that food will play at your event (deLisle 2009). If the sporting event is an all-day affair with many spectators, food may be a primary attraction during certain periods of the day. In contrast, an event with few spectators may receive little to no traffic at the concession stands.

Hospitality Services

Hospitality entails a relationship between a host and a guest. Because of the integration of sport and tourism, hospitality is an important component of event management. Since many events travel from market to market, the relationship between the host organization and the guest becomes increasingly important. Using hospitality as a means, destination marketing organizations (DMOs) such as sports commissions and convention and visitors bureaus (CVBs) spend considerable time cultivating relationships with event rights holders. For example, upon arriving at the host destination, event planners often find a gift in their hotel rooms that was provided by the DMO. During the site visit to the host destination, event planners are often "wined and dined" by the sports commission or CVB.

Sporting events such as golf tournaments have hospitality tents that are often sold to corporate sponsors such as Coca-Cola or Budweiser. Since 1993, MSG Promotions has been the exclusive corporate hospitality marketing and management company for the United States Golf Association's

U.S. Open Championship (MSG Promotions 2012). During the 1998 U.S. Open Championship at Torrey Pines Golf Course in San Diego, California, the U.S. Golf Association made more than $20 million on hospitality tents. The tents sold at various price points, including $110,000 for the Torrey Pines Village 30-by-30-foot (9 by 9 m) condo tents and $210,000 for the 40-by-40-foot (12 by 12 m) Ocean Village structure (Sweet 2008).

Many sport venues sell hospitality suites as part of their luxury ticketing inventory. For example, for $300 per game you can sit in the Lexus Presidents Club Suite at Nationals Park in Washington, D.C., home to Major League Baseball's Washington Nationals. The Presidents Club is an exclusive members-only club featuring all-inclusive food and beverages, MVP parking, and access to the closest seats to home plate. The benefits of purchasing include a complimentary chef's table buffet, a complimentary draft beer and house wine, a red-carpet rewards program, VIP parking, an invitation to view batting practice from the field, exclusive club programming, and autograph sessions with the players (Washington Nationals 2012).

WASTE MANAGEMENT SERVICES

A key factor of servicing an event is a sustainable program for waste management. One of the largest waste management providers is Waste Management, Inc., a $13 million Houston-based company that provides waste collection, transfer, recycling, resource recovery, and disposal services. The bid requirements for many events require host organizations to submit an environmental plan at the time of their bid submission. The International Olympic Committee (IOC) requires all host organizations to submit a candidature file as early as seven years before the event that highlights their plans for sustainability in terms of waste and other environmental issues such as conservation of carbon emissions, energy, water, materials, biodiversity, and overall environmental impact. The issue of managing waste systems is an important factor not only from an environmental perspective but also in terms of service quality at the venue. The proper placement of waste removal systems and a comprehensive plan for servicing these sites are imperative. For events such as the Olympic Games, environmental issues such as waste management are important because they influence the legacy of the Games. You can learn more about issues such as sustainability for the 2012 Olympic Games by visiting Learning Legacy (http://learninglegacy.london2012.com), a website that shares knowledge and lessons learned during the construction project of the Olympic and Paralympic Games.

CUSTODIAL SERVICES

Cleaning before and after a sporting event is a critical service factor. Depending on the type of event, custodial services may be outsourced or event planners may use staff or volunteers. Most of the time when an event planner contracts with a sport venue, the terms of the contract specify the requirements for keeping the venue clean. Some areas of a venue that may require cleaning include the following:

- Stadium and arena seating areas
- Stadium and arena concourses
- Concession areas
- Luxury seating areas
- Bathrooms and portable toilets
- Press box
- Parking lots, especially if the event includes tailgating
- Event field surfaces, especially after large mega-events that allow confetti

TRANSPORTATION SERVICES

Events that involve moving guests from one location to another can be a major challenge and may require various modes of transportation, including transit via air (e.g., private charters, commercial airplanes, helicopter), land (e.g., motor coaches, school buses, private cars, vans, limousines), water (barges, private boat charters, cruise ships), and trains. Allen (2009) suggests that event planners extend the same care and detail to guest enjoyment in the transfer phase as during the actual event. Transportation should be taken into account when budgeting for the event because there can be a number of hidden costs.

A key factor to consider is that transportation modes can be the first point of contact with the event for many attendees. Most events will employ some form of outsourcing. For example, many events require charter buses from companies such as Trailways, Mears, and local motor-coach fleets. Parking is another service that is often outsourced. For example, parking for golf tournaments such as the Masters and U.S. Open is outsourced to Country Club Services, a New Jersey company that offers a broad range of services, including valet parking, parking directing, shuttle and van operations, traffic control, and parking lot organization and security (Country Club Services 2012).

Allen (2009) suggests that event managers consider the following questions in regard to transportation for an event:

- When and where will transportation be required for each event element?
- What are the various transfer options? Event planners should look at conventional and convenience modes and consider creative transfer options as well.
- What are the choices for various routes?
- How can the transfer experience be enhanced? For example, can you include food and beverages during the transfer or some form of entertainment?
- How can you reduce the stress and confusion for passengers such as parking congestion and overnight airport stays?
- Where will the majority of your guests be departing from, and how can this affect their arrival time at the event destination?
- What is the estimated number of cars or arriving vehicles?

- Will factors such as rush hour traffic or other major events taking place at the same time have an impact on the event start time?
- Where is the closest parking to the event venue?

When considering transportation and parking factors, Goldblatt (2011) provides the following suggestions:

- Parking attendants help alleviate the problem of hazardous drivers who don't follow parking lot rules.
- Parking attendants can help separate unaware pedestrians and unsafe drivers.
- Signs should be posted in the parking lot to inform drivers to note the location of their vehicles. Event attendees often forget where they parked.
- Shuttle buses should be enclosed in the event of inclement weather.
- Ensure the parking area has sufficient lighting because dimly lit parking lots tend to promote criminal activity.
- Have a drop-off area for children where they can be safely secured so they do not run off while parents are loading or unloading the car.

LIGHTING

Lighting for sporting events is a critical component of safety and can even contribute to revenue generation (Sawyer 2005). For example, the addition of lights at Wrigley Field in Chicago in 1988 allowed the team to sell tickets and generate additional revenues from fans who could not make day games. Melbourne Cricket Ground is the largest stadium in Australia and holds the world record for the highest light towers at any sporting venue (Tabi 2010). The stadium has six light towers that stand approximately 75 meters high (equivalent to a 24-story building), and the power to the light towers is supplied off an 11-kilovolt electrical ring main into a transformer inside the base of each tower (MCG 2012).

Lighting needs for televised events are also important. According to Jeroen Jansen, Philips Lighting's general manager for Southern Africa, light represents less than 1 percent of many stadium and arena budgets, but it determines 99 percent of the effect seen on TV (van Mierlo and van der Laarse 2010). Illumination levels for baseball and softball fields are 20 foot-candles for the outfield and 30 foot-candles for the infield. The lighting requirements for other team sport fields such as field hockey, football, lacrosse, rugby, and soccer are at minimum 30-foot candles (Sawyer 2005).

VENDOR RELATIONSHIPS

Developing strong relationships with vendors is an important factor in event management. Event managers may interact with a number of different vendors depending on the type of event. Following is a partial list of the many vendors that event planners may form relationships with:

- Concession vendors
- Marketing and advertising vendors
- Media vendors
- Ticketing vendors
- Office supply vendors
- Industrial supply vendors (e.g., companies selling bathroom and cleaning supplies)
- Transportation vendors (e.g., rental car agencies, airlines, and charter bus companies)
- Accommodation vendors (e.g., hotels and motels)

Using outside vendors can reduce, but not totally eliminate, an organization's legal responsibility for safety and quality (deLisle 2009). However, event planners should be careful when selecting vendors because the reputation of the event will be affected by the products and services provided by the vendor. As some marketing studies suggest, often the relationship with the vendor firm's key contact employees is stronger than the relationship with the firm itself (Bendapudi and Leone 2002; Gwinner, Gremler, and Bitner 1998).

Event planners should continually work to cultivate the relationship with their vendors. In cases where the sporting event moves from place to place, the event planner should utilize the resources provided by the local sports commission and convention and visitors bureau. Often, these organizations are helpful in connecting the event planner with local vendors such as transportation providers or airlines that frequently fly into the local airport. When vendors change frequently, one of the challenges facing the event planner is the need to constantly educate the vendor about the needs for the event. However, when the event planner has cultivated a strong and lasting relationship, the vendor is able to provide a higher quality of service.

EVENT FACILITY SELECTION

Although event managers are not required to be experts, there is a fundamental need for them to understand certain components of sport facilities. This is especially true during the bidding process. During this time, the event manager may need to interact with the venue's facility manager regarding any necessary requirements and specifications for the event. For example, issues such as setup and teardown, equipment needs, temperature controls, field and crowd safety, dressing rooms, and field surfaces may require discussion. Fried (2010) suggests that facility managers must consider the following factors when selecting a site for a sport event:

- A review of feasibility studies (economic and political impact) for the site
- Permits (lease, license, or letter) and whether they can be obtained
- Site information (from environmental issues to historical concerns)
- Regulations (e.g., building codes and health ordinances)
- Community involvement
- Affordability and decision to lease or purchase facility
- Easements (will the neighbors have the right to cross the property)

- Zoning (cluster, flood plain, open space) issues
- Restrictive covenants that may limit who can purchase the land or how it can be used
- Aesthetic value of the site and whether there are beautiful views; many of the professional stadiums built today are designed for aesthetic beauty and face the skyline of the respective city
- Recreational opportunities; a criticism of some new football stadiums is that they do not benefit the community because they are used only for a handful of home games

Most likely the event planner will have one primary contact for each sport venue. However, there may be times when the event planner interacts with a wide variety of people. In the case of large sport facilities, several crews are responsible for functions ranging from ticketing, marketing, game operations, and mechanical and janitorial services (Fried 2010). Every event should have a facility manager on call for issues where maintenance or facility operations are required. In addition, the facility manager should be readily available in the case of an emergency, security issue, or life-threatening illness.

One of the key issues for the event manager is determining the physical requirements of the event. An important question is how many venues will be needed for the sporting event. In addition, the event planner must interact with the facility manager of the venue or venues to specify issues related to the field surface, seating requirements, sponsor signage, broadcasting facilities and equipment, and concession needs. In addition, many events also require food and beverage functions such as sit-down dinners, exhibit space, meeting space, and registration booths. The event planner will need to specify how much food is required for the sit-down dinner, the number of exhibits, the number of rooms for meetings, and the number of registration booths. These types of physical requirements should be written in the request for proposal (RFP) submitted to the sport venue during or before the initial site visit.

Restroom Facilities

The number of restrooms and hand-washing stations required for an event will vary according to local and state sanitary codes based on attendance levels (deLisle 2009). Some events may require additional portable restrooms to meet these requirements. Event planners should pay particular attention to several factors concerning restrooms during the initial site visit. First, is there a regular plan for cleaning restrooms? Cleanliness of the physical environment of the facility is an important factor for consumers. Are the restrooms well lit for evening events? The safety of event attendees should be of primary concern, and restrooms in dimly lit locations can be troublesome. Do restrooms meet ADA requirements for accessibility, and how far do event attendees need to walk to find the nearest restroom? Is there signage that points event attendees to the nearest restroom? Events that attract families will need changing tables or separate family restrooms.

Traffic Flow Considerations

The flow of traffic can be considered from two standpoints. First, as attendees enter the event in passenger cars, how will traffic flow into and out of the sport venue? Second, traffic flow refers to how you will set up the sport venue or points of purchase within the venue for the flow of spectators or participants. A number of factors must be considered in terms of passenger traffic. Some events will outsource parking services to help with the influx of traffic to the sport venue. In cases where parking is paid, the event planner should have a plan for moving traffic in and out smoothly with little interruption. Parking attendants should wear brightly colored uniforms so they are easily identifiable, and attendants should wear an apron or be housed in a booth for managing cash payments. Parking attendants should be provided with colored cones so they can reroute traffic before and after the event. Signage is also an important safety tool and should be readily visible and easy to read. Parking attendants should have two-way radio communication and be available to assist parking patrons with disabilities. Depending on the size of the event, local law enforcement can be contracted to assist with traffic flow. In some cases, major highway ramps may need to be blocked, and certain intersections will require police officers to assist with directing traffic.

There are many strategies for dealing with the flow of spectator traffic in the sport venue. Major intersections within the sport venue should be identified during the initial site inspection. Security should be in place to assist with intersections where sport participants come into contact with spectators. For example, before the race, jockeys riding in the Kentucky Derby at Churchill Downs walk from the dressing room to the paddock and must cross through spectator traffic along the way. Popular golfers on the PGA Tour also intermingle with spectators and often require security as they walk from one hole to the next.

Event planners should develop a plan for dealing with pedestrian traffic and crowd control. Crowd control is especially important during mega-events, championships, and rivalry games where spectators may rush onto the playing surface. The pedestrian traffic plan should outline specific areas within the sport venue that may require signage, cones, or stanchions as well as areas that may need to be roped off. Concession and ticketing lines often use stanchions to assist with traffic flow. Figure 11.2 is a sample parking and traffic flow map for sporting events.

Seating

The average sporting event lasts somewhere between one and three hours, so event planners should take into consideration the comfort of consumers. Of course, some sporting events such

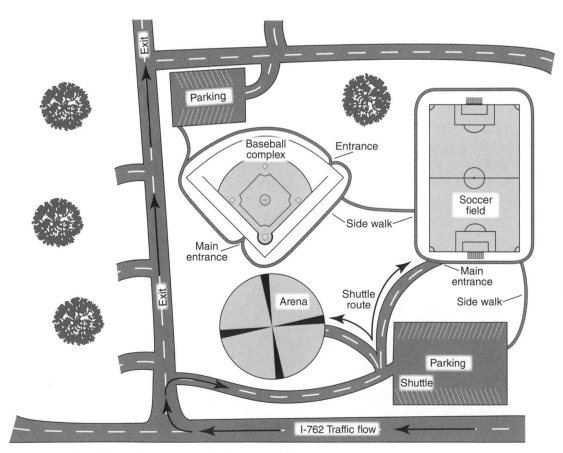

■ **Figure 11.2** Sample parking and traffic flow map for sporting events.

as all-day youth tournaments may last longer. Representatives of professional sport venues recognize the importance of seating, and many professional teams in the United States now have sport-specific stadiums. Coates (2008) reported the following statistics for stadium construction of professional teams in the United States between 1990 and 2008:

- Major League Baseball: 19 new stadiums and 3 under construction

- National Football League: 17 new stadiums; major renovations to 4 others; 3 under construction; and 4 more projects at various stages of planning and negotiations

- National Basketball Association: Opened more than two-thirds of its 30 arenas; at least three NBA franchises actively seeking new arenas

In addition, Savino (2011) reported a total of 12 soccer-specific stadiums before the end of the 2011 regular season playing host to 13 Major League Soccer teams. Many colleges, universities, and high schools have also upgraded their facilities and built new sport venues.

Seating is an important component of many new stadiums. For spectator comfort, almost all the seats at these new professional sport venues are wider and have chair backs and drink holders. Beyond general admission and reserved seating options, most stadiums and arenas also offer luxury and club seating with upscale amenities such as bars, bathrooms, televisions, upscale furniture, and full-service food and beverage menus with servers. Many of these luxury suites offer excellent sight lines for watching all the action on the field. The Dallas Cowboys Stadium has 300 suites over five levels. All the seats are on rails rather than bolted into the concrete. During the regular season, the seats are 22 inches (56 cm) wide; when more seats are required, those seats are removed and 18-inch (46 cm) seats are installed. In addition, the stadium has six party decks on each level of the end zones for standing-room-only crowds to gather (Barron 2009).

All new stadiums are required to comply with the Americans with Disabilities Act (ADA). The ADA requires new stadiums to be accessible to people with disabilities so they, their families, and their friends can enjoy equal access to entertainment, recreation, and leisure (U.S. Department of Justice 2012). Most stadiums and arenas also hire ushers who help spectators find their seats, answer questions, enforce seating policies, ensure people are sitting in the correct seats, wipe down dirty and wet seats, transport people in wheelchairs, and generally serve as friendly hosts. However, not all sporting events are held at new stadiums and arenas. For example, a beach volleyball tournament does not offer the amenities of new facilities. Transportable or temporary seating may be needed for such events. In addition, event planners should take into account the following factors:

- Will you offer tiered seating (e.g., general admission, reserved, box seats) with different price points, or are all seats the same with one general price?

- Where is a safe place for ADA seating that still allows people sitting in these areas to be close to the action on the field or court?

- Where can you place signage to help spectators find their seats?

- What are some ways to make the seating more comfortable?

- What safety considerations need to be taken into account? For example, spectators, especially children or the elderly, could fall from older mobile bleacher seats.

Sound Considerations

Sound-related factors should be considered throughout the entire event planning process and specifically evaluated during meetings with event facility managers. Although some sounds can be controlled by the facility manager, other sounds cannot. According to Fried (2010), recreational activity sounds are caused by normal facility use and cannot be controlled. One type of recreational activity sound is airborne sound, which is caused by facility users and may include whistles, voices, music, and cheers. Structure-borne sounds are those caused by direct impact with some part of the facility's structure, such as a bouncing basketball that vibrates and then is transmitted in the air. Mechanical sounds are produced by the machinery used to operate the facility and can be controlled by a facility manager. Thus, it is important that event planners meet with facility managers during the initial planning stages and provide details concerning their needs for each facility space. For example, if the event requires space for a quiet and focused board meeting, this should be mentioned in the initial meeting so that a quiet room can be scheduled.

There are a number of factors event planners should consider in terms of managing the sounds of a sporting event.

- What are some potential recreational sounds that may occur at the event, and what is the most appropriate course of action for dealing with them? For example, consider an event being planned at a venue next to a train track or an outdoor event next to a busy highway. What can be done to reduce the impact of the sound of a train whistle, passing trucks, or car horns? Some options include asking the train company if the trains can run during off-event times and not scheduling events during rush hour traffic.
- What are the needs in terms of a sound system for the sporting event, and does the sport venue have an appropriate system already in place?
- Does the sport venue provide all the necessary sound equipment needed for your event?
- Do some sport venues for your sporting event require portable sound systems? For example, some outdoor events require bullhorns or portable speakers and wireless microphones.
- What is the quality of the sound system at each sport venue in which your event will take place?
- What is the compatibility of your sound equipment with that of the venue?
- Who will be responsible for playing music and making any necessary public address announcements during the course of the event?

Sport marketers commonly use music to enhance the atmosphere of the stadium or arena, and it excites crowd emotion. Spectators often sing and dance in their seats when music is played. The public address system is used to announce event action and to make other types of announcements. Most sporting events in the United States begin with the national anthem and often include school or team alma mater or fight songs. The music at some events arises from crowds singing songs, anthems, and chants. Many cities have a noise ordinance that takes into account decibel levels and times for general "reasonableness" when it comes to loud music and sound (Manning 2012). These ordinances vary from locality to locality and can be a challenge for late-evening games that go well into the night.

Hotel Availability

As already discussed, the merger of sport and tourism is a considerable factor in the sport event industry. As more events travel from one destination to another, the participants and spectators follow along and are in need of a place to stay. Recent estimates suggest that event tourism is the fastest-growing sector of the leisure-travel market, and the demand for room nights now surpasses that for business conventions (Chalip 2004). Research by the World Travel and Tourism Council (2009) reports that travel and tourism is expected to contribute to 9.5 percent of gross domestic product (GDP) by 2019. A study by *SportsEvents* magazine of event rights holders who participate in events that move from one destination to another report that athletes spent $705 per competition in 2011 (O'Connor 2012).

Negotiating hotel contracts and room blocks is an important duty for sport event planners during site selection. Foster (2006) provides the following guidelines for negotiating hotel contracts:

- Ensure the room block is adequate to cover the needs for the event but not so large as to trigger attrition charges if attendees do not use all the guest rooms reserved in the block.
- Calculate as best possible how many participants will stay the entirety of the event,

how many local attendees will not need guest rooms, and whether attendees may stay at other hotels.

- The contract should specify the guaranteed room rates if the contract is signed one or two years before the event.

- Include a clause in the contract specifying that all rooms occupied by event attendees will count toward performance clauses based on room pick-up, regardless of the rate paid.

- Specify how reservations will be made by attendees (e.g., individual reservations, housing bureau, rooming list) and individual deposit requirements.

- Find out if there is an early departure fee if guests check out early.

- Ensure that the hotel will honor all reservations guaranteed by event attendees. You may have a public relations fiasco if the hotel decides to "walk" one or more of your attendees (i.e., not honor the reservation and kick the attendee to the street).

- Include a cutoff date in the hotel contract. The cutoff date specifies the last date the hotel will hold out of its inventory the guest rooms blocked for your event.

- Include an overbooking clause in the contract, thus protecting you from the hotel's selling any of your room block before the cutoff date.

- Carefully read the wording for the attrition clause that many hotels include in a contract. Attrition is the difference between the actual number of guest rooms picked up and the number of guest rooms or minimum amount of revenue guaranteed by the event rights holder in the contract.

Many factors related to hotel accommodation must be taken into account during the planning stages of the event. One of the toughest challenges is estimating the number of hotel rooms required. It is always helpful when you have a history of conducting the event at a certain destination because you can look at prior room pick-ups. However, this information is not available when the event is being held at a new destination.

Depending on your room block requirements for the event, you may be able to use one host hotel. The advantage of using one host hotel is that all your event attendees are confined to one location, and it is much easier to manage the event and convey information. However, when the room block exceeds the capacity for using one hotel, you will need to include additional hotels in your room block. The following are considerations when using multiple hotels:

- The distance between the hotels and the convenience and cost of transporting attendees

- The difference in cost between the hotels (the cost to event attendees may rise or fall depending on the types of hotel property you choose)

- The level of service and amenities provided by each hotel

CUSTOMER SERVICE

A service is an act, deed, performance, or effort (Berry 1980). Event managers work in a service-related industry, and the quality of service provided during the event can be a competitive advantage. A sporting event can be described as an intangible experience that must be carefully crafted by event planners, and each interaction with the customer must be analyzed. The service experience for active participants and spectators begins the moment they depart from their home residence and lasts until they arrive back home. The participants and spectators will judge the quality of the experience based on the difference between their expectations of what will be delivered at the event and the actual service. If their overall experience at the sporting event exceeds their expectations, then it could be said that a high-quality experience was delivered. In contrast, service failures, which are breakdowns in service delivery, can cast the event in a negative light. In October 2007, one runner died, 49 were hospitalized, and many others were denied the opportunity to cross the finish line at the Chicago Marathon because of 88-degree heat (31 degrees Celsius) and a lack of water and sport drinks. During the planning stages, it is vitally important to consider every area where the event process may break down and suffer a service failure such as the one just described.

The service quality delivered at an event is important because higher-quality service produces more satisfied customers who return to the event in subsequent years. Shonk and Chelladurai (2008) suggest that quality in event sport tourism is measured in terms of access, accommodation, venue, and outcome. Access quality refers to the accessibility of the destination, the sport venue, and the hotel. Accommodation quality refers to such service factors as customers' perceptions of the physical environment of the hotel, their contact with hotel employees, and the value the hotel provides. The physical environment at the sport venue, interactions with employees such as ushers and ticket takers, and the value of various pricing options are important components of venue quality. Outcome quality refers to the process of the contest (e.g., quality of officiating and public address announcements) and the actual outcome in terms of wins and losses.

Customer service must be a primary initiative of everyone involved in hosting a sporting event. Many events have customer service areas where event attendees can ask questions and have their problems solved. Event planners should develop a comprehensive plan for delivering high-quality service before the event and then communicate their expectations of what constitutes superior service to all event employees and volunteers. One of the challenges event planners face is controlling the level of service. For example, an event planner may have little control over the service delivered by a vendor that has been outsourced to serve concessions at the sport venue. However, human resource initiatives such as volunteer training along with clearly communicating service expectations can help solve some of these issues.

AWARDS CEREMONIES

Awards ceremonies are usually celebrated at the conclusion of an event. Championship events are notorious for having awards ceremonies. For example, the NCAA celebrated the University of Alabama's Football Bowl Series national championship win in 2012 with a trophy presentation at the 50-yard line after their win against Louisiana State University. Awards ceremonies may take place after a game or may be incorporated into a more formal event held at a hotel or other venue that includes dinner; entertainment; and plaques, trophies, scholarships, gifts, or cash awards for honorees. Event planners should consider the following factors when planning an awards ceremony:

- Do you have a fair and organized process for determining award winners?
- What technical equipment (e.g., wireless microphone, video) will you need for the awards ceremony?
- Are invitations necessary, and if so, who do you send them to?
- Will you invite the media to the awards ceremony? If so, what arrangements must be made to accommodate the media?
- What will award recipients receive (e.g., trophy, certificate, gift) during the ceremony?
- Who will serve as the master of ceremonies?
- How will you honor past award winners?

SUMMARY

Event planners are responsible for coordinating the logistics of a sporting event, which entails making sure the right people, equipment, and services are available in the right place and at the right time. An event timeline, starting with a research phase and followed by event planning, coordination, and evaluation phases, is a helpful tool for coordinating the logistics. Some of the logistical considerations that event planners must take into account include facilities, ticket sales, food and beverage operations, hospitality, waste management, transportation, custodial services, working with vendors, restrooms, traffic flow, seating, customer service, hotels, sound, and awards ceremonies.

LEARNING ACTIVITIES

1. Using the research and event planning phases as described in this chapter, please design a new and creative sporting event. The event may include the introduction of a new sport. Give the event a name, and describe the various activities that make up the event.

2. This chapter describes the logistical considerations of a sporting event, including facilities, ticket sales, food and beverage operations, hospitality, waste management, transportation, custodial services, working with vendors, restrooms, traffic flow, seating, customer service, hotels, sound, and awards ceremonies. Search for an article on the Internet about one of these logistical operations, and summarize the article in one double-spaced page.

REFERENCES

Allen, I. 2009. *Event planning: The ultimate guide to successful meetings, corporate events, fundraising galas, conferences, conventions, incentives and other special events.* 2nd ed. Mississauga, ON: Wiley.

Barron, D. 2009. $1.15 billion stadium gives the Cowboys braggin' rights. *Houston Chronicle.* [Online]. August 21. Available: www.chron.com/sports/texans/article/1-15-billion-stadium-gives-the-Cowboys-1730035.php.

Bendapudi, N., and R.P. Leone. 2002. Managing business-to-business customer relationships following key contact employee turnover in a vendor firm. *Journal of Marketing* 66:83-101.

Berry, L. 1980. Services marketing is different. *Business 30* (May/June): 24-29.

Carlisle, K.G. 2006. Taming the registration beast. In *Professional meeting management: Comprehensive strategies for meetings, conventions and events,* ed. G.C. Ramsborg, 359-374. Dubuque, IA: Kendall/Hunt.

Chalip, L. 2004. Beyond impact: A general model for sport event leverage. In *Sport tourism: Interrelationships, impacts and issues,* ed. B.W. Ritchie and D. Adair, 226-252. Tonawanda, NY: Channel View Publications.

Coates, D. 2008. A closer look at stadium subsidies. *The American.* [Online]. April 28. Available: www.american.com/archive/2008/april-04-08/a-closer-look-at-stadium-subsidies.

Country Club Services. 2012. About. Available: www.countryclubservicesinc.com/about.php.

deLisle, L.J. 2009. *Creating special events.* Champaign, Illinois: Sagamore.

Foster, J.S. 2006. Facility contracts in the meetings industry. In *Professional meeting management: Comprehensive strategies for meetings, conventions and events,* ed. G.C. Ramsborg, 627-648. Dubuque, IA: Kendall/Hunt.

Fried, G. 2010. *Managing sport facilities.* 2nd ed. Champaign, IL: Human Kinetics.

Goldblatt, J. 2011. *Special events: A new generation and the next frontier.* Hoboken, NJ: Wiley.

Gwinner, K.P., D.D. Gremler, and M.J. Bitner. 1998. Relational benefits in services industries: The customer's perspective. *Journal of the Academy of Marketing Science* 26 (2): 101-114.

Kartalija, J. 2011. Camden Yards gets 5-star dining for O's games. CBS Baltimore. March 23. Available: http://baltimore.cbslocal.com/2011/03/23/camden-yards-gets-five-star-dining-for-os-games.

Manning, A. 2010. Noise ordinances can be bigger headaches for communities than noise itself. *Columbus Dispatch.* [Online]. April 23. Available: www.dispatch.com/content/stories/local/2012/04/23/noise-ordinances-can-be-big-headaches-for-communities.html.

MCG. 2012. MCG light towers. Available: www.mcg.org.au/The%20MCG%20Stadium/Facts%20and%20Figures/Light%20Towers.aspx.

MSG Promotions. 2012. Events portfolio. Available: www.msgpromotions.com/MSG/events.html.

Myhill, M., and J. Phillips. 2006. Determine the success of your meeting through evaluation. In *Professional meeting management: Comprehensive strategies for meetings, conventions and events,* ed. G.C. Ramsborg, 17-48. Dubuque, IA: Kendall/Hunt Publishing.

O'Connor, T. 2012. 2012 market report: Trends & economic impact. *SportsEvents* (March): 25-32.

Savino, C. 2011. MLS still primary revenue source for soccer-specific stadiums. SB Nation. June 26. Available: www.brotherlygame.com/2011/6/26/2245290/mls-still-primary-revenue-source-for-soccer-specific-stadiums.

Sawyer, T.H. 2005. *Facility design and management for health, fitness, physical activity, recreation, and sport facility development*. Champaign, IL: Sagamore.

Shock, P.J. 2006. Food and beverage arrangements. In *Professional meeting management: Comprehensive strategies for meetings, conventions and events*, ed. G.C. Ramsborg, 399-417. Dubuque, IA: Kendall/Hunt.

Shonk, D.J. 2011. Event logistics. In *The encyclopedia of sports management and marketing*, ed. L.E. Swayne and M. Dodds, 482-484. Thousand Oaks, CA: Sage.

Shonk, D.J., and P. Chelladurai. 2008. Service quality, satisfaction and intent to return in event sport tourism. *Journal of Sport Management* 22:587-602.

Sweet, D. 2008. Hospitality tents a bonanza for U.S. Open: Corporations will fork over $20 million for a top-flight experience. NBCNews.com. June 12. Available: www.msnbc.msn.com/id/25104918/ns /business-sports_biz/t/hospitality-tents-bonanza -us-open.

Tabi. 2010. Top 10 world's largest sport stadiums. The Wondrous. April 2. Available: http://thewondrous.com/ top-10-worlds-largest-sports-stadiums.

U.S. Department of Justice. 2012. Accessible stadiums. Available: www.ada.gov/stadium.txt.

van Mierlo, M., and S. van der Laarse. 2010. Philips' sports lighting at South African stadiums set to enhance viewing experience. June 10. Available: www.newscenter. philips.com/main/standard/news/press/2010/20100610_ wc_africa.wpd.

Washington Nationals. 2012. Premium seating. Available: http://washington.nationals.mlb.com/was/ticketing/ premium_seating.jsp.

World Travel and Tourism Council. 2009. Travel & tourism economic impact: Executive summary. March.

CHAPTER 12

Event-Day Management

Chapter Objectives

After completing the chapter, the reader should be able to do the following:

- Understand the process of managing an event and what needs to take place to ensure a good event day.

- Appreciate the importance of communication in staging sporting events.

- Understand the challenges related to managing staff, participants, spectators, and sponsors.

- Develop a plan for managing staff, participants, spectators, and sponsors.

Nicole Averso is an event presentation and production assistant with the Kansas City Royals, where she is responsible for game scripts and pregame production. Before her work with the Royals, Nicole was a marketing assistant with the York Revolution Professional Baseball Club. Her duties with the Revolution included managing on-field promotions, pre- and postgame activities, and social media as well as helping to create marketing and promotional campaigns. Nicole has also worked with the Washington Nationals as an entertainment and production trainee and with the Washington Redskins as a corporate hospitality intern.

Q: Your job title suggests you are responsible for event presentation and production. So, what are your primary duties and responsibilities?

A: I develop and obtain all the necessary public address announcements and scripts for games and events. During a typical game, I run and help produce our pregame show with our in-game host. I also assist in executing pregame ceremonies, which include the presentation of colors by a color or honor guard, the singing of the national anthem, and the throwing of the ceremonial first pitch. We have three in-game entertainment groups that I work closely with, and I help oversee their movements during a game or event.

Q: Tell us about the logistics of one of your events, and describe in detail the planning that went into making this event happen.

A: Each event, whether it's a small press conference, a game, or an all-day event, is treated and approached in the same manner. First, each part of the event is planned and then broken down into very detailed time segments. From there, transitions on how to get from each phase to the next are added to the appropriate spots. Every moving part of an event has a distinctive beginning, middle, and end. Once the initial planning is completed, we hold rehearsals. We never show something without first running through it and executing it correctly. Rehearsals are also important because sometimes phases need to be changed around to ensure the event runs smoothly and projects the result we're aiming for. After rehearsals, we finalize our event's rundown. During this time, each person is assigned to certain segments, and we discuss the duties for that specific part. Finally, once we've gone over each phase and transition, we execute our event.

Event day is often the culmination of extensive planning and anticipation. For the event manager, event day typically starts early and ends very late because a number of significant tasks have to be managed in order to stage a successful sporting event. The event manager has to consider timing and coordination of event setup, the event itself, and event takedown. He also has to work with event staff, facility staff, and event organizers or sanctioning bodies in addition to dealing with participants, officials, spectators, and sponsors.

The number of tasks that need to be accomplished can be overwhelming; however, good event managers can make event day run more smoothly if they plan, anticipate, delegate, train and rehearse, and communicate.

• Plan: Detailed plans of action need to be in place for how everything will be accomplished throughout the event day. Address each contingency, and make sure everyone knows how to handle their tasks.

• Anticipate: Event managers need to put substantial thought into what could happen during the course of an event and have a realistic understanding of what it will take to execute the event. Also, things typically take longer than expected and consume more resources than expected. Make sure you anticipate any delays or overruns, and schedule buffers into the event so that subsequent activities will not be delayed.

• Delegate: Good event managers understand that although they may be responsible for everything, they cannot do everything themselves. They need to entrust staff to accomplish certain tasks. Delegating tasks and responsibilities also empowers staff to make decisions, freeing management to pursue other opportunities.

• Train and rehearse: The manager's job is to make sure the staff have a clear understanding of what their responsibilities are and to guide them through their tasks. When possible, do dry runs of various activities to ensure they can be run smoothly.

• Communicate: The event manager must be able to coordinate with multiple staff to make sure everyone knows what is happening and when things need to happen. Changes occur constantly throughout the day, so event managers need to

continually update their staff about any modifications or adjustments.

Fortunately, event managers have a number of tools they can use to ensure everything happens as it is supposed to happen and when it is supposed to happen.

• Schedules and checklists: Keep lists of everything that needs to happen before, during, and after the event. Checklists often include the task, location, and person responsible (see table 12.1).

• Contact lists: Contact lists ensure you can find the right person at the right time. Keep lists of performers, staff, or groups taking part in the event along with key contacts (table 12.2).

Delays and disorder can be disastrous when athletes and spectators are on site. Athletes don't like waiting around. Spectators don't like staring at an empty field. Although many of these delays may be short, audiences notice them and can quickly lose their enthusiasm (Supovitz 2005). As

Table 12.1 Sample Event-Day Checklist

	Person responsible	Completion time/date
PREEVENT		
Event schedules		
Contact lists		
Event rundown		
Event script		
Contingency plans		
Risk management plans		
Facility and equipment inspections		
ACCESSIBILITY		
Spectator parking controls		
Mass transportation drop-off and pick-up zones		
Access and parking for staff, officials, vendors, and VIP guests		
Disabled access and facilities		
STAFF MANAGEMENT		
Check-in and assignments		
Preevent briefing		
Communications plan and communications equipment		
Staff uniforms and clothing		
Postevent debriefing		

(continued)

(continued)

	Person responsible	Completion time/date
VOLUNTEER MANAGEMENT		
Volunteer check-in and assignments		
Volunteer briefing		
Volunteer contact assignments		
SPECTATOR MANAGEMENT		
Adequate facility entrances and exits		
Ticketing policies and procedures		
Appropriate directional signage		
Crowd control procedures		
First aid facilities and personnel		
VIP entrances and arrival arrangements		
VIP seating and accommodations		
PARTICIPANT MANAGEMENT		
Arrival arrangements for participants and officials		
Participant liaison		
Locker facilities		
Training facilities		
Postevent evaluation		
SPONSOR MANAGEMENT		
Sponsor hospitality		
Fulfillment plan		
Sponsor liaison		
Sponsor evaluation		
MEDIA		
Credentials and check-in		
Media work room		
Interview area		
Press kits		
Media seating and accommodations		

Table 12.2 Sample Contact List

Event	Group/performer	Contact
Honorary captain presentation	John Hughes	Bill Slatts
National anthem singer	University Choir	Bill Smith
Color guard	City High School ROTC	Col. Sharp
Halftime show	Slam Dunk Demons	Christine Cobb
Band	University Band	Mike Bezcal
Cheerleaders	Home Team Cheerleaders	Randy Edgar
Dance team	Superstars Dance Team	Suzy Sunshine

such, many professional teams have hired directors of entertainment to coordinate music, video, mascots, and various other activities to ensure spectators are entertained throughout the event. Timing and coordination are critical elements for running an event smoothly. To ensure everything happens on time, event managers often create additional documents that specify what has to happen at various points during the event:

• Event rundown: Document that outlines what has to happen during each stage of the event (table 12.3). The rundown includes specific times

Table 12.3 Sample Event Rundown for a Basketball Game

Time	Scoreboard	Event	Audio/Visual
11:00 a.m.		Event staff arrive	
11:30 a.m.		Game management meeting	
1:00 p.m.		Doors open	Highlight videos
1:18 p.m.	45:00	Court available for warm-ups	Prerecorded music
1:30 p.m.		Band begins playing	Band with live video
1:43 p.m.	20:00	Start 20-minute clock (TV)	
1:51 p.m.	12:00	Teams to locker rooms	Band with live video
1:52 p.m.		U.S. national anthem Honorary captain presentation	Singer P.A. announcer with live video
1:58 p.m.	5:00	Teams return	Band with live video
2:03 p.m.	0:00	Horn: teams to benches Visiting team intros Crowd build continues Home team intros Crowd build continues	P.A. announcer with live video Intro video P.A. announcer with live video Band with live video
2:06:30 p.m.		Horn: teams return to court	Tip-off video
2:07 p.m.	20:00	Tip-off	
1st half	1st TO	Cheerleaders Sponsor announcements	Band with live video P.A. announcer with logos
	2nd TO	Shootout promotion	P.A. announcer with live video
	3rd TO	Sponsored trivia question Facility commercial	P.A. announcer with logos Facility commercial
	4th TO	Cheerleaders Sponsor announcements	Band with live video P.A. announcer with logos
	5th TO	Cheerleaders	Band with live video
Halftime	15:00	Institution admissions video	Institution admissions video
	14:30	Dance routine	Recorded music with live shots
	11:00	Halftime contest	P.A. announcer with live Clear Floor video
	6:00	Teams return	Band with live video
	2:00	Warm-ups	Band with halftime stats
2nd half	1st TO	Cheerleaders Sponsor announcements	Band with live video P.A. announcer with logos
	2nd TO	Student promotion	P.A. announcer with live video
	3rd TO	Attendance quiz Sponsor announcements	P.A. announcer with logos P.A. announcer with logos
	4th TO	Cheerleaders Sponsor announcements	Band with live video P.A. announcer with logos
	5th TO	Cheerleaders	Band with live video

next to every activity that occurs during the event presentation.

• Event script: Document that outlines the information the public address announcer, host, or emcee will need to convey throughout the event. A script ensures that no details are missed.

EVENT FLOW

The flow of activities, vehicles, people (spectators, participants, and officials), and materials around the event site is one of the most important logistical areas (Bowdin et al. 1999). Consider a college football game. To the typical sports fan, it may appear that not much happens before the gates open. However, event managers have probably spent many hours orchestrating the flow of materials and personnel into the facility and to their appropriate locations within the facility. Food and drink supplies, television equipment, and staging equipment all have to be delivered to the site and then positioned. Police, security, and medical staff need access to the facility. Game staff such as ushers, concessionaires, and event staff all need to be checked in and situated. Closer to game time, media and game officials arrive and need access to special areas of the facility. Then players, coaches, and other team personnel have to be transported to the stadium. Once at the stadium, the logistical issue shifts to getting players from the locker areas to the field. On top of this, you must manage spectators entering the facility.

Lawrence and Wells (2009) suggest that managers conceptualize flow in a time sequence by asking who and what will be arriving and when they will be arriving. Further, managers should put themselves in the positions of spectators, participants, staff, emergency personnel, and vendors and walk through all the situations they may face, such as arrival, parking, check-in, setup, and so on. From this process, managers should be able to develop a natural progression from start to finish.

ALTERNATIVE PLANS

The importance of developing contingency plans is discussed in chapter 2. This also applies to the day of the event. Contingency plans should be in place to deal with anything that could disrupt the event or place participants, spectators, or personnel in harm's way. Despite how much you may plan and prepare, things can still go wrong, necessitating courses of action different from what you had planned. In these situations, it is the job of the event manager to swiftly assess the situation and be flexible enough to implement alternative plans. A cool head and a flexible attitude are essential to ensure people and property are protected and to proceed with the event with the smallest possible interruption.

A great example of flexibility comes from the 2008 Southeastern Conference men's basketball tournament. A severe storm damaged the roof of the Georgia Dome, causing the game between Mississippi State and Alabama to be delayed and the game between Georgia and Kentucky to be postponed. As the storm was damaging the facility, the facility's disaster plan kicked in. Players and coaches were sent to locker rooms to avoid falling debris, and spectators were moved from the upper seating areas of the stadium, where nuts and bolts were falling from the roof's torn section (Towers 2008). Considering the damage to the facility, organizers had to develop alternative plans for the remaining games. The games were moved to nearby Alexander Memorial Coliseum on the Georgia Tech campus, creating additional issues for television because equipment had to be moved and start times had to be changed. It also created other logistical issues since the arena held significantly fewer people; therefore new plans had to be developed to deal with ticketing and media access (Katz 2008).

COMMUNICATION

Whether the event is large or small, communication is vital. Information flow may be one of the most important elements of managing the day of the event (Solomon 2002). The purpose of a communication plan is to maximize how efficiently people communicate while minimizing unnecessary clutter (table 12.4). Two separate lines of communication need to be considered.

Table 12.4 Sample Communication List

	Radio	Contact	Cell phone number
Event staff	Channel 1	Event manager	XXX-XXXX
Facility staff	Channel 2	Stadium manager	XXX-XXXX
Security	Channel 3	Security chief	XXX-XXXX
Ushers	Channel 4	Guest services	XXX-XXXX
Medical	Channel 5	First aid center	XXX-XXXX
Maintenance	Channel 6	Maintenance shed	XXX-XXXX
Food service	Channel 7	Food services manager	XXX-XXXX
Press box	Channel 8	Sports information	XXX-XXXX

First, each unit (e.g., maintenance, concessions, security) needs to have a plan for how workers will communicate within that unit. For example, the guest services director needs to have contact with usher supervisors, who then communicate with ushers. Second, there needs to be a plan for how units can communicate with each other (e.g., guest services and maintenance) when issues arise outside their units. Consider an usher who notices a leaking pipe in the concourse. In this case, the guest services staff would need to communicate with maintenance to fix the problem.

To be effective, management and staff need to understand what needs to be communicated, who needs to be informed, and by what means they should be informed. To facilitate efficient lines of communication, each person has to know her contact person and how to reach that person (e.g., personal contact, two-way radio, cell phone). Staff must also understand how communication flow procedures may differ for routine issues than for emergency issues.

To facilitate contact between units, many events supply personnel with a list of contacts. In the case of larger events, a communication center may be utilized to facilitate the flow of information. For the 2008 Ryder Cup, each hospitality site involved a large number of different entities working together such as corporate sponsors, corporate event planners, concessionaires, guest services hosts, and the host organizing committee. To manage issues concerning hospitality, a hospitality hotline was set up. Regardless of the problem, people could call the hospitality hotline and their issue would be forwarded to the appropriate contact.

MANAGING STAFF

Given that the event manager cannot be everywhere and do everything, many responsibilities fall to the event staff. Your staff will be responsible for executing the event and will most likely have the most contact with participants, spectators, and sponsors; therefore, it is necessary to have a plan for how to manage staff on event day. Your goal should be to have knowledgeable and motivated staff dedicated to giving all your stakeholders the best experience possible.

• Arrival and check-in: Staff arrival should be scheduled to allow plenty of time for staff to receive duties, prepare for work, and acclimate themselves to the environment. Check-in serves several purposes. First, it provides a security point to control and limit access to authorized personnel. Second, check-in provides an initial contact point for informing staff of their respective responsibilities and tasks. Third, check-in procedures give management a quick account of no-shows, allowing time to make adjustments to cover the duties of anyone not present. Fourth, event managers may need to be able to account for who is present for legal or ethical reasons (Van der Wagen and Carlos 2005).

• Staff briefing: Staff briefings are meetings with staff before each shift. During the staff briefing, management reviews organizational or operational issues. In addition, management updates staff with any last-minute information or recent changes in operations. The staff briefing may include information pertaining to the following:

• Event considerations: Staff should be briefed on what will be happening during the event. An emphasis may be placed on activities that are outside normal operations such as pregame festivities, halftime events, and special guests. It may be helpful (especially for staff who interact with the public) to develop a fact sheet including basic details of the event, such as event schedules, ticket policies, emergency information, relevant statistics or facts about the event, VIP biographies, directions, policies, and facility maps.

• Facility considerations: Staff may be briefed on issues concerning the facility such as when gates open, areas that need to be avoided, and facility contacts.

• Chain-of-command: It is important for staff to identify supervisors and management and to understand authority. Each level of staff should know their immediate supervisor and understand their reporting responsibilities. Figure 12.1 shows a sample chain of command for an event using volunteers in the hospitality areas.

• Responsibility overview: Specific duties and expectations may be reviewed at this time. This information is much more important for events involving inexperienced or volunteer staff than it is for experienced, trained staff.

• Breaks and rotation: Given that many events last several hours, it is important to communicate the break schedule so that staff know when breaks are required and to ensure positions are covered during breaks.

• Problem resolution: With any event, problems or issues are likely to arise. Staff should be briefed on typical problems they may encounter and educated on how to deal with these situations. Further, staff should be informed of whom to contact in the case of unusual problems.

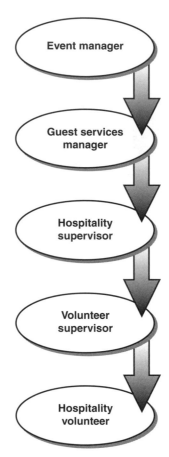

■ **Figure 12.1** Example of chain of command for a hospitality function.

• Positional assignments: Whether you are using paid staff or volunteers, each staff member has unique abilities, knowledge, and skills. The goal of the event manager is to find the ideal person for the specific job. Depending on the position, significant problems can arise when people are put in positions requiring abilities beyond their skill sets. On the other hand, when people have abilities well beyond the position they are assigned, you risk underutilizing their talents, and they may feel undervalued.

• Postevent debriefing: After the event, management and staff review the event, recognize what worked well, and identify areas of improvement for future events.

• Staff evaluation of event: Given that staff are often on the front lines of the event, they have a unique ability to identify problems. Ushers have the most direct contact with customers; therefore, they are likely to understand customer concerns. Ticket takers are most likely to understand customer ingress and bottlenecks. This type of evaluation is also beneficial when developing a risk management plan because staff working with customers or on the event floor are more likely to encounter facility issues or operational issues needing attention. Wolf and Wolf (2005) provide a list of tips for staffing success.

- Consider your staff when scheduling. Make shifts short and manageable.
- Schedule staff meetings before the event and during setup.
- Identify your best staff, and put them in positions of contact with the public.
- Overstaff. Make sure you have more than you need.
- Treat your staff with courtesy and respect.

MANAGING SPECTATORS

A common mistake of inexperienced event managers is to assume that once a spectator buys a ticket and the money has been received, the job is finished. However, good event managers realize that spectators require care throughout their experience. Your goal should be to give your spectators a satisfying and memorable time. You want your spectators to leave the event wanting to attend again and telling others to attend.

Customer Service

Numerous benefits are associated with providing excellent customer service. Primarily, good customer service helps you retain customers, increases positive word of mouth, and can differentiate your event from the competition (Lovelock and Wright 2002).

To provide good customer service, it is important to make customer service part of your organization's mission. Management must understand customers' needs and expectations, make meeting those needs a priority, and demonstrate a commitment to providing superior service. Frontline staff, who are more likely to come in contact with customers, should be trained and rewarded for providing good customer service. For example, in 2009 the Los Angeles Angels were named the most fan-friendly team in the NFL, NBA, NHL, and MLB. According to vice president of communications Tim Mead, this was possible because the team prioritized fan satisfaction by providing courteous service; affordable pricing; and a clean, safe, family-friendly environment (Saxon 2009). Similarly, the Somerset Patriots baseball team has been one of the most successful minor league teams because they strive to provide an exceptional customer experience through a nice facility, quality food and beverages, and friendly players and staff (Frassinelli 2009).

A popular method of enhancing customer service is to identify "moments of truth." Moments of truth are defined as any interaction between the customer and the core product, facility, and service personnel (Carlzon 1987). When Charles Steinberg went to work for the Boston Red Sox, he identified individual moments related to fans' experiences at a ballpark, listed them on a chart, and ranked the organization's success in each category (Collins 2004). This exercise allowed the Red Sox to formulate and implement simple changes that could significantly influence the fan experience.

A good example of identifying and preventing potential issues comes from the annual Rose Bowl game. Each January, the Rose Bowl attracts 90,000-plus fans to the stadium, many of whom are traveling to support their team and most likely unfamiliar with the stadium. To combat some of the potential problems, the Rose Bowl produces and distributes a game-day guide that provides customers with information on the following:

- Driving directions
- Parking information
- Ticket information (e.g., entry gates, ticket pick-up locations)
- Service locations (e.g., first aid, restrooms, ATMs)
- Stadium policies

- Security measures
- Stadium and area map

Similarly, Kentucky Speedway publishes a fan guide for its racing season. As part of its fan guide, the speedway provides a list of quick tips, covering topics such as what to wear at the track, what to bring to the track, what not to bring to the track, and how to survive a day at the track (drink lots of water, use sunscreen, and wear comfortable shoes). These tips are all provided to help ensure customers enjoy their day at the speedway.

Newer technologies assist in providing a high level of customer service with applications that supply information through PDAs, expedite concession and merchandise purchases, and collect spectator feedback. For example, in 2008 the Pittsburgh Pirates began allowing fans to add monetary value to their tickets; these "loaded tickets" can be redeemed by scanning the bar code at concession and merchandise stands. The goal is to add flexibility and convenience for fans. These tickets work well for the teams, too—research has shown that fans spend up to 70 percent more on concessions (Muret 2008). In addition, new technologies have changed the way fans experience events. Social networking sites allow fans to connect with each other through online communities. Teams are now supporting these services because they allow teams to connect with fans and potential consumers beyond the traditional boundary of their arenas (Coyle 2009). Many NBA arenas have a service where fans in the building can send a text message to the venue. If appropriate, the message is displayed for everyone to see. The teams benefit by capturing cell phone numbers and e-mail addresses for future marketing uses (Henry 2008).

Ticket Collection

Although it may seem simple, collecting tickets and moving customers into a facility can be problematic without careful planning. Event organizers have to consider how tickets will be collected and when. If it's expected that spectators will arrive over an extended period of time, a relatively small number of entrances and ticket takers may be sufficient. However, if spectators tend to arrive in a narrow time period, more personnel are needed to ensure there are no long lines of angry spectators eager to get into the facility. Other concerns include pass-outs (will people be allowed to leave and return), ticket scalping, ticket forgery, gate security, and box office security.

Technology is increasing the efficiency of event operations through specialized software and applications that assist in ticketing, online registration, league management, tournament management, and volunteer tracking. For example, technologies such as print-at-home ticketing and web-based secondary ticket sales have greatly reduced the number of walk-up (day of event) sales. Considering walk-up sales are unpredictable, these new technologies allow organizations to shift staff from ticket sales to other areas.

The recent trend in spectator sports is toward paperless tickets. Many NBA teams such as the San Antonio Spurs and Charlotte Bobcats are transitioning to paperless technology in the form of smart cards. The advantages of this technology include allowing customers to electronically transfer tickets to games they cannot attend to other fans and allowing customers to add value to cards to be used for merchandise and concessions. Further, the cost of the cards is about half of what the team would have spent printing hard tickets (Muret 2011).

Larger events can often create issues with ticket collection. Organizers of the 2006 FIFA World Cup in Germany realized the issues that could result from poor ticket policies and planned accordingly. Fearing complicated processes would lead to long lines, empty seats, and crowd unrest, organizers utilized a series of controls including trained security personnel, random identification checks, visual checks, and electronic scanners to limit ticket delays while ensuring ticket security (Starcevic 2006).

VIP Entrances and Seating

Many events are attended by spectators who warrant special treatment. These guests may be people important to the community such as government officials, celebrities, or other dignitaries. In addition, events may provide special treatment to key business partners such as sponsors, broadcasters, vendors, donors, or other key contributors. These very important people (VIPs) are often granted complimentary tickets, private entrances, premium seating, and other perks such as preferred parking or personal wait-service to express gratitude for their support or to lay the foundation for future support.

VIPs may have higher expectations for their experience at the event than other guests. In addition, a failure to meet VIPs' needs can be disastrous. Therefore, special care should be taken to ensure everything goes well for your VIPs. Check to make sure that every benefit promised has been delivered, and be prepared to deliver additional service above and beyond what has been promised. It is always a good idea to think *extra* with this group (e.g., extra staff to meet needs, extra tickets for last-minute requests, extra perks available only to VIPs).

Will Call

Will call is a delivery method in which spectators who have already purchased tickets can pick them up at a designated location before the event. This option is commonly used for spectators who have purchased tickets close to the event date and for spectators who wish to leave tickets for others. With the growth of telephone and Internet sales, will call has become a much more popular option.

Problem Resolution

When event delivery has not met customers' expectations, they may become dissatisfied or complain. This is problematic because dissatisfied customers are less likely to return to the event and are likely to tell others of their problems. Therefore, events should have policies for resolving customer complaints. Often consumers can be appeased by merely listening to their problems and providing an apology. Watkins (2007) describes a five-point method for dealing with upset customers:

1. Listen: Active listening allows customers to vent their frustrations and shows that you care. Passive listening or dismissive comments can actually make the situation worse.

2. Apologize: Apologies are not necessarily admissions of fault. Instead, they are a way to communicate that you are listening and are concerned.

3. Empathize: Putting yourself in the customer's situation allows you to understand the customer's experience and frustrations.

4. Explain: Without making excuses, try to provide facts that may help the customer understand why the unfortunate situation may have happened. Typically, customers do not understand the whole story, so explanations may help change their perceptions of the incident.

5. Act. If you can resolve the problem, take steps to do so. If not, try to identify alternative solutions that will at least demonstrate you are trying.

Under more serious circumstances, it may be necessary to practice service recovery by compensating spectators with a gift or discount. When approximately 400 fans did not have seats for the 2011 Super Bowl when a temporary seating section was not completed by the start of the game, the NFL had to come up with a solution to compensate those spectators who missed the big game. The league decided to offer displaced fans $2,400 (three times the face value of the ticket) or round-trip airfare, hotel accommodations, and tickets to any future Super Bowl (Sandomir 2011). Another example of service recovery designed to placate put-out spectators and minimize bad publicity comes from NASCAR's 2011 Quaker State 400 at the Kentucky Speedway, where as many as 20,000 ticket holders missed the race because of traffic congestion. Traffic was still backed up even as the race hit the midway point. Many others who reached the speedway were turned away because of a lack of parking. To try to make it up to those customers affected by the problems, the speedway's parent company, Speedway Motorsports, Inc., offered a ticket exchange good for free entry at any another Sprint Cup race held at one of their tracks and an equal number of tickets to one of two future events at the Kentucky Speedway (Story 2011).

Signage

Making signage easily visible is extremely important because you cannot assume spectators are as familiar with the facility as you are. Proper signage at entry points reduces backups at ticket lines, directs spectators to the correct entry points, and reduces spectator confusion. Signage should also direct spectators to basic amenities such as restrooms, concessions, merchandise, and customer service locations. Effective signage also plays an important role in spectator safety because it directs spectators to medical facilities and exits in case of emergency.

Disseminating Information

Informed spectators are more likely to enjoy their experiences and less likely to encounter frustration. Use tools such as public address systems, scoreboards and message boards, printed materials, and the media as well as face-to-face communication to convey important information. Consider issues spectators may have with access, parking, ticketing, or changes in event schedules, and devise methods for communicating to spectators any rules, policies, procedures, and changes. Plans must also be developed for how organizers can communicate with spectators during a crisis or emergency. Identify how you can speak directly to your spectators (alarms, public address messages, video) and how you can get vital information to staff that can be relayed to spectators.

Spectator Evaluation of the Event

Spectator evaluations allow organizations to learn about spectators' experiences and identify pressing concerns needing management's attention. Collecting this information allows management to prioritize initiatives to increase satisfaction or decrease dissatisfaction (Greenwell, Lee, and

Naeger 2007). Management may solicit spectator input through formal methods such as surveys, depth interviews, or focus groups. Figure 12.2 illustrates a sample spectator survey. Informal methods can also be effective. For example, many organizations provide comment cards to their customers or publicize e-mail addresses spectators can use to pass along comments, concerns, or complaints. Other organizations may encourage their ushers or event staff to converse with spectators to learn important information first-hand.

MANAGING PARTICIPANTS

The athletes are the core of a sporting event and require different care than spectators. Athletes, as well as their coaches and families, will have special needs throughout the event that must be addressed so they can concentrate on their performances. The event manager's goal is to create an atmosphere where participants don't have to worry about the little things. You want to create an environment where athletes can focus on being their best when they compete. Athletes remember great experiences and let everyone know when an event has exceeded their expectations. They also remember terrible experiences—and let even more people know.

Participant Arrival

Participant arrival is often the first contact point between participants and event organizers. As such, this is the first opportunity to create an impression—positive or negative—of the event. It is important to greet participants when they arrive at the venue. For small events a simple greeting from the event manager may be enough to welcome participants and orient them to the facility and event. For large events, participant arrival can be a complex process involving transportation to the host city, accommodations, and transportation from hotels to event sites. Once at the event site, movement of people and equipment to locker rooms, warm-up rooms, and the event floor; security; and special requests become the main concerns.

How did you learn about our event? _____

Would you attend again? ❏ Yes ❏ No Why? _____

Would you recommend this event to others? ❏ Yes ❏ No Why? _____

How would you rate ticketing? (1 = poor, 5 = excellent)	1 2 3 4 5

How would you rate ticketing? (1 = poor, 5 = excellent)   1   2   3   4   5

How would you rate the ushers? (1 = poor, 5 = excellent)   1   2   3   4   5

How would you rate the facility? (1 = poor, 5 = excellent)   1   2   3   4   5

How would you rate parking? (1 = poor, 5 = excellent)   1   2   3   4   5

How would you rate the souvenir stands? (1 = poor, 5 = excellent)   1   2   3   4   5

How would you rate concessions? (1 = poor, 5 = excellent)   1   2   3   4   5

How would you rate your overall experience? (1 = poor, 5 = excellent) 1   2   3   4   5

What can we do to improve this event next year? _____

■ **Figure 12.2**   Sample spectator survey.

One way to improve the probability of a smooth arrival is to communicate important information to your participants before the event. Send information packages with arrival instructions, hotel and transportation information, local maps, facility maps, restaurant and entertainment options, and contact information for additional questions. A website can also be used to provide up-to-date information that will help your participants make a smooth arrival.

Area Logistics

Depending on the event, participants may also have different needs ranging from locker and shower facilities, meeting rooms, hospitality areas, equipment storage, and warm-up areas. Further, the type of event may dictate the number of security personnel or staff needed. To prepare for these logistics, event managers should meet with team liaisons to understand the entire traveling party's needs and expectations.

Access to these areas as well as sideline, dugout, and bench areas is often controlled by issuing cre-

dentials to participants and the traveling party. As well as identifying the bearer, credentials should identify to which areas the bearer has access.

Communicating With Participants

It is important to keep participants and coaches up to date on key information. Specifically, organizers should make sure participants have been given the schedule of events and locations, registration or check-in information, facility diagrams, and contact numbers. In addition, it is important to note that participants may not be familiar with the area or the format of the event. Therefore, communication should be specific and detailed. Table 12.5 is a sample of information you might provide a team arriving for a basketball game.

Communication with coaches and participants comes in multiple formats. Key information may be provided in an information packet or posted in locker facilities. Signage throughout the facility provides information on locations, policies,

Table 12.5 Sample Participant Information Sheet: Basketball Game

Equipment delivery	Thursday: Delivery of sideline signage, 24 chairs, ball racks, and balls. Return to practice facility on Monday.
Band	Home and visiting bands can deliver equipment at 10:00 a.m. on game day. Delivery must be made at Cole Street Docks.
Training staff	Trainer will deliver equipment at 10:00 a.m. on game day. Equipment will be stored in locker room.
Will-call tickets	General public: Broadway ticket window Players: Broadway ticket window (tickets must be delivered no later than 90 min. before game time)
Parking	Visiting team bus: Park at North Cole Street Docks. Student buses: Drop off at entrance B. Game officials: Park at Cole Street Docks. Band and cheer: Buses park at Cole Street Docks.
Entrances	Public: Entrances A and B Booster club: Entrance B Home players: Broadway Central Entrance Visiting players: Cole Street Dock Media: Broadway Central Entrance Staff: Broadway Central Entrance Band: Cole Street Dock Cheer: Cole Street Dock
Locker rooms	Home team: Visitor's locker room South Visiting team: Visitor's locker room North Officials: Officials locker room B Home cheerleaders: Auxiliary locker room A Visiting cheerleaders: Auxiliary locker room B
Media	Interview: Interview room Media work room: Room 150
Booster club	Hospitality room: Room 140 (floor level)
Gates open	12:30 p.m. Central
Game time	2:05 p.m. Central

and timing of events. Public address announcements are utilized to inform participants about upcoming events or schedule changes. Event managers should also assign a participant liaison to each team or entity. This person becomes the key point of communication when questions or special needs arise. Larger events may set up a command center to centralize and integrate communications.

Participant Liaisons

Participant liaisons are key communications tools and are integral to the satisfaction of participants. Liaisons should be educated about event activities and prepared for questions or special requests. Often events will appoint a facility liaison. This person is responsible for assisting participants and event organizers with any issues with the facility or event.

Traveling Parties

Sporting events often have official traveling parties including coaches, administrators, and staff that may be as large as, or larger than, the number of participants. The needs of these people also have to be considered in order to create a memorable experience for all involved. Since team officials often make the decision whether or not to return to an event, their satisfaction is vitally important.

Locker Facilities

Changing rooms may be required for each team and officials. Additional changing rooms may be needed for support groups such as cheerleaders, dance teams, in-game entertainment, other performers, and family. A separate room may also be requested for use as a meeting room or office area. Typical changing rooms include lockers and showers, but participants may also require additional amenities such as laundry services, athletic training equipment, or multimedia devices. Event organizers also have to consider personnel needs related to locker facilities. It may be necessary to provide security, custodial, or laundry staff depending on the event and the needs of the participants.

To ensure this aspect of the event moves smoothly, it is imperative that organizers specify what will or will not be provided and communicate those specifications to participants. A lack of communication is likely to cause confusion and dissatisfaction. Be specific so that teams know exactly what to expect and can prepare accordingly. For example, event organizers may provide the following information to participating teams before an event:

- Locker facilities will be open two hours before game time and one hour after the event.
- Each locker room has an attached training room that is available to teams.
- Ice and water are available in each training room.
- No towels or locks will be provided.
- Locker rooms will be available to team members and the traveling party only.

Participant Departure

There should be a plan for participant departure that covers exits, transportation, and safety. The departure plan should also account for participants' equipment and traveling parties.

Participant Evaluation of the Event

A participant's final evaluation of the event is often the determining factor as to whether or not she intends to participate in future events. Considering that many events depend on attracting top competition, events often create inventive programs to ensure participants enjoy their stay and want to return. For example, the 2005 Canada Summer Games did a great job entertaining participants, leaving most athletes praising the event. Organizers provided great food, massage therapy, nightly entertainment, and an athlete lounge featuring video games and an arcade. In addition, volunteers were on hand around the clock to assist athletes (Canadian Press 2005). Participant satisfaction is especially important for PGA tournaments because these events need to do all they can to attract key players. For example, many PGA Tour events provide extra touches for participants including courtesy cars, gourmet meals, gifts for players' wives and children, child care, and personal maid service. At the 2009 Mercedes Championship, golfers and their families enjoyed a Steve Winwood concert in addition to other perks such as whale watching and zip-lining (Morfit 2009).

To gather information about what participants think of an event and to collect ideas about how the event can be improved, many event organizers create a postevent participant survey. Figure 12.3 is an example of a survey for examining runners' perceptions of a marathon. Results from these surveys can be used to identify strengths and weaknesses of your event in order to suggest changes for future events. In addition, participant evaluations can help planners determine how participants will respond to proposed changes to an event, estimate the economic impact of an event, or gather information to share with sponsors.

MANAGING SPONSORS

Selling a sponsorship is just the first part of the process. Events and sponsors have to work together to ensure sponsors receive maximum

How did you learn about our marathon?_____

Would you participate again? ❑ Yes ❑ No Why? _____

Would you recommend this marathon to others? ❑ Yes ❑ No Why? _____

How would you rate registration? (1 = poor, 5 = excellent)   1   2   3   4   5

How would you rate the course? (1 = poor, 5 = excellent)   1   2   3   4   5

How would you rate the staff? (1 = poor, 5 = excellent)   1   2   3   4   5

How would you rate the water stations? (1 = poor, 5 = excellent)   1   2   3   4   5

How would you rate the postrace (1 = poor, 5 = excellent)
   awards ceremony?   1   2   3   4   5

How would you rate the participant gifts? (1 = poor, 5 = excellent)   1   2   3   4   5

How would you rate your overall experience? (1 = poor, 5 = excellent) 1   2   3   4   5

How far did you travel to get here? _____

How many nights did you stay in town? _____

What can we do to improve this event next year? _____

■ **Figure 12.3** Sample participant survey for a marathon.

benefits from their association with the event. Special care must be taken to ensure sponsors are satisfied, as the best way to recruit a sponsor is to retain an existing one. To accomplish this, events should strive to deliver all promised benefits, protect sponsors' rights, and develop relationships with sponsors. It is much better to exceed sponsors' expectations by delivering more than what was promised than to fall short on promises. In other words, you should underpromise and overdeliver.

Hospitality

Hospitality should exceed sponsors' expectations. Catering, facilities, and special functions should be managed to provide sponsors with a unique experience they will remember. For the 2012 Super Bowl, the National Football League created NFL House—a hospitality facility open to spon-

sors—to provide an enhanced experience for the purpose of making their sponsors feel special.

Signage

Signage is a benefit sponsors commonly seek from sponsorship programs. The facility should be carefully evaluated to find the best locations for sponsors' signage. Look for spots that provide the best exposure to participants, spectators, and the media. Identify locations such as sidelines, backdrops, and finish lines that will maximize exposure.

Promotions

Many event sponsorships involve sales promotions that may include premium giveaways, contests or sweepstakes, product sampling, point-of-purchase displays, or other special events. Timing and execution are important to ensure all activities meet sponsors' expectations.

Deliverables

Organizers should develop a fulfillment plan for each sponsor that ensures the event is honoring each contractually obligated component of the contract. Summary sheets outlining the specific deliverables promised to a sponsor can list activities that need to take place, people responsible for these activities, and deadlines for completion.

Sponsor Liaisons

One person from the organization should be appointed as the sponsor liaison (for a large event you may have multiple sponsor liaisons in order to cover all responsibilities). This person serves as the sponsor's primary contact and should develop relationships and have the authority to make decisions (Geldard and Sinclair 1996). The NFL recently undertook a research project to better understand what sponsors felt about their working relationship with the NFL. Results revealed that sponsors desired better communication and more clarity about sponsorship assets (Lefton 2009).

Sponsor Evaluation of the Event

As opposed to philanthropy, sponsors are typically looking for a return on their investment or a return on their objectives. Event organizers should identify sponsors' objectives before the event and show a commitment to delivering on those objectives. After the event, sponsors should be provided with reports detailing how the sponsorship was fulfilled (e.g., attendance figures, media coverage, advertising value, public relations value, direct sales). Care should be taken to illustrate the value the sponsors received in exchange for their investment.

EASILY MISSED DETAILS

Experienced event managers learn that missed details can cause big problems for an event. Double-check everything on your lists. Think of everything that could go wrong and try to plan for even the most unlikely event. Logistics can be a crucial factor in whether your event succeeds or fails (Graham, Neirotti, and Goldblatt 2001). Think of how some minor details could affect how the event is perceived by participants, spectators, sponsors, and staff:

- You begin the event with the singing of the national anthem, but there is no flag in the arena (or you play the wrong national anthem).

- You set up a great buffet for your VIPs but forgot eating utensils (forks, knives, spoons).

- You are running a volleyball tournament, but the equipment manager forgot to bring game balls.

- Sponsors or VIPs names are mispronounced (or you misspell one of their names on a sign) because you did not rehearse the script with the PA announcer.

- The halftime show is ready to begin, but the sound engineer cannot cue the music (dancers without music tend to be very awkward).

- There are no towels in the locker rooms for teams to use because someone forgot to properly stock player areas.

- Important people cannot get into the arena because the guest list, pass list, or credential list was not double-checked, and key names were left off.

As you can imagine, these details can cause quite a headache in addition to creating a bad image for your event. The Houston Dynamo soccer team's first MLS game is an example of what can happen when several minor details add up to a major problem. Management underestimated crowd size and did not adequately staff the box office, resulting in many fans having to wait up to 30 minutes to pick up tickets. Consequently, the team had to delay the start of the game. In addition, concession, traffic, and parking staffs were smaller than required for a crowd that size, resulting in long concession lines and displeased customers (Fallas and Davis 2006).

SUMMARY

The day of the event is when all the planning and preparation come together. Numerous tasks must be accomplished throughout game day; therefore managers need to anticipate, plan, delegate, and communicate in order to ensure everything gets done in a timely manner. Event managers should make use of various tools such as checklists, contact lists, event rundowns, and event scripts to help coordinate activities.

Event managers need to coordinate the staff entrusted to accomplish all these tasks. They also have to deal with the needs of spectators, participants, and sponsors. For each group, the manager's goal is to leave them satisfied and wanting to return to future events. This undertaking is made easier if event managers understand each party's needs and commit to delivering experiences beyond expectations.

LEARNING ACTIVITIES

Identify an event, and put yourself in the position of being responsible for event day.

1. Create a list of things that need to happen, from an operations perspective, for the event to be a success.

2. Create a checklist of necessary activities for each functional area, and identify when those activities need to happen or be completed.

3. Prepare an event rundown for this event. Think of the coordination necessary to make everything run smoothly.

4. Prepare a public address script for one segment of the event (e.g., pregame, halftime).

REFERENCES

Bowdin, G., J. Allen, W. O'Toole, R. Harris, and I. McDonnell. 2006. *Events management*. Oxford, UK: Butterworth-Heinemann.

Canadian Press. 2005. Food great at Canada Games. *Guelph Mercury*, August 17, B6.

Carlzon, J. 1987. *Moments of truth*. Cambridge, MA: Ballinger.

Collins, J. 2004. Sox appeal: How the Red Sox front office reversed years of arrogance to finally make Fenway friendly. *Boston Magazine*. [Online]. August 17. Available: www.bostonmagazine.com/articles/sox_appeal.

Coyle, P. 2009. Social networking can help teams find way to fans' hearts. *Street and Smith's SportsBusiness Journal*, April 13, 23.

Fallas, B., and R. Davis. 2006. Play on the pitch was top notch. But before the game, some were getting restless— Fans hope Dynamo's not feeding them a line. *Houston Chronicle*, April 4, 14.

Frassinelli, M. 2009. Patriots owner makes sure team's fans always come first on 10th anniversary, ballclub is still a hit. *Star-Ledger*, March 8, 27.

Geldard, E., and L. Sinclair. 1996. *The sponsorship manual: Sponsorship made easy*. Olinda, Victoria, AU: The Sponsorship Unit.

Graham, S., L.D. Neirotti, and J.J. Goldblatt. 2001. *The ultimate guide to sports marketing*. 2nd ed. New York: McGraw-Hill.

Greenwell, T.C., J. Lee, and D. Naeger. 2007. Using the critical incident technique to identify critical aspects of the spectator's service experience. *Sport Marketing Quarterly* 16:190-198.

Henry, G. 2008. Fans, teams are benefitting from the wireless industry. *Augusta Chronicle*. [Online]. February 16. Available: http://chronicle.augusta.com/stories/2008/02/17/nba_187670.shtml.

Katz, A. 2008. Storm forces SEC tournament move, unusual twinbill. ESPN.com. March 14. Available: www.usatoday.com/printedition/sports/20080326/c11_update26.art.htm.

Lawrence, H., and M. Wells. 2009. *Event management blueprint*. Dubuque, IA: Kendall/Hunt.

Lefton, T. 2009. NFL improves communication scores on sponsor evaluations. *Street and Smith's SportsBusiness Journal*, October 26, 9.

Lovelock, C., and R. Wright. 2002. *Principles of service marketing and management*. 2nd ed. Upper Saddle River, NJ: Pearson Education.

Morfit, C. 2009. The Mercedes Championship fills the downtime between whale-watching and zip-lining, and kicks off the 2009 PGA Tour season. Golf.com. January 7. Available: www.golf.com/golf/tours_news/article/0,28136,1870091,00.html.

Muret, D. 2008. Loaded tickets catch on among MLB teams. *Street and Smith's SportsBusiness Journal*, March 10, 12.

Muret, D. 2011. Spurs giving season-ticket holders the option to go paperless. *Street and Smith's SportsBusiness Journal*, December 12, 11.

Sandomir, R. 2011. A suit of Super Bowl seats. *New York Times*, February 10, 19.

Saxon, M. 2009. Angels—no. 1 for fans by fans. *Orange County Register*, July 2, AC.

Solomon, J. 2002. *An insider's guide to managing sporting events*. Champaign, IL: Human Kinetics.

Starcevic, N. 2006. Germans promise to prevent long lines at World Cup. *Erie Times-News*, May 13, 6.

Story, M. 2011. Kentucky Speedway trying to make amends. *Lexington Herald-Leader*, October 2.

Supovitz, F. 2005. *The sports event marketing and management playbook*. Hoboken, NJ: Wiley.

Towers, C. 2008. Dogs play at noon Saturday at Georgia Tech. *Atlanta Journal Constitution*. [Online]. March 14. Available: www.ajc.com/sports/content/sports/uga/stories/2008/03/14/ugagameburst_0315.html.

Van Der Wagen, L., and B.R. Carlos. 2005. *Event management for tourism, cultural, business and sporting events*. Upper Saddle River, NJ: Pearson.

Watkins, K. 2007. 5 practical techniques to sooth upset participants. *SportsEvents* (May/June): 12.

Wolf, P., and J. Wolf. 2005. *Event planning made easy*. New York: McGraw-Hill.

CHAPTER 13

Postevent Details and Evaluation

Chapter Objectives

After completing the chapter, the reader should be able to do the following:

- Describe activities of importance after the conclusion of the event.
- Provide techniques for securing postevent media coverage.
- List ways to follow up with sponsors after the event.
- Explain various ways of evaluating the sporting event and its effectiveness.
- Understand the concept of return on objectives.
- Describe how to measure economic impact.

Industry Profile ▶ Linda Logan, Greater Columbus Sports Commission

Linda Logan has been the executive director of the Greater Columbus Sports Commission in Columbus, Ohio, since its inception in 2002. Linda previously worked as the director of sport marketing for the Greater Columbus Convention and Visitors Bureau and the director of sales and services at the Greater Columbus Convention Center. Before moving back to Ohio, Linda spent 10 years in Kansas City, Missouri, working for the Kansas City Convention Center, the Big Eight Conference, Kemper Arena, and the Kansas City Comets of the Major Indoor Soccer League. She also worked for the Milwaukee Does of the Women's Basketball League and the Cleveland Nets of World Team Tennis. Linda is a past national chair of the board of the National Association of Sports Commissions.

Q: What are some ways that you evaluate the success of an event?

A: When we evaluate the success of a sporting event, we consider a number of factors. One important factor is attendance at the event based on the turnstile count. Another big factor is the hotel room block and the actual pick-up of the block by all the stakeholders who attended the event. After the event, we consider the budget and match the actual budget figures with our earlier projections. We check that we met the requirements of the event as expressed by the sport property that owns the rights to the event. In this regard, our service motto is to underpromise and overdeliver so that we exceed the expectations of the sport property and all other stakeholders. We want to ensure the group believes we have provided the best experience possible. Very few cities have done a good job of using a formal citywide survey to evaluate events, and at this point we do not have this in place. However, we are looking into the possibility that we will have this type of instrument one day.

Q: How does your organization measure economic impact for a sporting event?

A: We do not measure economic impact per se, but rather measure visitor spending while attending an event. Visitor spending may include spending on hotel rooms, food, rental cars, and local attractions, plus other monies spent with various businesses in and around the Greater Columbus area. When measuring visitor spending, we try to err on the side of calculating a conservative estimate. Destination Marketing Association International (DMAI) has a spending calculator universally used by convention and visitors bureaus, and in the near future they will be rolling out a sports calculator. Once all sports commissions have access to the sports calculator, it will help ensure that destinations are consistent in measuring the same factors.

Q: Why is economic impact important to a sports commission?

A: Economic impact or visitor spending is important to us as an organization because it helps tell a story of the value of Destination Columbus. It also helps us provide justification to our founders about the need for resources to help us stay competitive within the industry. Economic impact is also a valuable way to demonstrate the importance of our industry. Many taxpayers may not be aware of this fact, but Franklin County residents in the Columbus region would pay an extra $1,800 per year of taxes were it not for the Greater Columbus Sports Commission and the convention and visitors bureau.

Q: What is involved in your job in postevent follow-up?

A: Depending on the event, we conduct a debriefing shortly after the conclusion of the event, either in person or via a conference call. During this time we get critical feedback from various stakeholders, and we ask the group owning the rights to the event to provide a testimonial. We also conduct internal meetings among our staff to better understand and recap what transpired during the course of the event. We are seeking to understand areas of improvement and opportunities moving forward. We consider whether we will bid on this event again and brainstorm ways to overcome any obstacles we may face in doing so. In addition, we conduct follow-up reports with hotels to better understand our occupancy reports.

After every event there is usually some type of cleanup to restore the facility to working order. Events that require meeting space and food and beverage breaks need services such as vacuuming of the meeting room, washing the dishes, and resetting the tables and chairs. Sporting events such as a baseball game require field maintenance such as raking and covering the mound. In addition, the seating, concession, and ticketing areas must be swept and cleaned thoroughly. In cases where a vendor is allowed to operate in the sport facility, standards of cleanliness should be set and clearly communicated along with a deposit taken in the event you need to pay a third party to clean the area (deLisle 2009).

Many other factors besides cleaning must be considered during breakdown. Some events use rental equipment such as computers, printers, two-way radios, sporting equipment, telephones, food and beverage equipment, and audiovisual equipment. These items must be inspected and then returned to the rental agency before the end of the contract date. It is important that this equipment be inventoried before the event and secured in a safe location after the event. The setup and breakdown portion of any event can be chaotic, and valuable items are susceptible to being stolen or easily misplaced.

Once an event is over, sometimes it is difficult to find staff to help with the breakdown and cleanup. Many facilities employ a housekeeping team or event staff members who are responsible for cleanup. If vendors are involved, event planners should include specific language in the contracts negotiated with vendors in terms of the requirements for cleanup. Some jobs within the sport industry require a large amount of work during the cleanup phase at the conclusion of the event. For example, an equipment manager is responsible for postevent duties such as laundry, equipment maintenance, and inventorying along with the transport and storage of equipment.

POSTEVENT PROMOTIONS

Communicating with the audience is important even after the sporting event is over. Promotion is defined as communicating with and persuading defined user groups (Irwin, Sutton, and McCarthy 2008). By reaching out to these defined user groups through postevent promotions, the event planner stays in touch with the primary consumers of the event. Postevent promotion can take many forms, such as sending out newsletters, following up on contests or sweepstakes that occurred during the sporting event, posting photos or videos on social media sites, sending certificates and awards, implementing customer service surveys, and sending out promotional information about next year's event while the consumer is still thinking about this year's. Event planners should remember the importance of aftermarketing—the process of providing continuing satisfaction and reinforcement to past or current customers in order to create lasting relationships (Irwin, Sutton, and McCarthy 2008).

POSTEVENT MEDIA COVERAGE

Sport is widely popular in North America, and there is strong demand from the general public for information. Fans of a sports team who just won a championship game want to continue the celebration and demand immediate media coverage with analysis by players and coaches. Media coverage is often built into the estimated economic impacts of a sporting event (Dwyer et al. 2000). Depending on the type and impact of the event, securing some form of postevent media coverage may or may not be necessary. For example, postevent media coverage after mega-events such as the Kentucky Derby, NCAA Division I championships, NFL Super Bowl, NBA Finals, MLB World Series, and Olympic and Paralympic Games is not only expected but also eagerly anticipated by avid fans.

Although most event planners will not have to deal with the media scrutiny that accompanies mega-events, every event should capitalize on some form of public or media relations. Media relations programs maximize favorable publicity and minimize unfavorable publicity for the sport organization. For smaller events, it is not difficult to invite a local newspaper or television station to write a human interest story about an event participant. Statistical information about the event can easily be reported to the media. Postevent media coverage often takes the form of short, spontaneous interviews of players and coaches or postgame press conferences that are more widely planned. Sports Media Challenge (2012) offers sport executives the following tips for media relations:

- Choose the spokesperson wisely, and ensure she is media savvy, believable, and equipped with all the facts.

- Get your coaching staff, administrators, and athletes involved in some sort of media training. The media will try to find the person who gives the most "colorful" sound bite, and this person is not always the most informed.

- Determine the main message you want your department to convey, and stick to it. Make sure that message is communicated throughout the entire organization so you're all saying the same thing.

Sports Media Challenge is a company based in Charlotte, North Carolina, that specializes in preparing athletes, coaches, and administrators in the areas of media and presentation skills.

News Conferences

Stoldt, Dittmore, and Branvold (2012) suggest the goal of a news conference is to "disseminate noteworthy information from an organization to its targeted publics" (p. 181). One of the key components of sporting events is the emotion that emanates from the competition. This emotional component has led more than one athlete and coach to mutter words immediately after the contest that they would later regret. Thus, event planners should factor in a time period, after the event and before the news conference, in which coaches and players can decompress and cool down from an emotional standpoint. The event planner may need to serve as the liaison between the media and the teams during this cool-down period. Irwin, Sutton, and McCarthy (2002) suggest setting up the press conference facilities at least one hour in advance, and they provide the following checklist to ensure success:

- Blackboard, easel, screen, and projections
- Chairs and tables for principals
- Designated place for video cameras
- Floor microphones for questions if room is large
- Full staff at entry door to greet media
- Lectern brackets for press microphones
- Organization logo displayed (normally projected in background)
- Outside directional signage indicating room location
- Podium height and lighting
- Posters, graphics, and artwork
- Press kit or handouts at registration desk
- Public address system, including microphone and speaker
- Registration desk or book
- Schedule of photos for house photographer
- Sufficient chairs for reporters
- Technical service operator for all equipment
- Water glasses for speakers

Impact of Social Media on Postgame Media Coverage

It is important to understand the impact of social media on sporting events. Many professional and some collegiate athletes use Twitter to reach their followers and thus bypass more traditional media routes. Both sports participants and spectators can deliver newsworthy information at the click of a button via various social media sites. Photos can be taken using mobile telephone technology and immediately uploaded. One of the strangest examples of the instantaneous nature of these social media sites was a live tweet in April 2012 by former NFL great Deion Sanders alleging he was being assaulted by his wife. He posted photos of himself and his kids filling out police reports; the photos were later removed.

The Mashable Entertainment (2012) website reports that more than 80 percent of sport fans monitor social media sites such as Twitter and Facebook while watching games on TV, and more than 60 percent do so while watching live events. In fact, certain players may be trending on Twitter, which suggests they are the most popular topics being discussed on Twitter. Mashable reported that more than 9,000 people per second tweeted about Tim Tebow during the 2011-2012 season after he threw an unexpected touchdown pass in the NFL playoffs. Another example is New York Knicks guard Jeremy Lin, who gained more than 550,000 Twitter followers in a single month because of his NBA success in 2012.

SPONSOR FOLLOW-UP

The relationship with corporate sponsors does not end once the event is complete. In fact, all sponsorships should be evaluated throughout the entire process, and a postevent follow-up is both expected and imperative. The follow-up procedure is important because it not only helps the sponsor fulfill its goals and objectives but also allows the rights holder to identify problem areas or points of dissatisfaction. According to Irwin, Sutton, and McCarthy (2008), an entire audit of the event sponsorship should be conducted at the end of the campaign to determine how well the goals and objectives were met. If the sponsorship was conducted effectively, it is more likely the sponsor will reactivate or renew during the follow-up meeting.

Shortly after the conclusion of the event, contact the sponsor and schedule a meeting. During this meeting, the sponsor representative should be given a number of metrics that are helpful in measuring the success of the sponsorship. Lynde (2007) suggests that some elements of a sponsorship package such as media rights, signage, and tickets are easier to quantify because a market rate has been developed over time. Other elements, such as category exclusivity, use of intellectual property, and pass-through rights, are more difficult to quantify. As Lynde states, it is easier to evaluate a sponsorship package when the true value of the sponsorship assets can be quantified and emotion is not involved in decision making. With some sporting events, emotion plays a big part when sponsorship decision makers are fans of a certain team.

POSTEVENT DEBRIEFING

A postevent meeting or debriefing with the most important stakeholders involved in planning the event is an important opportunity for event planners to gain feedback about the event. Key personnel who may be in attendance at this meeting include facility managers, security personnel, event organizers, hotel managers, and representatives from destination marketing organizations along with other people involved in planning the event. It is also advisable to invite members of traffic and safety agencies because they can provide feedback that will help improve future traffic management plans (deLisle 2009). The debriefing may take place at the sport venue, host hotel, or any other location convenient for all stakeholders. Depending on the schedule of the various people involved, as well as facility availability, the debriefing may include a food and beverage function such as a luncheon.

Event planners may ask the various stakeholders to complete a report that highlights findings from the event and provides recommendations for improving future events. For example, a report from traffic coordinators may highlight key times when traffic congestion detracted from the event and offer suggestions for better handling the flow of traffic filing into the sport venue and the corresponding departure. Event planners may also use some form of survey research during this phase. Online or paper-and-pencil surveys may be distributed to stakeholders requesting their feedback for improving the event. Both open-ended and closed questions may be included on the surveys, which can be administered before, during, or after the debriefing.

The debriefing can take many forms. At one extreme, Masterman (2009) suggests the debriefing is simply a celebration of the event and a postevent party. In contrast, the debriefing can be simply one meeting, submeetings, or a series of meetings, and the agenda should address all aspects of the event. Another question to consider is when the debriefing takes place. Final evaluative reports for some events are not completed until many months or years after the conclusion of the event. Masterman recommends holding the debriefing within a week of the event so that memory does not detract from the process. When conducting the debriefing, all stakeholders should be given an opportunity to report their findings from the event. It is important that the tone of the debriefing not be too celebratory, but attendees should also avoid highly critical personal attacks. The primary purpose of the debriefing is to record important institutional knowledge that was gained from the event and to use it for future planning purposes.

EVENT EVALUATION

One of the weaknesses within the sport event industry is the lack of evaluation by event planners. An evaluation of a sporting event allows the planner to better understand if the objectives of the event were accomplished. It also shows the various areas within the event that need to be improved. This section discusses the various levels of evaluation as well as several evaluation methods.

Levels of Evaluation

In the meetings industry, Myhill and Phillips (2010) outline up to six levels for evaluating objectives for a meeting or convention, which are listed here. These levels can also be applied within the sport event industry.

- Level 0: Statistics, scope, and volume; this level collects data such as the scope and volume of attendance, press coverage, website traffic, and other similar statistics.

- Level 1: Reaction, satisfaction, and planned action; this level gathers information on what stakeholders thought of the planning process, marketing efforts, facilities, and so forth.

- Level 2: Learning evaluation measures the extent to which principles, facts, techniques, skills, and professional contact have been acquired during the meeting. Similar types of learning take place at a sporting event and can be applied in a similar manner.

- Level 3: Application measures the extent to which skills, knowledge, and professional contacts learned at the meeting were applied on the job or in the personal life of attendees.

- Level 4: Business impacts monitors organizational improvement of business measures such as sales, cost savings, work output, and quality changes. Within the context of sport event management, business impacts would refer to sponsor impacts.

- Level 5: Return on investment (ROI) for the various stakeholders of the meeting, calculated as the ratio of benefits to costs.

In a similar manner to the meetings industry, the sport event industry can use these levels of evaluation to determine ROI. In addition, event planners can use evaluative methods such as in-game evaluations, staff and management evaluations, budgeting, and attendance as evaluative measures.

In-Game Evaluations

There are a number of ways to evaluate an event during the contest itself. Participants and spectators can provide feedback using a street intercept methodology whereby people are surveyed as they enter or exit a sport venue. Street intercepts are useful in cases where you want feedback from hard-to-reach people in a real-life situation. One of the key factors to keep in mind when conducting any type of survey research for evaluative purposes during an event is to be brief because participants and spectators are not in attendance for the purposes of completing your survey, but rather to participate in or watch the event.

Both qualitative and quantitative types of research can be conducted for evaluative purposes. Quantitative methods include short questionnaires or surveys distributed during the event. If you conduct a quantitative survey, here are some key factors to consider:

- Where will you distribute the questionnaire or survey? Will it be at an entrance or exit? If you distribute at an entrance, you should consider timing because people arriving early may be more likely to respond than those running late. If you are distributing the questionnaire at the end of an event, what time does the event end? Will people leave the event early?
- You should provide a pen or pencil for completing the questionnaire.
- Will you offer an incentive for completing the questionnaire (e.g., future tickets to an event or souvenir merchandise)?
- Who will help you distribute the questionnaire, and how many people do you need to help in order to get a good response rate?

One form of qualitative evaluation is participant observation. This unobtrusive form of evaluation allows you to learn more about active event participants or spectators within the real setting of the event. The disadvantages of using participant observation to evaluate an event include the following:

- It is time consuming for the observer.
- The observer cannot be everywhere at once.
- The observer can affect the behavior of the person being observed.

Individual interviews and small focus groups can also be used to evaluate various aspects of an event. Interviews ask for individual opinions, perceptions, beliefs, and attitudes about the event. Focus groups do the same; however, the interview is conducted with a small group of people. Timing is critical for both these forms of qualitative evaluation because participants do not want to

be interrupted at key times during the event. You should consider this form of evaluation at points when your subjects have discretionary time, such as in between innings at a baseball game, during intermissions, or before or after the event.

Staff Evaluations

Evaluation of staff members is a good way to maintain control over the success of the event and is helpful for professional development. Observation during the course of the event can be more useful if staff members are trained beforehand (Masterman 2009). The use of benchmarking is advocated as a way to achieve a level of standardization in the evaluation process (Allen et al. 2002). Partovi (1994) defines benchmarking as "the search for the best industry practices which will lead to exceptional performance through the implementation of these best practices" (p. 25). Benchmarking has also been described as a continuous and systematic process for evaluating products, services, and work processes representing best practices for the purpose of organizational improvement (Spendolini 1992). A number of event management areas may be benchmarked in terms of staffing. For example, an event planner may benchmark event staffing in relation to the following:

- Uniforms for staff members
- Number of staff members placed at each point of purchase
- Salaries or pay rates for part-time and full-time staff members
- Shift hours for staff members
- New and creative types of staff positions

A second way for event planners to evaluate staff members is to engage in a technique called management by wandering around (MBWA). MBWA was made famous by Tom Peters and Robert Waterman after their visit to Hewlett-Packard in the late 1970s and later discussed in their book *In Search of Excellence*. Peters and Waterman (1982) defined MBWA as "the business of staying in touch" (p. 288). The idea behind an MBWA program is to get a manager out of the office and onto the floor to make contact with employees (Amsbary and Staples 1991). If you have ever watched the popular television show *Undercover Boss*, you have witnessed this technique. A high-ranking executive in a company (often the president or CEO) alters his appearance and gains an alias so he can work in an entry-level position within the organization for a week. During this time, the boss works in various areas of company operations and with many employees, often with a different job and at a different location each day. This gives the undercover boss a better appreciation for the work being done by his staff. At the end of the show, the undercover boss summons these employees to the corporate office, at which time his true identity is revealed. In the end, the boss learns more about the day-to-day operations of the company and either rewards hardworking employees through promotion or financial rewards or provides additional training or better working conditions. The idea here is that event managers should be critically involved in the operations of the event. In other words, by employing MBWA, the event manager knows if concession employees are serving hot and high-quality foods, and they can monitor the length of time it takes to wait in line at a concession stand. Furthermore, the event planner can monitor if ushers and ticket takers are friendly, helpful, and reliable.

Another way to conduct staff evaluation is to administer a quantitative or qualitative survey to consumers of the event. Some of the questions should measure customer service components such as employee helpfulness, product knowledge, empathy, caring, friendliness, reliability, responsiveness, and assurance. Other items on the questionnaire may measure whether employees keep the facility clean and can also gauge consumer perceptions related to the atmosphere of the facility. This type of quantitative analysis can help identify service touch points where consumers are dissatisfied or highly satisfied. It can also help reveal areas where the event may experience a service failure.

Finally, qualitative questionnaires can provide event planners with more in-depth knowledge of certain areas where consumers are experiencing satisfaction or dissatisfaction. This type of questionnaire asks for more detailed information from the consumer, and often the questions are open ended (figure 13.1). Open-ended questions may ask, "How can the sporting event be improved?" or "What was your favorite part of the event?"

Management Evaluations

The evaluation of an event should not focus only on the performance of frontline staff members such as ushers, concession workers, and ticket takers; it should also examine the management of these employees and the processes for helping them complete their work. For example, sales staff may be responsible for selling event inventory such as signage, broadcast commercials, print ads, and other forms of sponsorship. However, management evaluations may pertain more directly to the effectiveness of staff members such as the director of marketing, who supervises these employees. Areas of evaluation may include the following:

- How well does the supervisor communicate with employees under her supervision?
- Does the supervisor provide employees with the necessary resources to perform their jobs in an effective manner?
- Is the manager clear in his communication of the expectations for the position?
- Does the manager possess strong leadership skills that help her motivate subordinates?
- Is the manager knowledgeable about the organization and its various products and services?
- Does the manager cast a strong vision for the event to subordinates?

Event managers should also consider conducting 360-degree evaluations, which allow subordinates to see themselves from multiple perspectives. Weigelt and colleagues (2004) describe a 360-degree evaluation as a self-assessment and an assessment by coworkers (peers), staff supervised by the person, and the people who supervise him. Formal feedback is provided to the person from all sources of evaluation. The program should invest

POSTEVENT EVALUATION SURVEY

Thank you for attending our recent event. We'd like to hear your impression of the various aspects of the event so we can continually improve the experience for all attendees.

1. Overall how would you rate the event?

   Excellent

   Good

   Fair

   Poor

   Terrible

2. Please rate the following aspects of the event.

	Excellent	Good	Fair	Poor	Terrible
Scheduling and timing					
Entertainment					
Food and beverages					
Parking and directions					
Invitations and guest list					
Choice of facility/venue					
Cost and pricing					
Vendor management					

3. Based on your experience at this event, how likely are you to attend future events?

   Very likely

   Somewhat likely

   Not likely

4. What was your favorite part of the event?

5. What was your least favorite part of the event?

6. Do you have any other suggestions or comments to help us improve future events?

■ **Figure 13.1** Postevent evaluation survey.

Adapted, by permission, from Web Survey Master. Available: www.websurveymaster.com/t/29/

20 percent in data and 80 percent in designing, training, and coaching.

Budget Evaluations

As Allen (2009) suggests, do not wait until you get to the end of the event to find out that you have exceeded your budget projections. The budget should be reconciled throughout the event process and updated each time you receive new costs or make adjustments or changes. One way to evaluate the event is to compare its cost to its usefulness or value in monetary benefits, which is commonly referred to as the event's return on investment (Myhill and Phillips 2006). Destination Marketing Association International (DMAI), an association for destination marketing organizations, provides an event impact calculator that measures the economic value of an event and calculates its return on investment (DMAI 2012). DMAI is currently working on a sports calculator that will provide a more valid and reliable estimate of economic impact for sports commissions across the United States.

The term *return on event* (ROE) was coined by Aggarwal and Goldblatt to identify the percentage of earnings returned to an organization sponsoring an event based on marketing efforts (Goldblatt 2011). Goldblatt suggests that if you increase attendance by 25 percent through e-marketing strategies for a small event of 100 persons, you may save a significant amount of money and generate a sizable net profit directly attributable to this e-marketing activity. See figure 13.2, which illustrates how to measure the return on event.

Hanson (2010) suggests that successful budgeting is dependent on the amount of detail put into the budget, and managers must continually ask the question "What other expenses can I expect?" Hanson claims that "clumping" and "miscellaneous" are two of the most common mistakes made by managers. Clumping occurs when 12 to 15 possible expenses are put into one administrative category rather than being broken into separate line items. Allocating a number of items into a Miscellaneous or Other category is also easy to do, but it often becomes too large and not very beneficial to the manager. Following are some common budget categories that Hanson outlines for events:

- Accommodations
- Administrative
- Ceremonies
- Contingency
- Exhibitions or trade shows
- Food service

	Year 1	Year 2
EXPENSES		
Advertising • Newspaper • Radio • Television	$30,000 $25,000 $65,000	$40,000 $30,000 $80,000
Direct mail • Design and printing • Postage	$3,000 $7,000	$4,000 $8,000
Internet	$8,000	$10,000
Promotions	$3,500	$4,500
Public relations	$4,500	$5,500
Subtotal	**$146,000**	**$182,000**
INCOME		
Ticket sales	$125,000	$150,000
Sponsorships	$50,000	$50,000
Subtotal	**$175,000**	**$200,000**

■ **Figure 13.2** Measuring the return on an event.

- Hospitality
- Insurance
- Marketing
- Media and public relations
- Medical
- Merchandise
- Officials
- Participant services
- Printing
- Rights fee
- Salaries
- Site visits
- Transportation
- Venue
- Volunteers

Attendance Evaluations

Attendance can be a valuable form of evaluating the success of your event. For a single one-off event, the event planner can compare attendance from year to year. Events with multiple activities may also be evaluated based on the attendance at each of the separate activities.

Two common ways to count attendance at a sporting event are paid attendance and turnstile counts. Paid attendance or paid registration counts every person who bought a ticket or registered for the sporting event regardless of whether they attended or not. Thus, it could be stated that a sporting event that sold 25,000 tickets in 2011 and 50,000 tickets for the same event in 2012 doubled its attendance in a year. However, the challenge of evaluating an event based solely on paid attendance is that it does not indicate how many people were actually at the event and thus contributed to the atmosphere of the event. In contrast, turnstile counts measure how many people actually attended. Many event planners employ turnstile counts using bar-code scanners or the more antiquated system of having a ticket taker manually use a clicker as each spectator enters the facility. More recently, sports teams such as the Houston Astros and Houston Rockets are using paperless tickets that allow consumers to simply swipe their credit cards at the gate upon entry.

Although attendance can be an effective way to evaluate an event's success, some precautions must be taken into consideration. First, event planners representing the rights holder of the event should ensure they have control over any public announcement of the attendance. Second, there does not seem to be an industry standard for the correct way to count attendance. Some teams count both paid attendance and the turnstile count, which inflates the numbers. Many professional and collegiate teams have been known to inflate their numbers in this way to appeal to sponsors. Third, simply calculating attendance without considering other relevant factors can be misleading when evaluating an event. For example, consider the impact of the following scenarios on attendance:

- The event was held at the same time as another big event in the area.
- Inclement weather prevented many people from attending the sporting event.
- The event was held on the same day as a religious holiday.
- The event was rushed, and there was inadequate time for marketing and advertising.
- The sport does not have a large following in the geographic area where the event was held. (For example, lacrosse is widely popular in the northeastern regions of the United States but less popular in other areas.)

EVALUATING OUTCOMES AND OBJECTIVES

Event planners are increasingly using return on objectives (ROO) as a more comprehensive measure of event effectiveness in comparison to ROI. Instead of calculating the impact of the event based solely on revenues, ROO measures success based on whether key objectives for the event are met. Arnold (2012) provides some guidelines for measuring ROO:

1. Talk with key stakeholders, and ask them some of the following questions:
   - Why are you holding the event?

- What type of outcome do you want from the event?

- Who do you expect to attend? Are they the right people?

- At the end of the day, how will you measure success? This may vary for each stakeholder. For example, success for sponsors may be related to name recognition, but success for the rights holder is winning the contest.

- What is unique about this event? Consider the Kentucky Derby, which is branded as "the most exciting two minutes in sport." Not many sporting events can make this claim.

- If something could go wrong, what is it?

2. Next, analyze the conversations with stakeholders and come up with a few succinct objectives. It is important to keep in mind the SMART acronym. Whereas goals are normally broad statements, objectives should be specific, measurable, achievable, realistic, and timely.

3. Determine how your objectives translate into monetary deliverables. The more business-related your objectives, the easier you will be able to translate them into dollars. Although ROO is not focused solely on revenues, all events must be cognizant of the bottom line.

4. Factor in the fact that every dollar spent on the event should somehow be tied to the objectives of the event.

5. Using quantitative or qualitative measures, set up a simple and consistent way of measuring success based on your objectives.

MEASURING ECONOMIC IMPACT

Measuring the economic impact of an event is a somewhat controversial but very important topic within the industry. Event planners must have a keen understanding of this topic because of the political nature of economic impact. Many scholarly studies have shown that bringing an event to a certain destination does not always equate with enhanced economic impact for the region. However, at the same time, economic impact is widely used by both event planners and government officials to sell key stakeholders on bidding for and hosting an event in their region because of the positive impact the event will have through economic growth of local businesses, increased job growth, enhanced infrastructure, and overall community pride. There are a number of ways to measure economic impact within the sport event industry.

The total estimated economic impact of a sporting event is made up of the direct, induced, indirect, and implicit benefits (Depken 2011). According to Depken, *direct spending* is the dollars spent specifically because of the event; it reflects only money that would not have been spent but for the event, called *new spending*. The National Association of Sports Commissions recommends that event planners measure economic impact using only direct visitor spending. Direct spending may include lodging, food, local transportation, access to the event, and other spending in the local market for tourism and entertainment venues. The new spending on hosting the event that would not have occurred if the event had not taken place is called *induced spending* and is generally undertaken by entities such as a sports franchise, convention bureau, sports commission, and host city. For example, the city of Beijing spent considerable money on facilities such as Beijing National Stadium (referred to as the Bird's Nest) at a cost of $423 million for the primary purpose of hosting the Olympic and Paralympic Games.

The money spent outside of the local economy by consumers is called leakage. Some events (e.g., mega-events such as the Super Bowl) employ the use of *multipliers* when calculating economic impact. Depken suggests that multipliers account for the additional spending created after the direct and induced spending has been completed. It is important to use a multiplier of correct magnitude. The appropriate multiplier for direct spending is different from that for induced spending based on factors related to leakages and tax structures. Economists suggest that multipliers be less than two, but some studies use multipliers as high as five.

The indirect benefits of hosting a sporting event may include additional tourism to a destination or enhanced reputation. *Implicit benefits* are those that enhance the destination's image and may include quality of life advancements, civic pride, and advertisements for the destination. These types of benefits add value to the host destination and are difficult to measure.

SUMMARY

After all the planning and the actual implementation of an event, it seems natural that event planners could relax at the event's conclusion. However, a number of important activities must take place even after the event is complete. This chapter discusses the importance of cleanup and breakdown as well as postevent media coverage. Sponsors must be contacted, and some time must be set aside to review the strengths and weaknesses of the event. Postevent evaluation is critical to the success of future events and must not be dismissed. Evaluation allows the event planner to identify if objectives were met and to provide feedback to stakeholders who are vitally involved in the event.

LEARNING ACTIVITIES

Measuring Economic Impact

1. Go to the following YouTube video titled "Measuring the Economic Impact of Sporting Events with Jon Schmieder" at www.youtube.com/watch?v=025YBECRfE8. Listen to the interview, and describe the differences between how the National Association of Sports Commissions (NASC) recommends measuring economic impact (EI) in comparison to how some mega-events actually measure EI.

2. Think of a recent event you attended. Using a form of participant observation, evaluate the event by describing what you liked and did not like.

3. Watch the YouTube video "Oklahoma State Football Coach Mike Gundy Upset" at www.youtube.com/watch?v=aoMmbUmKN0E. After reviewing the section about press conferences in your text, list the positive and negative aspects of this press conference.

REFERENCES

Allen, J. 2009. *Event planning: The ultimate guide to successful meetings, corporate events, fundraising galas, conferences, conventions, incentives and other special events.* 2nd ed. Mississauga, ON: Wiley.

Allen, J., W. O'Toole, I. McDonnell, and R. Harris. 2002. *Festival and special event management.* 2nd ed. Queensland, AU: Wiley.

Amsbary, J.H., and P.J. Staples. 1991. Improving administrator/nurse communication: A case study of "management by wandering around." *Journal of Business Communication* 28 (2): 101-112.

Arnold, K. 2012. *How to create a return on objectives (ROO) for your next meeting.* Official newsletter of the Arizona Sunbelt Chapter of Meeting Professionals International. Available: www.naylornetwork.com/maz-nwl/articles/?aid=16810&projid=1243.

deLisle, L.J. 2009. *Creating special events.* Champaign, Illinois: Sagamore.

Depken II, C.A. 2011. *Economic impact study.* In *Encyclopedia of sports management and marketing,* ed. L.E. Swayne and M. Dodds, 428-435. Thousand Oaks, CA: Sage.

Destination Marketing Association International. 2012. Event impact calculator. Available: www.destination-marketing.org/page.asp?pid=417.

Dwyer, L., R. Mellor, N. Mistilis, and T. Mules. 2000. A framework for assessing "tangible" and "intangible" impacts of events and conventions. *Event Management* 6:175-189.

Goldblatt, J. 2011. *Special events: A new generation and the next frontier.* Hoboken, NJ: Wiley.

Hanson, B. 2010. Budgeting for sports events—Part 2. Available: http://sportscommissions.wordpress.com/2010/10/25/budgeting-for-sports-events-part-2.

Irwin, R.L., W.A. Sutton, and L.M. McCarthy. 2002. *Sport promotion and sales management.* Champaign, IL. Human Kinetics.

Irwin, R.L., W.A. Sutton, and L.M. McCarthy. 2008. *Sport promotion and sales management.* 2nd ed. Champaign, IL. Human Kinetics.

Isaacs, E. 2010. 360 degree project evaluation for a dance performance or event. DANZ. Available: www.danz.org.nz/resources_360evaluation.php.

Lynde, T. 2007. *Sponsorships 101.* Mableton, GA: Lynde & Associates.

Mashable Entertainment. 2012. How social media is changing sports [Infographic]. Available: http://mashable.com/2012/04/27/sports-social-media-2.

Masterman, G. 2009. *Strategic sports event management.* 2nd ed. Oxford, UK: Butterworth-Heinemann.

Myhill, M., and J. Phillips. 2010. Determine the success of your meeting through evaluation. In *Professional meeting management: Comprehensive strategies for meetings, conventions and events,* ed. G.C. Ramsborg, 691-710. Dubuque, IA: Kendall/Hunt.

Partovi, F.Y. 1994. Determining what to benchmark. *International Journal of Operations & Production Management* 14 (6): 25-40.

Peters, T., and R. Waterman. 1982. *In search of excellence.* New York: Harper & Row.

Spendolini, M.J. 1992. *The benchmarking book.* New York: AMACOM.

Sports Media Challenge. 2012. Media relations tips for executives. Available: www.sportsmediachallenge.com/solutions/getarticle.php?s=executives&a=Media%20Relations%20Tips%20for%20Executives.

Stoldt, G.C., S.W. Dittmore, and S.E. Branvold. 2012. *Sport public relations: Managing stakeholder communication.* 2nd ed. Champaign, IL: Human Kinetics.

Weigelt, J.A., K.J. Brasel, D. Bragg, and D. Simpson. 2004. The 360-degree evaluation: Increased work with little return? *Current Surgery* 61 (6): 616-626.

INDEX

Note: The italicized *f* and *t* following page numbers refer to figures and tables, respectively.

ABOUT THE AUTHORS

Courtesy of Christopher Greenwell

T. Christopher Greenwell, PhD, is a professor in the department of health and sport science at the University of Louisville in Kentucky. He has taught event management since 2002 and published several articles on unique aspects of the service environment at sporting events and how these can be used as an effective marketing tool.

Greenwell has direct experience as an event manager, having planned and coordinated the event management, promotions, and game operations for all athletic events in an NCAA Division I athletic program. Events under his management set attendance records in men's and women's basketball, volleyball, and women's soccer. Greenwell was also an event volunteer for major events such as the Ryder Cup, NASCAR, and the World Equestrian games.

Greenwell and his wife, Donna, reside in Louisville. In his free time, he enjoys watching mixed martial arts and playing fantasy football.

Courtesy of Leigh Ann Danzey-Bussell

Leigh Ann Danzey-Bussell, PhD, is an assistant professor of sport management at the University of West Georgia in Carrollton. She has taught event and facility management courses since 2006. In 2008 she was named Outstanding Professor of the Year as recognized by Sigma Phi Epsilon, Gamma Chapter, at Ball State University in Muncie, Indiana.

Danzey-Bussell has over 25 years of experience working in the sport industry in various capacities in NCAA Division I, II, and III and NAIA programs as well as in the nonprofit sector. She has served as the executive director of Team Clydesdale International, Inc., a nonprofit organization responsible for hosting national and world championships in various events. She also worked as the media relations coordinator for the United States Golf Tour. Danzey-Bussell worked as a sport information director responsible for event management and promotion at the University of Alabama, University of South Alabama, and Northeast Louisiana University. Danzey-Bussell serves as one of the co-chairs of the North American Society for Sport Management Teaching & Learning Fair and is a member of the Finance Committee for the North American Society for the Sociology of Sport.

Danzey-Bussell has volunteered for local, regional, and national sporting events including American Heart Association Heart Walks, Southeastern Conference gymnastics championships, two NCAA Final Fours (Indianapolis and Atlanta), NCAA Swimming and Diving Championships, and the 2012 Super Bowl in Indianapolis. She also served the University of Alabama as the Alumni Chapter President for the state of Indiana for 10 years.

Danzey-Bussell enjoys attending and watching sporting events, sharing movies with her family, and cooking. She and her husband, Timothy, and daughter, Sophie Grace, reside in Carrollton, Georgia.

Courtesy of David Shonk

David J. Shonk, PhD, is an associate professor in the School of Hospitality, Sport and Recreation Management at James Madison University in Harrisonburg, Virginia, where he conducts research in sport event management and has taught a course in sport facility and event management. Shonk has worked as a meeting and event planner in both professional sport and the nonprofit sector. During that time he was responsible for planning a range of conferences, tours, and events including concerts, on-field promotions, and special events, such as the Carolina League All-Star Game. He also worked as marketing director of the Salem Professional Baseball Club and director of development at DECA, Inc.

In 2011, Shonk founded the Harrisonburg-Rockingham Sports Commission, where he serves as the executive director of this all-volunteer organization. He is also a member at large of the North American Society for Sport Management Executive Council.

Shonk lives in Harrisonburg with his wife, Jennifer, and their children. He enjoys coaching his children's sport teams, traveling with his family, and staying fit with cardio workouts.